BIRMINGHAM BLITZ:
OUR STORIES

**Birmingham
Air Raids
Remembrance
Association
presents**

BIRMINGHAM BLITZ:
OUR STORIES

**Compiled by
Brian Wright**

BREWIN BOOKS

BREWIN BOOKS
56 Alcester Road,
Studley,
Warwickshire,
B80 7LG
www.brewinbooks.com

Published by Brewin Books 2014

Reprinted November 2016

© 2014 Birmingham Air Raids Remembrance Association and contributors

ISBN: 978-1-85858-524-6

Printed and bound in Great Britain
by 4edge Ltd.

Contents

Birmingham Blitz: Our Stories

THE importance of Birmingham as an industrial centre, had world renown well before the war. This fact alone, guaranteed Birmingham special attention from the Luftwaffe. Birmingham endured 365 alerts and 77 raids resulting in over 9000 casualties of which 2241 died, statistics second only to London. The first raid was in August 1940 the last in April 1943. Despite this, post war reporting of the Blitz rarely mentioned Birmingham. It was for this reason Marjorie Ashby began a personal campaign to set the record straight. During the 50th anniversary of VE day (1995) a plaque was unveiled in the Peace Gardens in Birmingham. Marjorie felt this to be insufficient to the memory of those that died. In December 2000, Marjorie with the assistance of Dr Carl Chinn (now Professor) held a service remembrance at St Martin's church.

From this service the Birmingham Air Raids Remembrance Association (BARRA) was born. With a small group of 13 members led by Jean Purser the Association set about raising funds for a more fitting memorial. The association was and still is supported by Carl as President. The association was also honoured by the Patronage of Mr Alex Henshaw who was senior test Pilot at Castle Bromwich during the war until his death in 2007. Membership steadily grew over the next 4 years. In early 2005 I became Chairman of the Association with my vice chairman Barbara Johnson. With help from the Liverpool Blitz Memorial Fund our Association goals were rewritten and a successful application was made to the charities commission. Our charity status was instrumental in securing several large donations, the biggest of which was the memorial itself. The association had been in discussions with the Halcyon Gallery to base the memorial on the work of Lorenzo Quinn (son of the Actor Anthony Quinn), it was agreed that his work the "Tree of Life" would indeed be used. Councillor Ian Ward had been working hard on our behalf to obtain planning permission for the memorial. It was no surprise to us when Ian requested that I and Barbara attend a meeting at the council house on Tuesday 6th September 2005. At this meeting we met with Paul Green of the Halcyon Gallery, we were both stunned and delighted to receive the news that Paul and his directors had agreed to fund the memorial and its installation in Edgbaston Street. Paul went on to insist that our current funds should be used to preserve our blitz history by the education of Birmingham's People. The Tree of life memorial would be unveiled on the 8th October 2005 at our annual service. The Memorial would include the names of the civilian dead shown by the Commonwealth war graves commission. After the unveiling a further 76 names were identified by June Eastlake (BARRA Archivist), these have now also been added to the memorial.

Left Prof. Carl Chin and myself in 2005; Centre Tree of Life memorial in 2013; Right BARRA chairman Barbara Johnson lays a wreath 2013.

I stepped down as chairman of BARRA in 2006, to be replaced by Barbara. Barbara continues to educate by organising visits to schools and local history events and was instrumental in the creation of this book. This book contains the memories and views of those that experienced the Birmingham Blitz at first hand. I have attempted in many cases to accurately transpose stories from hand written accounts, if any errors are noticed by the authors I apologise in advance. Some stories have appeared elsewhere but all the writers have expressed a wish for all the stories to be brought together in one record. As the compiler of the stories I hope that this book helps retain the memories of the Birmingham people when war was thrust upon them. I also hope you as a reader find the stories of interest and inspiration.

Brian Wright

Our stories begin

We must remember

As a member of the Birmingham Air Raids Remembrance Association, I would like to tell you what BARRA means to me.

In 1940 my sister Gladys aged 8 and myself aged 5 were evacuated to Evesham. I can remember my mom giving us both a kiss and she was crying. We both went off holding hands and carrying a small case each and our name labels pinned to our coats.

When we got there we were taken to a school hall and people were coming in and choosing who they wanted. We were almost the last to go because there were two of us. We didn't know what life was going to be like. But it was terrible. We just wanted our mom and dad.

As time went on I started to wet the bed and the people were very cruel to us. Mr. C. always gave me 2 or 3 lashes with his belt every time I wet the bed. In the end they would not let me sleep in the bed so they put me in the coalhouse on a bag of straw with a pillow and a blanket. I just sobbed and was very frightened.

In September 1941 my mom came to fetch us back home. What we didn't know was that our cousin Allen had been killed, aged 19 months on 23 November 1940, when my Auntie Dora's house was bombed in Clissold Street, Brookfields.

When we were on the bus coming home to 10, Richmond Terrace, Bridge Street West, Hockley we were very happy because mom told us she had got a big surprise for us both when we got back home. Our surprise was we got a new baby brother John. He was lovely. He was born on 2 June 1941 but in December 41 John died of pneumonia.

It was terrible because we didn't have him for long and I can remember when he was buried my Nan and granddad came and went with mom and dad and they went together in the same car as the tiny coffin.

We also had an older brother but he went to Wales and didn't come home till later. His name was Billy. Every night mom and dad used to put on our coats, shoes and gasmasks and waited for the sirens to go and get us out of bed. On the 27th July 1942 we were all in the shelter and my dad was fire watching. He came to the shelter and told my mom that Roseberry Street had been hit. That's where my Nan and granddad lived. My mom just panicked. She got out of the shelter and left us with Mrs. Patrick, a neighbour who lived opposite us in the terrace.

When the all clear went we were taken into her house. We didn't know where mom and dad were. Mom had gone. When mom came home we were taken back over home. My mom was in the chair with two neighbours who lived in the terrace and were trying to get mom round with smelling salts and tapping her face. I was so frightened I thought my mom was going to die. Later that day mom and dad told us that Nan and granddad had gone to heaven. My Auntie Daisy and cousin Jimmy aged two were in hospital. I cried and cried because I loved my grandparents so much. We used to go every Saturday and I knew I wouldn't see them again.

Harry and Louisa Gregory

My grandparent's names were Harry and Louisa Gregory. They died on 28th July 1942. They had seven daughters and two sons. It was a day I shall never forget.

That's why I joined BARRA. I want to do this, get a memorial, for them and my mom who is no longer with us. But through all this I have suffered with my nerves. All I want now is to live long enough to see a fitting memorial for them.

**Barbara Johnson nee Haden,
Bromford, Birmingham
Current chairperson of BARRA**

National Fire Service, the Story of a Firewoman in Wartime 1939-1945
Jacqueline. M. Wilde (nee Neighbour) 859397
"C" Division HQ Birmingham Area 24

I was a fire woman in the fire service C division headquarters, Cambridge Street in Birmingham which was area 24 from 1939 to 1945. I was also the divisional instructress for Squad Drill and RE. In 1938 I joined the ARP which was air raid precautions and it was being formed to protect the home front, so if war was declared, and we had bombs or fires or anything over here it was the civilian population helping out with the forces. It was purely a voluntary organisation and I and many of my friends joined this. Later on in the year which was May 1939, I heard that the fire service were hoping to recruit people, they needed civilians to help out in the offices and back up the firemen when they went to fires. They wanted civilians for admin jobs, office jobs, cooking, switchboards, transport and help with training. So I rang up to see if I was qualified enough to help and the age limit was 18 but because they were in such need of people they said if I filled in the form and sent it in, by the time war was declared I'd be 18 and eligible to join. So I filled the form in sent it in and when war was declared on the 3rd of September. We were told on the radio to mobilise and to go to the nearest station or posts or whatever we had volunteered for.

Some weeks I continued to do my office job during the day and going to the fire service in the evening and working until late. They'd had a lot of civilians who used their cars they were called dispatch riders although they weren't on motorcycles they had their cars and they took messages from here to there. They took people who were working late on night duty home: in case the buses had stopped, they picked them up if it was difficult for people to get into the fire stations. These people with cars generally made themselves helpful taking messages from fire station to fire station. The fire stations were the regular fire stations, the big fire stations that we have today, and then each division (the city was made up into several divisions) and each division had about 8 auxiliary stations which were made up from large houses, and there they had vehicles which could tow the pumps. These were put onto the back of private cars like trailer pumps, they had people standing by with cars, they had auxiliary firemen which weren't regular brigade men but they'd been trained, they'd gone through training and they were qualified to go out with the firemen and put out fires. This took quite a few months to organise but in the end there were 11 stations on our division including three which were main fire brigade stations where they kept the big escapes and later the turntable ladders which are now the Simon Snorkles containing ladders which you see going up to the roofs. We didn't have a uniform to start with so we wore slacks. As I was working during the daytime I used to come home and have a quick meal and then go into Cambridge Street in town and take over the switchboard for the night shift. Well this was a bit strenuous so after a few weeks of doing this I was asked if I'd like to become a full time fire woman and not have my job during the day. This entailed earning £3 a week for the whole time. This meant I went in every day; there were three shifts from 7am-3pm, 3pm-11pm and from 11pm-7am the next morning. So that way the switchboard was covered. I was the first firewoman to be recruited for C division and after that there were quite a few girls, about 12 of us altogether to cover the switchboard.

The switchboard was on the ground floor of a very old building in Cambridge Street, it belonged to the ARP people and they had got all their equipment and pumps in there, so we took over the first floor and the top floor. Down in the cellar they had made a control room with maps on the wall so that we knew just where every fire engine or auxiliary pump was, just by looking on the board. The switchboard they couldn't unfortunately take down into the control room and so outside our window we had stacks and stacks of sandbags piled up and they had built around our switchboard an Anderson shelter that was a metal structure about 6 feet wide by about 8 feet long. And they just stood it over the top of the switchboard and clamped it to the floor and the firemen used to come in and put little notices on it, like "Please don't feed the rabbits", because it looked just like a rabbit hutch but anyhow we were assured that if a bomb did strike the building it would protect us.

Part 2
During the early part of the war, the first time the sirens went off we put our gas masks at the ready, thinking that the bombers would be overhead because

we were told that they were going to drop gas and we'd had all our instructions what to do and the different types of gas bombs that would drop down. But fortunately gas was never used to my knowledge during the war on the civilian population, so we never really had to use our respirators but they were great things, not like the civilian ones, they were large, they had two round glasses for the eyes, where you could see through, and a long nozzle which went from the nose into the respirator part which you had strapped in front of you. Normally, you just had a brown bag like a case which you carried over the shoulder, but when it was in use you'd been trained to have it in the front of us so that the tube, which was very much like a Hoover tube, went from the case to your nose and so therefore you could breath safely through this. The mask completely covered your face and you were able to breathe quite normally.

One time when I was travelling to my job, it would be about seven in the evening the sirens went and stopped all the buses, we had to get off the buses and walked from then on. I walked with two soldiers because the soldiers if they couldn't get back to the barracks they had to notify the nearest police station so that the police station could notify the barracks that they were unable to return either because the trains had stopped or the public transport had stopped. We were walking along Great Hampton Street when we heard this enormous rattling sound and the two soldiers pushed me into a doorway and flung themselves on top of me and down came a large fire bomb, which we called a Molotov Cocktail because when it reached the floor it exploded and went in all directions and also they used to send these down and then send high explosives down afterwards when the fires were going merrily and they could see what was happening down below. This came down and we stayed put for awhile and we saw lots of figures coming out: extinguishing the fire there would be the different air raid wardens with their stirrup pumps because they were all trained to put out the fire bombs as well as deal with explosives. When everything was clear we went on our way again. Hearing the high explosives which dropped down a few minutes after we'd passed this place and blew up the road in front of Lucas and it pitted the whole building. I think to this day you can probably see the marks on the brick work where the explosive went off so we were lucky. It was a very bad raid this particular day and instead of going to the end of Colmore Row I decided to go up Great Charles Street. I had difficulty in getting up because the raid was so heavy. My fire station were worried because they knew I normally came along Colmore Row which had been hit with high explosive bombs and most of the buildings were down, The Grand Hotel was hit and all along St. Phillips Churchyard.

This one day I came up Great Charles Street. I was able to collect shrapnel which had fallen. It was hot when you picked it up and I picked up some to take with me and when I got to work they were all very relieved because if I had come the normal way which was along Colmore Row, I should have probably been blown up with the building, so I was a very very lucky.

Part 3

Another time when I came on duty in the morning the central fire station had dropped down on the switchboard and a quiet voice said "I have a message for you". There had been a heavy raid the night before and the switchboard was jammed with calls from the control room, as they were so busy downstairs they asked me to take messages. So I said to central "yes go ahead I'll take your message" they said "we have to inform you once again that a bomb has fallen at the rear of your building. Please take action immediately". Well I wrote the message down and read it back. I had to put the hooter on quickly. The alarm, which was a Klaxon hooter, and made an awful lot of noise and the assistant divisional officer came running in and I handed him the message, he said "that's strange we had this message last night". We searched the building and we couldn't find anything at all. Then he said he'd go have another look. At the back of our building there was a canal with telephone wires above and apparently the large land mine, it was about 6 feet across, had come down on a parachute that had got caught in the telephone wires which were very high because there were high buildings on either side of the canals which were the factories and warehouses, so it was very high up in the air but where the bomb had swung, it was so heavy it had caved in the whole side of the building. The bricks had gone in but of course in the night time, when they'd searched the building, no one had thought to look up in the air over the canal. We thought it would have landed on the ground. So we evacuated the building and I was left on the switchboard phoning round all the fire stations – notifying them that we were going to secondary control room which was in Hagley Road. Everything each day was copied from the boards downstairs in the control room to the duplicate one in Hagley Road so that we knew where all the fire engines were and what fires there were and where they'd been sent out to. This was done everyday so it was quite up to date. I was left on the board phoning round the stations and I thought I'm sure I can hear something ticking. The divisional officer kept me company and the fire stations kept ringing back to see if I was alright and they said "never mind Jackie. You'll have a union jack over your coffin". I wasn't worried about the union jack over my coffin I just wanted to get out of the building. When I had finished ringing round the 12 fire stations, we got into the car and locked the front door. Why we locked the front door I really don't know and went off to the secondary control room. But when we got there we'd found that in the emergency they'd forgotten one of the best pieces of equipment we had got and that was 'Millicent'.

Now 'Millicent' was our fire float. These fire floats; there were only three in Birmingham. And we were lucky in having one because we got the canal at the back. They were used for canal fires and they had what was called radial branches in them. They were very powerful hoses more powerful than the normal hoses that were on the fire engines, they had to be held in a clamp because they were so powerful. They were able to get right to the top of the buildings which were three to four to five stories high. So the Water officer, with the Transport officer, (who was later my husband) made their way back as fast as they could to Cambridge Street to get the fire float and bring her out of danger. We all kept our fingers crossed because we thought at any moment the bomb would go off. The whole area of the city centre had been evacuated because when a land mine went off it flattened a block of shops and offices and buildings. They did get her safely away and we heard next day that a soldier, who was on leave, had come along and said what's the matter because the whole place was surrounded by police and they said there was an UXB (Unexploded bomb) and were waiting for the bomb disposal squad to come, he said he belonged to a bomb disposal squad and he climbed up and diffused the bomb and then went on his way. We never knew to this day what his name was but we were all able to go back when it had been diffused to our building and to our control room.

Part 4

Another time we had a very heavy raid at night and when I came off duty I couldn't get back home, the buses had stopped running and they couldn't spare anyone to transport us home. So we had to stay in the building, they had made the top floor into a canteen and it had got little rooms with beds in so if you had done a long spell of duty and couldn't get back home you could always go there and have a rest or a sleep for a few hours. But this particular night it was very heavy and all the fire engines on our stations were occupied with fires in the city centre and around and we had to send to outside Birmingham for the fire engines to come and stand in. Different places in the country which weren't bombed if they had got fire engines they'd send them into the cities that were under fire and they'd stand in at the stations so that no fire station was completely empty. That meant that they'd always got a machine in the event that if any new fires started or the crews could go to help relieve the firemen who had been fighting a fire or damping down after the fire.

They had probably been there for eight or ten hours without a break so these fire engines were coming in from outside the Area and not a lot of the drivers knew the ways to the different fire stations so I was sent out to stand at the top of Great Charles Street and direct the traffic, its not traffic like you see these days with lots of cars, because cars weren't allowed As soon as the air raid warnings went off it was only the official vehicles that were allowed, the fire engines, the ambulances and vehicles like that. So I had to go and stand there and when I saw the fire engines coming in I had to direct them to the different divisions and fire stations or wherever they should go. On the outskirts of each city on the different main roads they had a fire station which had a chequered board outside which looked like a draughts board with black and white squares, and this chequered board was a rallying point so that fire engines coming in from outside Birmingham would stop there to get their orders, on where to go, then they would send them into the city centre. I was directing the traffic so that when they got into the city centre I could send them on to the different fires where they were needed. I was only seventeen or eighteen at the time and it was quite exciting directing traffic. I'd got my helmet on and my uniform on and was just hoping that there wouldn't be a direct hit or a bomb come down near me while I was there. Anyhow I stood there for about three hours doing this and then went back to headquarters and took a couple of hours sleep until the raid eased off and somebody was going home my way.

Part 5

Some two years after the war had been on, I accidentally burned my hands and so I was taken off operational duty, which was switchboard, and put on administrative duties which was more nine to five. Our division decided to have a training officer so they asked me if I would like to help the training officer and be his training clerk. The training had always been done through the Central Fire Station but now each division was going to have its own training because when there weren't raids they had to do so much drill each day on hose drill or pumping drill they had various things to do so they had to keep trained up for the latest piece of equipment so that they didn't get rusty. We had to make a note of all the hours training each fireman did on the division each day. Well they never had this before, so they gave us a table and a chair and said that is your office start from scratch. One of the regular brigade firemen had been made up to a Company officer and he was my boss. So we set about making rules, regulations and we had to make the cards that the training hours were put on. We had to absolutely start from scratch.

After we had been going a few months and got the hang of it, it was decided we could have a training school and so a large private boys' school with grounds all around it was taken over in Edgbaston, I think it was called Penryn School. It was taken over by the fire service and we then had a proper training school, before then we just had an office in a house on the Hagley Road on the corner of Norfolk Road, which was our secondary control room. We outgrew Cambridge Street offices and they just kept Cambridge Street, for its very large garage at the back for all the trailer pumps because not only did we have fire engines but there were a lot of private cars and vans which had trailer pumps on the back of them so they had towing brackets fitted and they could get these little pumps out so if it wasn't a large fire they sent these little pumps out at the beginning of the war which helped considerably. Anyhow, we went to the training school at Penryn. They used to have courses for the firemen and the officers and this went on for a good many years. I enjoyed the training because I used to go out with my boss to where they were doing the training either by the canals or the pumping stations and clock up the hours for the different firemen so it got me out of the office and I was able to travel round. Sometimes in the evenings when

Penryn Training School Edgbaston. My Squad 1943
(I can be seen sitting 3rd from left on the front row)

there weren't raids on we'd play table tennis and this was something I liked very much and I was good enough to get into the area team of the fire service and we used to go round to other areas playing table tennis

this was when we were off duty of course. So that if there was a raid it was immediately cancelled. I quite enjoyed being in the fire service, I was in for five and a half years and the companionship and the friendliness and the helpfulness amongst it was really something.

Part 6

From the Auxiliary fire service it became the National fire service and then just before D-Day when they expected the German planes to bomb our ports they sent the different fire brigades down to the coastal areas to stand in because they knew that the bombing would be very very heavy at the ports. We all had to go, they just kept a skeleton staff and we weren't told where we were going but we had to all assemble at the Central Fire Station in Birmingham with our kit bags and we were put on trains. It was called the "Colour Scheme" and it was very hush hush. My boss was put on the train and he went down to Plymouth on the Overseas column, the Overseas column was standing ready in case they needed firemen abroad and they would send them abroad with the army. I didn't see him at all and he went back to being a regular fire officer after the emergency was over. It lasted about a year.

When we got down as far as Bristol on the train this was all at night and we didn't know where we were because in those days if any of the enemy landed over here there weren't any names on the stations and of course the blackout kept it so that it was very difficult to see anything at all because we only had glimmers of lights. All car lights had metal pieces with narrow slits cut into them so you could only get a narrow slit of light coming out and no lights were able to be seen at all. Everybody had to have blackout curtains, so it was very difficult in the train to see where we were because the blinds were down. When we got to Bristol we were then told where we were going whether we were going down to the south coast or whether we were going to Wales. I wanted to go to the south coast because I was born on the coast and I liked the south very much, but as it happened I was one of them that went to Wales and I'd always thought that in Wales you saw coalminers going along with pickaxes on their shoulders. I was there for a whole year and I never saw one miner with a pickaxe on his shoulder at all. They were lovely people and they made us very welcome and I was very, very happy while I was there.

We slept on bunk beds in a nissen hut which was not very comfortable at all and this was November time and it was very cold and a nissen hut is very cold unless you've got a fire in it. They'd got these coke stoves in it and the first morning we woke up with headaches feeling really awful and we found that you can die if you've got a coke stove without any ventilation so we had to sleep with the windows open which wasn't very pleasant. After a few weeks of this the lady that worked in the canteen of the fire station, who was a cook, said she had a spare room vacant and her house was opposite the fire station, so one of the girls and I shared a bedroom in her house and she made us most welcome. She used to cook us the most gorgeous things even though we'd got ration books and you couldn't get a lot of things. She managed to get them and she managed to make lovely food and things. We were very happy there.

This was at Caerphilly, we travelled by train each morning to Llanishen, which was a few miles outside Cardiff and we worked at a lovely old house called Brooklea. It was the Area headquarters, and then you had an area with so many divisions and the Birmingham area was a different area to the welsh area so this was their headquarters. It was a lovely house right on top of the hill with a lot of grounds around it so that when we were off duty we could sit in the grounds and different times of the year we'd have sports to keep ourselves occupied when there weren't any raids because unlike Birmingham which had raids night after night, down there they didn't have an awful lot, they had them around the dock areas but the cities weren't bombed like Coventry, Birmingham and London were.

So we had quite a lot of spare time and as we were administrative, we worked nine to five like an office would do. The only thing with Wales was that once if started to rain it never stopped, and it went on for hours and hours and hours. That's the only thing I could fault with.

Part 7

The city of Cardiff was very nice and clean with a beautiful university there as well, and after I'd been there six months I got married up in Birmingham on two weeks leave. They made a great fuss and were very, very kind to my husband who had left the fire service because when the raids were over they sent the soldiers back into the army again. First of all he was a fireman and then in 1940 he went into the army and when the raids were on in Birmingham, they sent all the soldiers who had been firemen back to the cities because they were needed more in the fire service than they were in the army. Then finally when the raids after D day calmed down, they sent the firemen back into the army again so they became soldiers again. At this point he was a soldier and was stationed just outside Aldershot at Crookham so we both went up to Birmingham to meet or he came to me at Cardiff. We got married from Birmingham and had a fortnight's leave which we spent in London.

Although there were bombs and raids going on you couldn't get to any of the ports because all the ports were occupied by the navy and of course they had barricades all round the beaches just in case there was an invasion. There were blocks all along the seafronts so that you couldn't get anything through the blocks and then down on the sand on the shore there were angle iron, there was barbed wire and everything like that so there was no point in going on holiday to the sea, so we spent it in London.

Although we had several raids and had to get up in the night and go down into the lounges it was quite enjoyable and we were able to see some of the shows, one was by Irving Berlin and it was called 'This is the Amy' and that had all American army personnel so it was very interesting and it was up to date as well, very topical and very patriotic. Also Ivor Novello in 'Perchance To Dream'. The famous Windmill Theatre boasted that "it never closed". Not even for the raids.

Part 8

During the time I was in Birmingham I had applied to go on an instructor's course, they wanted instructors for squad drill and physical training so I volunteered and I went on two courses for PT instruction and I got a Grade A, so I was made chief instructor for the division and twice a week I used to take the girls for squad drill and PE and this went on for quite a few years and I used to go to the training school. Although I worked at the training school at the time I used to have my own squad there but when the students came to do their training there I would take them in squad drill and I would take them in PE.

About this time they were trying to recruit fire women for the fire service. Most of the young women either went into the army or RAF or the navy or the land army so they were hoping for more fire women so they chose six of the girls. I was one of them and we posed for the newspapers so they could put pictures of us either on the fire float or holding the hoses in the newspapers with an article hoping that it would get more fire women to join the fire service and this was quite a success.

One amusing story that I remember we had a course on first aid and we had two first aid instructors, and the one always seemed to get his students through the courses, there was no cheating at all it was just that they got through, and the other instructor seemed to have some failures, though the one time my training officer said I think I'll go and listen and he listened at the door, and he

found the instructor that got all his students through the courses used to tell them stories about any particular part of the course that he wanted them to remember. He used to illustrate it with a rude joke and they'd all have a good laugh about it, and then when they were sitting at their exams and they came to that particular part they'd remember what he wanted them to remember, because of the joke he told them, and this way they all remembered and did well in their exams. I don't know whether that would apply today but at least it got them through their first aid exams. The majority of the firemen had to have St. John Ambulance badges so that they had to have knowledge of first aid, so if they went to the fires and people were affected by the smoke or gasses or whatever they could administer to them there.

Part 9

Another funny story was the fire engines they had in those days, some of them were self-propelled ones and they weren't like the fire engines of today large and enclosed. The firemen had to hang on the outsides of them, so when the alarm bells went and they came down the pole all their clothing was usually put in a line and all they had to do was jump into it, the leggings were draped over and the boots that they wore and everything was all ready to put on. On this one particular night a friend of ours, he was a regular fireman and he decided to have a bath although he was on duty and he was in the middle of having this bath when the bells went down. He had to leap out of the bath without drying himself and one of his friends grabbed all of his equipment his boots, leggings and put it on the fire engine, and he had to leap on the fire engine completely naked and go along the road getting dressed in full view of everybody that was there but as everybody was fully occupied because there was a raid on nobody seemed to notice. I don't think it would be allowed these days for a naked fireman to get dressed on a fire engine, in any case I think they're covered in these days so it wouldn't have been all that cold for him.

Part 10

Another funny incident that occurred in Handsworth and on the Soho Road, there was a Peacocks and Peacocks had a direct hit with a fire bomb and they sent several fire engines to it and because I lived opposite we made lots of tea and took it across in jugs to the firemen. Because some of these fires went on for three or four hours before they could get under control and then if they started up again they still had to remain there to damp down, to see that there was not a scrap of embers left that could catch fire again and start, they would probably be there all night long. But of course there was no one to relieve them so I had to help hold the hoses with another fireman, while the other fireman had his drink of tea because of the water and they couldn't get out of the area very easily, half the water from the hoses would go in their cups of tea and make it cold but apart from that it was something to quench their thirst and it gave them five minutes rest before they went back again to the intense heat and holding the hoses, which was no mean feat because the pressures that come through the hose is really terrific and some of them had to be held by two men not just one. Needless to say when they had a break they came across to the house and sat down for five minutes, and had a cigarette or another cup of tea or a piece of cake or whatever we had got in the house to give them, at least it was a break for them they could have a wash or go and spend a penny or whatever they needed to do and then go back to the fire again.

Part 11

When I got married we were only allowed twenty five people at the reception, because food was on ration and in any case you had to give up your ration books. You were only allowed twenty five because of the food rationing, so therefore the majority of my friends were unable to come. For a bridesmaid dress, you had to have something that you could use afterwards so really a wartime wedding (you've probably seen the pictures of it) is very basic and nothing lavish at all, like you get today.

Everything was in short supply. If you heard there were new shoes coming in you would queue up at the shop and wait until they were delivered. In the windows they would put little high heel shoes but if you went in to ask for them they would say 'I'm sorry they are only two and half' or 'they are a size three'. My mother had very small feet and she wore a lot of high heels so she was able to go in.

They didn't like to get them out of the window you see they liked to get people to come in thinking that they'd got those shoes but they hadn't really. So she would go in and say yes I take a size two and a half so they were compelled by law to take them out of the window but this didn't happen very often because people didn't have such small feet as a rule. They liked to keep these little model shoes in the window, the same with rugs if you knew a furniture shop would have some rugs in you'd have to queue up beforehand until the supply came in and then hoped by the time you got into the shop that there were still some rugs left.

All films for cameras were used by the RAF and for the planes, so if you heard of a camera shop that was going to sell films, you queued up again and, for my wedding, I managed to get two films so I haven't got many pictures of the wedding at all and very few pictures were taken because, for one thing, it wasn't allowed because of the defence regulations and also the majority of people didn't really take holidays because they were too busy working for the war effort.

You also had coupons for sweets and cigarettes and the people who didn't smoke used to swap with the people who didn't eat sweets. I didn't smoke and my husband didn't smoke so we used to swap our cigarette coupons for sweet coupons. And if you went round to peoples houses for cups of tea you'd take a packet of tea with you. If you had got it to spare and they'd think that was something marvelous.

Part 12

When I was in the fire service on a Sunday night there was a club in Birmingham for the forces personnel it was called the Queensbury Club and you could go there and get in free providing you were in uniform and you could dance to one of the top bands and musicians. It would start about six o'clock on a Sunday evening and go on until 12 o'clock, or if there was an air raid until the air raid stopped but usually they didn't stop it. They told you the warning had gone and you were left to decide whether you wanted to take cover and go down into an air raid shelter or you wanted to go on dancing and after a while people used to go on dancing. There were overseas forces the Polish Navy and the Army there was the Czechoslovakian Army there were the Americans and the French and all the different nationalities that came over here to help us fight the war. So there were a lot of very nice people and a lot of lovely uniforms, all different types of uniforms and we used to enjoy ourselves and a lot of friendships were made from these dances, they were on a Wednesday and a Sunday because I was on duty most of the time it was only the Sunday that I was able to go.

Part 13

My father was a theatre manager first and when cinemas came in he became a cinema manager and his cinema was over the other side of the town, and he hadn't got a car so that if the buses stopped when the air raid started he had to walk all the way into the city centre. From the city centre he had to walk to Handsworth and if I was coming off duty I used to meet him there at about 10 o'clock at night in one of the public shelters. The public shelters were built under some of the big stores like Lewis's and Greys, places like that. Downstairs some of them had two basements and they turned them into air raid shelters with seats, they would hold 400 hundred people. Even more than that people in the area used to either go and take their blankets and stay there the night. If they were passing through Birmingham and there was an air raid they would take shelter in these and there was one at Greys which is no longer there now, but it was on the corner opposite to Lewis's, downstairs in the basement and I used to meet my father and we would go home together.

This one particular night it was rather a heavy raid and the buses had all stopped and they were all in lines drawn up to the kerb just outside Greys. I was standing at the top of the basement steps with my father and all the people were still sitting either in the buses or were downstairs in the shelter, and suddenly one of these noisy bombs started to come down, the noise was terrific they rattled and the people heard this high explosive coming down and they rushed off the buses and they just knocked my father and I clean over in their frantic effort to go down into the shelter. I was knocked down the stairs, fortunately I only had bruises but it was a bit scary because the high explosive was very near and it landed and we saw the explosion a road away. When the all clear went people came out again and got on the buses and they went on their way, trying to avoid the craters that were in the road where the bombs had dropped. We went to Snow Hill got on a bus back to Handsworth, but they stopped about 11 o'clock in those days, we didn't have all night buses at all so after that you had to walk.

Part 14

Around about November 1944 all the firemen and women were sent back from Wales to the cities from which we came. By this time I was married and I wanted to join my husband down by Aldershot at Fleet. I asked permission if I could be discharged because I had burned my hands badly a few years earlier. I had done five and half years with the fire service and they said I think you've done your bit and we knew that the war was coming to an end. They released me from the fire service and I went to live down at Fleet by Aldershot in Hampshire.

My husband was stationed there and he was an instructor in the army, he was also in the corps band because he was a musician. It was very nice down there, it was very different to these days, at night-time you could go and walk through the lanes and it would be absolutely full of army personnel. The Canadians were stationed down there and the Americans and also our own boys. But you could walk along these dark lanes and be perfectly safe nobody would accost you, you could leave your door open when you left the house nobody would go in and steal anything. If you went down the shelters and forgot to lock your front door you'd never have to worry because nobody would ever think of stealing anything. You were perfectly safe walking the roads at night.

Down in Hampshire there were no street lights because of the lanes so you just walked along and people would say 'good night' to you. From Fleet we used to go on the bus to Aldershot and there we used to go to the cinema, then we would come back on the bus to Fleet and we would have a meal which was a cup of tea, an egg on toast and a cake at a barn that had been turned into a café by a farmer. He did this for all the soldiers and people that wanted a snack at night. And for that we paid one shilling and sixpence for that meal, the cinema would cost us nine pence and so for a half a crown we would have a meal each, and would go to the cinema and travel on the bus for that. The army pay was a pound a week and three pounds if you were married and for four pounds you lived quite well. We used to go to the cinema twice a week or the Garrison Theatre that was the theatre that was run by the army and was free.

So we were fully occupied most of the evenings and all that for just four pounds a week. My husband and I lived out of barracks, so we had a bedroom and we shared the living room with this old couple in this house. We paid fourteen shillings rent the rest was spent on food.

We woke up one morning when we were in Hampshire and found that all the tanks and the army that had been hidden in the forests around there had all disappeared down to the coast. That was when we had the D-Day. The planes at night that used to go across looked just if all the stars were moving across the sky. These thousand bomber raids were going over to Germany but it looked just as though all the stars were moving from the sky.

When the war was over we celebrated in the barracks down there and went up to London and joined all the celebration that was in the city centre.

Jacqueline Wilde Firewoman 859397

Whilst standing by my Mum's garden gate one night, I looked at the sky which was bright red, not many miles away the bombs were dropping. I thought thank god its not us – next morning we heard that they had almost took Coventry off the map.

Next night we had a twelve hour raid, didn't have time for a cup a tea or anything to eat straight from work – down the shelter, things went very quiet during the night. So I told Mom I had managed to get TWO tomatoes, and would go back to the house and make a sandwich – then the bombing got worse, I ran back to the shelter – gave mom her sandwich. The funny ending to this story is Mom asked me "Did you bring the salt?"

Agnes Weblested

IN MEMORY OF MY BROTHER DOUGLAS WELLAN MILLS BY ANNE COURBÊT

Photo 1, taken in 1940 at the commencement of the Second World War. It features ARP Wardens taken outside Bordesley Green School. Douglas Mills is pictured third from the left. He was eighteen years of age.

The Mills family lived at 78 Churchill Road, Bordesley Green, and residents somehow felt protected from attack because the road was named

after our great war leader (I think it was named after the Boer War). Very little damage occurred, but a landmine caused great devastation and loss of life at the Bordesley Green end of the road, when the war was in its final stages.

Equipment issue Record Card   *Ministry of Labour Card*

Photographs 2, 3, and 4 depict scenes outside Bordesley Green School of Wardens, commandeered "ambulances" and a rescue exercise. These photographs were also taken in 1940.

Anne Courbêt

DIRECT HIT

On the Wednesday night of the 11th December 1940, at about 7pm, 23, Capcroft Road, Billesley, the home of my parents, Harry & May Smith, received a direct hit by a High Explosive bomb during an enemy air raid on Birmingham.

Living at home at the time were Harry & May, son Aubrey age 20, triplets Hilda, Elwin & Louis age 11, & daughter Hilary age 5. Also a friend of Aubrey's, Alan Board age 19. Alan and Aubrey were young Railway Engine Firemen, working from G.W.R. engine sheds Tyseley. Alan was on duty, should have been coming off duty at about 10-30 pm. I, Aubrey, was due to report on duty that night at about 11-00pm.

At about 6-45pm my father came into my bedroom and suggested that I should get up as things were looking bad. This I did, and because the Anderson Shelter, situated at the bottom of the back garden, was full of water Harry had moved the dining table so that two right angle sides were against the walls of the house, and under the table was my Mother, Hilary and the Triplets. Dad was standing in front of the fire, I sat down on the box curb beside him and scrounged a woodbine. It was then that it happened, ALL HELL LET LOOSE. I know I went up into the air because I had slippers on my feet and they were sliding off, I did not want to lose them, but I did. When everything stopped and went silent I was trapped under the rubble and could not move a muscle. I could hear voices shouting, but they seemed far away [I found out later that they had gone down to the shelter to investigate]. Eventually I could feel the pressure of people walking over the top of me and I started shouting, those brave, kind people soon had me out and on my feet. I was the first. Elwin & Louis were the next two. I hung around to try and help, but with nothing on my feet I was no help so they bundled us three off to a First Aid Centre. Elwin & Louis seemed to be free of any cuts, just bruises; I had a gash on my forehead over my right eye, that is all. Some time later Hilda was carried into the Centre. She was slightly concussed and badly bruised. We remained in the Centre until midday when one of the kind ladies took Elwin, Hilda & me to her home and gave us a cooked lunch, Louis remained in the Centre. When I returned to the Centre I learned that Harry, my father, and Hilary had been killed and my mother was in hospital with head wounds.

Relatives took the triplets and dispersed them among other relatives and friends in Leicestershire. I went to lodge with an uncle, easy for me to get to Tyseley Sheds. I was given 3 days leave in order to sort myself out and report back for duty. When my mother was discharged from hospital she too went to live with relations in Leicestershire. But due to our English values, our disciplinary way of life, and May's motherly driving force, we were soon back together as a family unit, facing more air raids. This kind of thing happened a hundred fold then, and people of all ranks were willing to bend down and help those in need. Do you think there would be the same response today?

Aubrey Smith

ERNEST GEORGE WILLIAMS 1890-1942. EVENTS OF 28 JULY 1942

We were the Williams family living at 103 Pineapple Road, Stirchley, Birmingham: my father Ernest, my mother known as Hilda, my sister Joan aged 12, and myself, Audrey aged 9. It had been some time since we had had an air-raid but when the siren sounded we soon fell into the well-rehearsed routine. We all went downstairs and my sister and I went under the Morrison shelter. This was a huge brown steel table with a spring underneath to support a mattress. Our Anderson shelter, which was dug into the back garden, tended to fill up with water, so we had the Morrison in the sitting room. It was very good for board games and jigsaws, but didn't leave much room for other furniture. My father bent down to speak to us before going out to join the other men on fire-watching duties. He had been badly injured in the First World War so was unfit for service in the forces. My sister got out from under the shelter to sit in an armchair. Suddenly there was a huge explosion and the glass from the windows shot across the room. A piece of shrapnel travelled over my sister's head, passed through a picture on the wall and buried itself in the wall. There was a knock on the back door. My father was injured and my mother was taken to him. A neighbour took my sister and me into their house and after the all-clear we were put to bed. The next morning we went home to hear that our father was dead. It was 28 July 1942 and schools were open during the holidays to allow mothers to work in the factories, so I walked to school at Colmore Road. As I left the house there was a large hole in the road surrounded by barriers. At the base of the oak tree, which played such a big part in our street games, was a pool of blood, covered with sand. That image haunts me still.

My father was not a victim of an enemy bomb. It was an anti-aircraft shell fired from an AA site between Cartland Road and Vicarage Road, roughly where King Edward's school stands today. I was too shocked to tell my teacher what had happened, and anyway children didn't converse with their teachers in those days. She only knew when I was having the day off for the funeral. It seems ironic that his coffin was placed on top of the Morrison shelter before it was put in the hearse. His coffin was covered with the Union Flag, but we picked some of his own roses and honeysuckle from the garden as a small floral tribute. One of the funeral cars was driven by the father of one of my school friends. I can still see the tender look of pity on his face as he helped me into the car. My over-riding memory of the journey was, as we turned into Bristol Road at Selly Oak to make our way to Lodge Hill Cemetery, a man removed his hat and saluted the flag. I don't know who he was but I have been forever proud of my father's sacrifice and of this unknown man's tribute. In modern times we would say my father died from 'friendly fire' but he gave his life willingly for King and Country.

Audrey Watson

THE WAR YEARS 1939-1945

"What's all that metal and stuff for, Dad" I asked. "That's an Air raid shelter duck we've got to build one at the top of the garden". I was ten years old and soon to find out we were at war. When the German bombers came over, that's when my dad said "get down the shelter quick". He knew by the hum they made they were loaded. One day me and some friends were playing in a field near the Old Mill, that was then on the Priory Rd., when a great lorry came in and started to drop its cargo. Oh boy was we lucky. It was getting rid of rubbish from bombed buildings in Birmingham, and guess what we found when it had gone, mounds of sweets, stuck together that had obviously been burned.

As my friend lived very near this spot in Slade Lane, she was able to run home and get some newspapers which we used to wrap packets of sweets together which we sold at school for a halfpenny a packet. We kept a very close watch on this spot for future finds but telling no one. It was our secret. One time I remember which left a bit of a scar, was being told by the Headmistress, "If the sirens go lunch time and isn't followed by the All Clear, do not come back to school, on the other hand, if the All Clear does go, you come back, understand". Great. Me and my pal were going home, the sirens went, "Lets go down to Trittiford park" we decided. The only thing that went haywire was the sound of the All Clear. Silly us, it was a lovely afternoon, and we were having a great game of Tig, in the bushes, when voices were heard. Our teacher had decided to bring the class out to the park for a refreshing stroll in the sunshine. Me and Rosie hid in the bushes all afternoon. If only we had gone to school. It was the only time we ever played truant, never again. On leaving school, because I had no 11 plus, I went straight into a munitions factory, but that's another story. If on leaving work the Sirens had gone, transport was stopped, so it meant walking home from the City to Yardley Wood. Very dark, no lighting allowed, no noise of buses going by, but wait a minute, what's that we hear, music loud and clear coming from a public air raid shelter. If any one had a musical instrument, that went into the shelter with them.

All the misery going on outside, was exactly that, outside, inside "all together now, do you know this one", Great. We stopped at every shelter on the way home and joined in the fun. An evacuation plan was put into practice, and as there were seven of us children, two of the children were chosen to go. My brother Maurice and sister Margaret. My brother went to a Lord and Lady Derby and became a stable hand, my sister, to a farm near Lichfield. That farm made my war years a most wonderful pleasure. When my Dad took me to visit my sister on a coach, as I was growing up then, I was nearly 14, dad said I could go on my own in future. The smell and touch of the animals to me was sensational. The maid of the house brought me a pair of boots and putting them by the farm gate for my arrival meant I could get straight on with the mucking out, or whatever else needed doing. Milking, cleaning out Pig Stys, whatever. When you walked into the farm scullery, that was the maid's territory, all thoughts of wartime food rationing were really something to think about. There were sides of bacon, hams, half a sheep, pigs and pigs heads all hanging around the ceiling. Really unbelievable when one thought of the meagre amounts allowed to us with the handing over of our ration books. They didn't know there was a war on down on the farm.

Mr. Tom Blood and his two son's Tom and Henry and the maid Miss Bella Salt. I well remember one day collecting all the fallen fruit and hiding it in a bag in the hedge so that on going home I could take it home to the family. Silly me, when it was time to go Bella handed me a bag filled to the brim with chicken, cheese, butter, eggs you name it, it was in it. I could barely carry it, Tom carried it to the Bus stop for me, but to this day I wonder if when ploughing the field they wondered what a bag of fruit was doing under the hedge. I had an older brother who served in the Welsh Guards during the war, and for some time my mom was very worried because she had not had a letter. We had better than that, when my dad came in with the mail on his way home from work, because there on the front page was a picture of my brother sitting on a captured German ammunition dump found by our troops.

I wrote to the Mail telling the story of my missing brother and their front page item, and they sent us a beautiful picture of my brother which had the place of honour on my Mom's wall for a long time. I must admit on looking back, that one of the regrets I have about the war was, one day sitting on the front gate when a blonde headed young man passed on his bike. He gave me a lovely smile and I gave him one back. Telling my dad about it he said "No more smiles my love, he's a German prisoner of war". That did it, they were evil every one said so. I saw him often when he stopped to look around in the road. All he got from me was a scowl and nasty look, whilst pulling my tongue out. Poor soul, like our young men in our forces, he was called up to do a job whether he wanted to or not. He was still some mother's son.

If only I had said something nice to him instead of looking at him with such dislike. Oh well, that's war, as we call them the good old days. I think not.

Beatrice Samuels

A WHOLE NEW WORLD – A summary of a life changing day for two Birmingham schoolchildren in wartime

Having endured (& survived) 16 nights of consistent air raids in the garden Anderson air raid shelter, my sister Shirley and I went to school on the Tuesday morning. Shirley was approximately 3 years younger than me and I remember feeling responsible for her. I should explain that the reason I feel it was a Tuesday was because we had been down to our cousins, to play, at Stirchley, together with Mother. We must have travelled the short distance down by tram, and we were making our way back walking through Stirchley. As we turned the corner into the main street, just past the public house (The Oak?) the air was filled with the rat a tat tat of a machine gun. The sirens gave the alarm, Mother bundled us together with many others into the nearest shop for cover. This finest cut to the fresh fish shop, and the passage way that we huddled in was partly filled with wooden boxes of fish in ice. Before we were pushed further in, I clearly saw a German plane being chased by a fighter. I can still see the cross on the plane as it swerved way ahead over the Breedon Cross.

It seems that the German plane still had a bomb left, which it jettisoned to gain speed. The bomb landed amongst houses to the rear of Kings Norton railway station, and the house damaged was lived in by one of the managers of the engineering works where Dad worked, down Laurel Road. Within a few minutes everyone left their fish smelling shelter and carried on. We soon arrived home quite safe. Back to the School assembly on the Tuesday! For whatever reason, after the usual hymn, in the school assembly hall (Cotteridge School) we were not sent off to our classrooms. Nothing was explained to us, as I recall, but we walked back the short distance home, with a policeman! The knock on the front door was answered by mother who passed out a small cardboard suitcase each, and joined us with the policeman, to make our way down the road to the factory where our Dad worked. The Policeman disappeared inside, to reappear with Dad, who signed a piece of paper, and off we set again to Cotteridge School.

I have no memory of saying good bye to Dad or Mother who made her way back home. I knew we never went back into the house, which I thought rather strange. At the school some trams lined up waiting, but again we had to wait in the school. After a long time all the children with some teachers, boarded some double decker buses (the trams were still waiting, but not used). The buses made their way into Birmingham – years later it was said that it had been intended to evacuate by train but New Street Station had been damaged in the night raids, and there was an air raid taking place right then. The buses joined onto the main tram route further into town, there were three churches quite close to each other along Bristol Road. All three had been damaged at some time, but one was still burning. Across the road from the church, lorries and cranes were pulling a tram, what was left of it, out of the ruins of a shop window. The main streets were full of lorries and people, I can visualise them now pushing the remains of vehicles and rubbish into massive bomb craters. Trams in line, all with smashed windows were not able to move, no track left. I don't know the details of the bus journey, but we headed across country so to speak. Eventually arriving at the same railway station where we would have come originally by train. Many years later I came across the same station, Rolleston-on-Dove, near Burton on Trent. Now it is no more, due to the railway cuts.

We were all given mugs of tea and something to eat before our final move of the day.

Shirley, myself and the Simkin brothers from next door at home, and one or two others were put into a car (and really not very large we were all so crushed). We made a couple of stops, until there were only the four of us left. Next the Simkin brothers were taken up to a little house. When the man got back into the car, I remember him saying "I'll keep you two together if I can". The car travelled on along the country road for quite a while, Shirley and I sitting in the rear seat, clutching our gas mask and suitcase each. Coming to a stop at the gateway to yet another little house (a cottage, as we found out later) we were ushered indoors. An elderly couple were both in bed in the small front room bedroom, so we were told to "wait here while we get dressed".

Thus we two city children were literally dumped on a bed ridden couple. The billeting officer (for that is who he actually was) called at a farm house just down the road, and then came a rather upset lady, in a big apron. She came back to the house some time later with some sandwiches. I asked where the toilet was (big mistake), She took me outside to the toilet, where I had my first experience of an "Elson" chemical earth toilet (HORRIBLE). The couple in bed had a doctor's note exempting them from having evacuees, totally ignored. The lady from down the road (a Mrs. Hall) was a widowed farmer's wife with a family of her own. Mrs. Hall had been interrupted in the middle of evening milking. She appeared later and put us to bed, in a big double brass or iron bedstead with the aid of a candle in a candle stick. So we were introduced to the ways of country life. No one could have forecast that from these traumatic events grew such a happy childhood, at least for myself. Shirley returned home to Birmingham way before me. I stayed until after the RAF Fauld munitions depot explosion in 1944. I returned to the cottage after my military service, with my parent's agreement. I eventually bought it, but this leads to another chapter in my story!

Brian Johnson

EXPERIENCE OF MY EVACUATION

At the height of the blitz, when aged 9, my brother and I were among a number of children who left Birmingham. We and our parents had no knowledge of where we were destined. In late 1940 we left by a special train from Brighton Road station on the Camp Hill line and travelled via Whitacre, Nuneaton to Ashby De La Zouch.

At the reception centre, a couple from a village called Osgathorpe, Leicestershire selected us from the group. We lived in a house in its own grounds near the crossroads. Whilst there the aerodrome at Castle Donnington was built with squadrons of Wellington bombers stationed. Today, it is the East Midlands Airport. We did not experience any local bombing, but certainly much activity from whining aircraft overhead and distant gun fire from 'BIG BERTHA' at Derby. Distant fire glows in the sky could be seen where bombing was taking place. We returned home after April 1943 when bombing had almost ceased. The couple we stayed with were very pleasant. They looked after our welfare and the accommodation was excellent. I kept in contact with them till the lady passed on, in May 1974 and her husband in July 1993. Occasionally during a lull in the bombing we went home for a break and my parents would relate the damage caused by the bombing. No relatives killed or injured and only superficial breaking of the window panes to the house in Edgbaston by blast.

Some Historical notes on the Carlton Cinema. The building on the corner of Taunton Road and Dennis Road is recorded in Kelly's Directory for 1940 as Gordon & Co. Motor car body builders. It is now a carpet warehouse, as you may know.

In the book on cinemas in Birmingham. The Carlton is described as a Picture Theatre. It was designed by Horace G Bradley and opened in May 1928. It was the only city cinema with a lift between the foyer and the circle.

Following the bombing in October 1940, it was repaired by A.W. Rogers of the Victoria Playhouse Aston. The cinema finally closed 1968. It became a Bingo hall and then an Asian cinema until Christmas Eve 1981, when it became a venue for reggae concerts.

Brian Stead

BLITZ MEMORIES OF AUNT NELL

It would have been November 1941, the night of the big air raid in Birmingham. My Aunt, Rose Ellen Fowkes, known as Nell, was in the kitchen at the back of a terraced house in Belgrave Road, when the air raid siren sounded. She was in no particular hurry to leave the house to go down the shelter, and decided to risk it and finish what she was doing first. The back of the house took a direct hit from a bomb, and the house collapsed, taking Aunt Nell with it as she fell through the house into the cellar with the whole house on top of her. She was several months pregnant at the time. Hours later she was brought out of the rubble and laid for dead on the pavement. Her husband was away at the front, but her family was aware that she was missing, and checked the local listings of the dead, only to find her name was indeed amongst those lost that night.

As Nell's body lay on the pavement, awaiting collection along with the many others, a rescuer saw her eyes flicker, and an alert was shouted that someone here was still alive. An ambulance arrived and took Nell out of the city to the safety of a hospital in Bromsgrove. Her condition and the fate of her unborn baby were, at this stage, unknown. Her husband Reg, who was away fighting with the Army, was contacted immediately and given compassionate leave. He arrived by train at Birmingham a few days later, and although he was aware that his wife had been taken to Bromsgrove in Worcestershire, he had no means of transport and probably little or no money. It was late at night, snowing heavily – and it was during the blackout. He had no option but to walk – all the way to Bromsgrove in his army uniform.

He had no rations or water, so in desperation he stopped en-route at a pub in the early hours and knocked at the door. The landlord opened the bedroom window, but sent him on his way – no-one felt able to trust anyone during those difficult years, everyone was afraid of who a stranger might be, perhaps an armed German spy? He had no option but to melt some snow in his hands to quench his thirst. Eventually, after many hours on the road he arrived at the hospital. His wife had broken her back and was in a metal case in hospital for the rest of her pregnancy, but the baby, miraculously, had survived the ordeal and was born perfect, a girl called Jean, the following July. Aunt Nell also recovered and walked again, although always suffered from back problems. Aunt Nell had no belongings or baby clothes whatsoever, all lost in the raid. She has always talked of her gratitude to the American Red Cross, who sent parcels of baby clothes and other supplies, without which, trapped in hospital and her husband away at the front, she would have been virtually destitute. Aunt Nell is now 89, and lives comfortably in a nursing home – by coincidence in Bromsgrove near her daughter Jean, after living in Selly Oak, Birmingham with husband Reg for many years before that.

Carolyn Taylor

THE WAR (1939-1945)

I was with my family listening to the wireless when the news of the war was given out. It was September 3rd, Sid and I were courting at the time and Sid came around on his bike and we watched the first barrage balloon go up in Heybarn's Rec. Little did we know how long it would last. It was not long before Sid had joined up and was in the RAMC. We were not that serious when he went away but he started writing to me and when he came home on leave, on May 24th 1941, we got engaged. When he went back he was placed on a Hospital Ship. Leave was scarce and I did not see him very often. His Mom and Dad were bombed out and had to move to another house. We had an incendiary fall on our house and we had to put the fire out. It was down to the shelter every night and the habit was to take our tea with us. I worked at Wilmot Breeden who made all sorts of things like, mine-horns, cartridge belts and aeroplane parts.

I worked from 7am till 7pm. We planned our wedding for the 14th of February 1942. Sid had a weekend pass and we were married at St Benedict's Church at 12 o'clock. My dress cost 5 guineas; my Mother thought this was far too much to pay for a wedding dress. I had three bridesmaids, Sid's two sisters and my little sister. The bouquets were made of velvet roses; mine was in red and the bridesmaids in pink. My ring was 9 carat gold. Sid wore his uniform, as it was free. The reception was at Sid's sister's house in St Benedict's Road. The cake was chocolate sponge. We had to take a taxi to Lacey's Shop on the Coventry Road to have the photographs taken. After the reception we walked home to my Mom's as we were staying with her in Small Heath. After a grand weekend Sid went back on the morning of the 16th of Feb. We had lots of air raids as the war went on and on. It was very sad when we got into work and heard which work-mates and friends had been killed. Before going to Wilmot Breeden I had worked at Tuckers but it was bombed so everyone had to move to another factory. Sid's ship hit a mine on D Day and they had to abandon ship. They were picked up by another ship and returned to England. Everyone had to spend the night in prison as there was nowhere else to go. All I received was a piece of paper saying he was safe. I didn't get any letters for a long time. We still pull his leg about spending a night in prison. I had my first daughter on the 25th of January 1945. Sid was still in the army and he didn't see his daughter until she was 8 months old. We were in rooms for some of the time; we paid 5 shillings a week rent.

When Sid was demobbed we moved into a prefab in Hall Green. I had my second daughter on the 2nd of October 1947. Then after the war I had a son, Robin. We were so glad that the war was over and that Sid was home safe and sound. Now after 55 years married we still celebrate.

Daisy Harvey

AN EVACUEE

I was evacuated on the outbreak of war on the third of September 1939. For ages I had looked forward to going to Camp Hill School and now, having passed the exam, I still was not actually going to the school. It was some compensation to be going on a train journey for we didn't often do this in fact hardly ever. Little did I realise that I should be seeing a lot of locomotives during the next three months. So, although we met in the school at Camp Hill, off we went down Sandy Lane to Bordesley station, there to board a train to Warwick. From the train we walked to the junction of Broad Street and Wharf Street on the Emscote Road and congregated on a small island there while a master read out the names of foster parents and the addresses of billets. I was to stay with a Mr & Mrs Hayward and their five year old son Peter at 5 Guy's Cliffe Terrace. Next door, No 4, at Mr & Mrs Webbs were Gerald Harding and Mick Hodgson. My memories are mixed, as I didn't really get on with the Haywards although, in retrospect they were very good to me. I spent as many evenings as possible next door where there was a billiards table. What I didn't like was having to sleep in the same room with

Peter Hayward; he had a proper bed whilst I had to make do with a camp bed. There was some compensation though in the location of the house as I could sit on the doorstep and watch the trains go by. I also spent many mornings on Warwick station train spotting. To assist goods trains in particular up Hatton incline there was a tank locomotive in a siding alongside the main platform. Our delight was to help stoke its boiler and have a ride on the footplate up and down the platform. We used Warwick School in the afternoons whilst they had the buildings in the morning. All the first form was in Junior House. My form was 1b; we were allocated according to age. As far as I can remember the form list started: Adamson (Guy who was at Hall Green with me since the infants), Allen, Apps, Edkins (John who was in Miss Eddon's class with me and worked for Lloyds Bank), Fisher (Tom who was billeted at the corner of Guy's Cliffe Terrace and Broad Street at a wood merchants named Wise, became a school teacher), Freeman (his name was Peter but we called him Wig because he was always scratching his head), Gatty, Greatrex (Ron and Mike, both at Hall Green), Green, Harding (Gerald who lived in Wheelers Lane, Kings Heath), Harris, Haynes, Hickson, Hodgson (Mick), Hughes.

Most weekends were spent at home, We left school at 6.00pm and had just about enough time to run from the Myton Road to catch the train, There is a long approach from the Kenilworth Road to the station which would be lined with foster parents laden with dirty clothing (to be washed at home) and something to eat on the train. We picked this up in the same way that marathon runners take up drinks. On one Friday evening my father took me on the bus to Sparkhill to see my grandparents and I thought it strange that the inside lights had to be shielded. Much as I appreciated coming home, my parents came to see me some weekends. We would stay in Leamington in one of the beautiful Georgian houses in Newbold Terrace just off the Parade, which sadly no longer exist. I was allowed to stay up a little longer than usual and we often had fish and chips at the Cadena restaurant in the Parade. These weekends were highlights in my life. The only other time we visited Leamington was on a school visit to the swimming baths, which were next to the Pump Rooms. After changing back into our clothes we had to walk past the deep end. One day a boy was diving down to retrieve pennies as we watched him from the side, to this day I swear that someone pushed me, but I leaned over too far and fell in. About three people dived in to save me and the baths had a laundry where my clothes were dried and ironed. It was many years later when I learned to swim. In the autumn of 1940 my father thought that my safety was assured if I was evacuated overseas so plans were made for me to go to South Africa. All my kit was bought but I could not tell anyone where I was going for security reasons. On the day before I was due to leave, having said goodbye to all my school friends, we had a letter to say that the sailing was cancelled due to the sinking of another ship carrying children. It was not easy to return to school and there were times when I regret not having had this experience. My attitude to apartheid could have been influenced.

Derek Hickson

July 1940 I had my 5th birthday, and during august we had the first of many air raids. Our Anderson shelter was approximately two yards from the house so we did not have far to travel. My father worked during the day as an engineer producing shell and bullet cases. My mother also worked at the same company. Every evening when he was not fire watching he would be on duty as a member of the ARP (Air Raid Precautions). Later in 1942 he was made senior fire guard. Each evening as the Air raid siren started up mother and me, plus our nearest neighbour and her children took up residence in our small shelter. During one of the early raids an incendiary bomb fell next to our standpipe from which we collected our drinking water each day. In attempting to extinguish the fire, my father put sand into the hole made by the bomb, and used a neighbour's wooden line prop to pack down the sand.

In doing so he burnt the end of the prop. The lady who owned it was most upset with Dad for burning the prop, but offered no thanks for him for probably preventing her home from being damaged. The standpipe was out of action for a day so we had to use the one in the next yard. Several nights later a large bomb fell behind our house completely destroying the house it fell on, fortunately for us it failed to detonate. Soon afterwards a police officer came and told us we would have to evacuate our shelter in case the bomb exploded.

For the next two days we stayed with my grandparents who lived in Goodrick Street, while the bomb was diffused. During another raid a bomb landed at the entrance to our yard on the brow of the hill in Duddeston Mill Road opposite Vauxhall railway station (close to the junction where Melvina Road and Duddeston Mill Road now meet). My father and his mate went over to the bomb and once again dealt with it as they would any other incendiary not knowing that on impact with the road the bomb had fractured the gas main, causing it to leak gas. Thinking they had successfully dealt with the situation they proceeded to walk back towards our yard when the heat from the bomb ignited the escaping gas, it must have been a miracle that no one was killed or seriously injured.

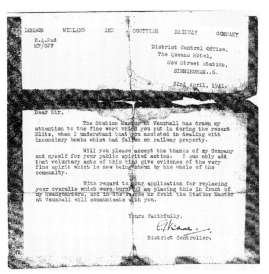

Reproduction of letter sent to Derek's father from LMS Railway Co.

London Midland and Scottish Railway Company
E.A.Pad
MF/CJV

District Control Office,
The Queens Hotel,
New Street Station,
Birmingham 6
22nd April 1941.

Mr. Samuel Simcox,
4/34 Duddeston Hill Road,
Vauxhall.

Dear Sir,
The station master at Vauxhall has drawn my attention to the fine work which you put in during the recent Blitz, when I understand that you assisted in dealing with incendiary bombs which had fallen on railway property.

Will you please accept the thanks of my Company and myself for your public spirited action. I can only add that voluntary acts of this kind give evidence of the very fine spirit which is now being shown by the whole of the community.

With regard to your application for replacing your overalls which were burnt. I am placing this in front of my Headquarters, and in due course no doubt the Station Master at Vauxhall will communicate with you.

Once again we were told we had to vacate our shelter and a police officer found us shelter in a nearby yard. I can still picture the flames coming from the gas main as they reached up to into the night sky and the memory has stayed with me all my life. Once again we were not allowed to return home after the all clear had sounded, so it was off to grans again, but on this occasion only for one night. Another incident I can recall happened after the all clear had been sounded. We had not long been in bed when I heard the drone of an aeroplane, and I knew it was German because their engines made a very distinctive sound. I called to my parents in their bedroom and told Dad what I could hear.

My father listened for a short time and told me to get dressed but before we could get down the stairs the sirens started up again and we all got back into the shelter again. Fortunately this time it was only a short stay before the all clear sounded and we all returned to bed. My father later told me that the plane we had heard was probably trying to make its way back to base after a bombing raid somewhere over England. Christmas 1940 my parents gave me the usual Beano, Dandy and film fun albums together with a fort and several dozen lead soldiers. How they had managed to acquire them at such a difficult time I never found out. Shortly after Christmas the air raids resumed and one particular night the bombs seemed to be falling thick and fast.

One bomb when it exploded appeared to be very close and someone in the shelter thought it may have hit one of the houses in our yard. On hearing this I turned to my mother and said I hope it isn't ours because my fort and soldiers are under my bed. My mother then said to the folk in the shelter did you hear what Derek just said, 'There's bombs dropping all over the place and all he's worried about is his fort and toy soldiers under the bed'. Thankfully no-one was injured or any property damaged in our yard that night.

Derek Simcox

THE TUDOR FAMILY

I, Doreen Elizabeth Howarth (maiden name Tudor) lived with my parents George Raynor and Elsie Annie Tudor, together with my four sisters Florence, Mary, Dorothy and Georgina, my last address being 30 William Street just a stone's throw from the hubbub of the city center. Little did I know then what life would have in store for me and also for thousands of others up and down the land during those war years and the repercussions would accompany me throughout the rest of my life. We were a happy, lively family and I remember Florrie, Mary and I going to St Thomas' Church and the school. It was September 1939 and I was six years old and Florrie, Mary and I were evacuated to a farm somewhere in the country – I have no idea where it was and on that farm we had to work picking apples and fruit in the orchard and carrying large white enamel buckets filled to the brim. We found it very strict there and the two women were quite uncaring and very menacing. I don't think we were there for very long and we went home to my

lovely mother and the two small sisters. I particularly remember missing my mother and Dorothy who was 4 years old.

I slept in a big bed with Florrie and Mary; bath nights were in front of a roaring fire in a galvanised bath and large shadows danced on the walls, which seemed to be very scary to us as small children. It must have been 1940 and then we were very much aware that there was a war on and in fact we were bombed out of our homes three times. The aftermath of these air raids I remember vividly was to see heaps of rubble where buildings had been bombed, trees adorned with pillows and bed linen, which had been hurled into the branches. After the third time we were bombed out we were all dug out of the debris by ARP men and taken to a police

Dorothy aged 4 yrs, Mother Elsie Tudor (killed 11th December 1940), Uncle Charlie (Hughes) – brother of Elsie. Photo taken in Birmingham 1940

station where we spent the night on benches and rough coconut rugs. I also remember the nights we spent in air raid shelters after being alerted by the air raid sirens which in themselves were very frightening. We heard the deafening sound of aircraft, bombs and incendiary devices; after the sound of the "all clear" we saw the awesome sight of searchlights lighting up the sky and the barrage balloons floating in the sky. These are the memories of a 6 year old. During the "peaceful" times I remember my mother who was a very beautiful lady and who I loved dearly; she spent time with us cutting "dancing ladies" out of newspaper and making jam in the kitchen. We had two dogs, some chickens and a horse upon which my father would lift me, and which in turn terrified me because I was so high up. We went to Dudley Zoo and fed the elephants. I adored my maternal grandfather, Henry Hughes who called me "Tuppence" and he would take me to his club and ply me with ginger beer, which I hated because it was "smokey". He lived in Bolton Road Small Heath and would take me down the garden to see the trains go by. I don't know when it was when we were evacuated again – Florrie, Mary and I, were taken to the railway station presumably by the schoolteachers, together with my mother. We took a few things in brown paper bags and had labels pinned on us giving our name, address and date of birth. I remember vividly even to this day leaning out of the carriage window of the train with my arms around my mother's neck, never wanting to let her go with the train pulling away and my mother running along the platform until she managed

Doreen aged 7 yrs with Mathilda Wallis (Aunt Til)

Doreen with Jim Wallis and his sister Elsie Wallis. Evacuated 1940. Pictures taken in Moira, Leicestershire

to free herself and telling me that "she would come and fetch me". I felt I had been torn away from my lovely mother and I felt a terrible feeling of loss and it was so bad I felt myself drawing into myself.

We eventually arrived in Moira a small mining village in Leicestershire being taken into the village hall (St Hilda's) near the tollgate. There was a spread laid out for us comprising food and drinks with a magician in attendance and I marveled at the doves coming out of his top hat and flying around the room.

Then people, mostly women, came into the hall and all the evacuees were lined up to be "picked out"; Mrs. Wright and her daughter picked me, together with a girl called Grace and we were taken away to a cottage in Stone Row. Florrie went with another woman and Mary to yet another woman, so we were separated and sent to three different places. I was put in a bath and scrubbed then put to bed with Grace. I felt very lost without my mother and my sisters. It was dark. A little time later I was fetched out of bed and taken downstairs where there were two other ladies. Mrs. Wright said to them 'you can have this little one; she won't be any good to me. I was dressed and taken down to another cottage a few hundred yards down the road. It was very dark no lights, cloudy sky, very quiet and the trees seemed very tall and frightening but one lady held my one hand and the other lady held my other hand. I was taken into "Coombes", Measham Road, Moira by these ladies one who I learned the next day was Aunt Til (the other one was her sister, Rose) and sitting in the small sitting room were two men, one of whom I found out the next day to be Uncle Jim the husband of Aunt Til, the other man being Rose's fiancé Wilf who was in a sailor's uniform.

Aunt Til (who of course was no relation) remarked that it was wicked to take a little gel away from her mam. They put me in a bath and scrubbed me again (no doubt because I was brown as a berry with dark eyes and hair) and they thought I could do with a bath! I slept that night in between Aunt Til and Rose.

I had no idea where Florrie and Mary were but I learned later that they were both billeted in separate homes in Stone Row near where I had first been taken. The next day Uncle Jim came home black as the grate and I was convinced he was out of the 'Water babies' – the sweep I guess, but I later learned that he was a miner. I went to Moira Council School, the complete number of pupils being about 20. I saw my sisters very rarely but I relished living in the glorious countryside, wandering the fields and making friends with the village children. So rustic and pastoral compared to the war-torn muddle of England's second city. My headmaster, Mr. Callier, who taught the juniors was my hero, he would invite me to have lunch with him one day in the week, which I chose to be a Monday because that was the day we had cold meat and mashed potatoes with turnips, and rice pudding, and as it was washday I felt really put out. With no rugs down on the lino floor because they had been taken up. Aunt Til cooked the most delicious meals on a Triplex green fireplace with the fire red hot with a kettle hanging above it on a hook and an oven on the left-hand side and a small oven (for puddings) above it. The sitting room was quite small by today's standards but I loved every inch of that cottage. The square oak table was in the middle with a one-arm sofa under the window, two dining room chairs under the table, a sideboard opposite the sofa with the other two dining chairs on either side. The sideboard boasted a Westminster chime clock, which chimed every quarter of an hour, and I loved it.

The kitchen was really a pantry wide enough to have white sink and running water with shelves on the wall covered in a wipe down material, which was cut on the edge to make a pattern. There was a thrawl, which was cold to the touch and served as a refrigerator. The place always smelled deliciously of cucumber and onion in vinegar.

A photograph of George and Elsie Tudor on their wedding day.

A newspaper report on the wartime deaths of George and Elsie Tudor.

There were three small bedrooms, the main one, and then my bedroom with just a bed in it and the box room, which always smelled of carbolic soap. One day two men came from Birmingham, they were my father's brothers but I never saw them; they had come to take us all back to Birmingham. My Aunt Til asked them to leave me with them, so off they went taking Florrie and Mary with them. It was to be many years before I saw them or heard from them again.

I used to write to my mother every week and give the letter to Aunt Til to post. I asked her every day when Mommy was coming and she always told me that because of the war, Mommie wasn't able to come. Daytime was all right; I was a normal happy little girl enjoying the countryside, going to school, playing with my friends. Nighttime was the worst, I was always looking for my mother and hearing her calling me but I could never find her. I wandered downstairs to find her but she wasn't anywhere to be found.

I was about 9 years of age, when I was given a box of chocolates by Mr. Callier my headmaster, these having been sent by the New Zealanders. When I finished school I was going back home when I was told by one of my school pals that the only reason I had been given a box of chocolates was because my mommy was dead. I pushed the box of chocolates into her hands, telling her to have them, then I ran home to Aunt Til who immediately knew something was badly wrong because I had changed from brown to white. I told her that Phyllis Sherratt had told me because I had been given a box of chocolates it was because my mommy was dead. Aunt Til took me on her lap, she felt soft and warm, and told me that mommy had gone to Jesus.

My mother, father and two small sisters were killed in a shelter in Holliday Street on 11th December 1940, during an air raid. I had a wonderful childhood with Aunt Til and Uncle Jim, they gave me the security I needed and I cared for them deeply. All the family embraced me as one of them. I attended Moira Methodist Chapel where life revolved around it. We had new clothes and shoes once a year to attend the 'Anniversary' whatever that was. Last year's new clothes were worn in the morning and the new ones in the afternoon and we all sat on the "platform" thinking our new clothes were the very best, my particular favorite being a dusky pink dress with coat and hat complete with long ribbons (to blow in the wind) and patent shoes.

We sang carols at Christmas. The first Christmas I was at Moira I sang at all the properties a little song I had learned at school in Birmingham and which went like this:

> God is our Refuge
> Be not afraid
> He will protect you
> During an air-raid
> Bombs may be falling

Danger is near
He will protect you
'Til the "all clear"

I went back to my Aunt Til's cottage, with my pockets bulging with pennies, tuppences, threepenny bits and sixpences. I was growing up and happy with Aunt Til and Uncle Jim.

Underneath the facade there was dreadful grief and sadness. After the war unknown to me arrangements had been made for me to go back to Birmingham to live with my maternal grandfather. The first I knew about this was when a children's officer and a great-aunt (Violet) came to collect me. Again, I felt that awful loss and the tearing apart of everything I knew and loved; the very same was when my mother was running along the platform those many years before. I was taken to my grandfather's house in Bolton Road Small Heath. I could remember him and he was shocked to see how much I was like my mother, his beloved daughter. There were strangers there and I didn't like the city – I longed to be back in Moira in the countryside and my beloved Aunt Til and Uncle Jim, all the families I knew and my friends. I don't know how long it was, I was with granddad, then with various aunts; suddenly the children's officer came to where I was living and took me across the city to Edgbaston where I was taken into a house where there was a man and woman and I was left there not knowing what I was doing there and who I was with. The man sat me on his lap and I knew then he was kind and gentle but I never took to the woman. I will not say too much about her but she was very, very strict and very cold and unloving. It was like walking on eggshells to be in her company. I was like Cinderella who never went to the ball. I was up early every morning getting the breakfast to take to her in bed. I did all the heavy housework, washing, going to school and shopping on the way back. I never knew what it was to have a meal on the table. I had to get something myself. I did all the washing and ironing. If I displeased her, always for no reason, I was locked in the dark pantry under the stairs. My life was a nightmare, full of despair, and grief. Pop was kind but he was unable to defend me against her wrath. I was well over 16 years of age and coming home from school one Friday afternoon I decided I could stand no more and would run back home to Moira and to my beloved Aunt Til and Uncle Jim. Saturday morning, my spirits soaring, I went to town down to the coach station, found the bus, which went near Moira and got on it. Having no money I told the conductor that Uncle Jim would pay the fare when we got there. I was taken off the bus into the Inspector's office, the police were called and I was taken back home. I was "grounded" for a month but during that time I ran errands to make enough money to get back to Moira. Again I ran way and did manage to get to Moira. I walked the three miles from Measham to Moira, I knew every blade of grass and ran to get there as quickly as possible. At the cottage, the home where my heart was, and the people I loved and cared for. I had never seen a man cry; they both cried and so did I, the first time for many years. They sat me at the table with something to eat and drink and I told them that I had come home and please don't send me back. I suppose it must have been quite some time later that day that the children's officer, a policeman and the dreaded guardian arrived.

I was sent upstairs out of the way. They took me back to Birmingham. I subsequently had a new children's officer who made sure I did not run away again. My school was informed and I was in a lot of trouble with "the guardian". I asked the children's officer where were my sisters and I was about 19 years of age, when Mary and I were reunited. She had been living with my father's sister since leaving Moira. It took until the early 1970s before I met Florrie – she had put an 'ad' in the paper asking my whereabouts. Mary and I have quite a good relationship but the years we had been apart have never been bridged. We have coped with the loss of our whole family but the three left, Florrie, Mary and I still remain the living victims of World War II.

In 1952 my guardians went to Australia, leaving me to fend for myself. I was nineteen years of age and decided again that I would go back to Moira to my Aunt Til and Uncle Jim who I had kept in touch with all over the years, seeing them as much as I was able. However my boyfriend decided that I would marry him, so I never did get back to live permanently in Moira. My guardians came back to England from Australia after 18 months, poor Pop dying not long after their return. She went into a residential home.

I was very happy being married and after four years my wonderful son Robert was born, followed two years later by my lovely daughter Jayne. Terrible tragedy was to follow, I lost my wonderful son Robert to a brain tumor at the age of 30 years (the same age as my father) and he too, leaving three little girls the same age as my sister and I when we lost our parents.

I continued to visit Aunt Til and Uncle Jim all of their lives, my Uncle Jim dying at the age of 64 (he was 30 when I first went to him) and my Aunt Til died at the age of 82. My 'roots' are still at Moira and I visit there still as Aunt

Til and Uncle Jim had a daughter in their 'old age' and she is Doreen also. We are like sisters. I was the daughter of their youth and Doreen is the daughter of their old age. It was a long, long time before I was told that Uncle Jim went to every court in the land to keep me, but was unable to do so as my grandfather was my next of kin and I was under the jurisdiction of the Social Services until I was 21 years of age.

Doreen Grocott (nee Tudor)

As a post-script to my memoirs I would like to add that I knew that to enjoy a good future, I needed a good education and I worked hard. Eventually I enjoyed a wonderful career in the West Midlands Police as a civilian secretary working for Maurice Buck (assistant Chief Constable Crime) and of course in the 1970s I was very much involved in the work concerning the IRA bombings in Birmingham, particularly those in November 1974 when the 'Tavern in the Town' and the 'Mulberry Bush' were bombed. It was then, as a mother, I realized the full extent of what my own mother must have gone through during the war and of the fear she felt for the safety of her children. I shall never be able to know and understand how she felt when she saw three of her children being taken away as evacuees all those many years ago; she has never been able to tell me. For myself, I will always remember that she promised to fetch me – I am still waiting for her to fetch me to this very day.

All my life I have remembered that little song I learned as a small child during those horrific war years –

God is our Refuge
Be not afraid
He will protect you…

Doreen Elizabeth Grocott

MARY'S WARTIME EXPERIENCE

I would like to pass on to readers my experience of the last war. I was barely five years of age when the war broke out. I was the middle daughter of five girls. The air raids used to really scare me and I dreaded the nightly sirens sounding, listening to the aeroplanes flying overhead and hearing bombs falling and people crying and shouting and dreading that we may be hit in our air raid shelter, in fact, we were bombed on three separate occasions. The third time we were all buried and luckily for us my uncle Ernie who knew we were in this particular air raid shelter, rescued us with a team of colleagues. We were taken to a local police station and spent the night trying to sleep on rough coconut matting. Not long after this incident, with my two elder sisters, Florrie and Doreen we were evacuated to a small village called Moira which is in Leicestershire. I can still visualise my mother crying bitterly (as we were) when she waved us goodbye. When we arrived at Moira we were lined up and 'chosen' by different ladies and taken away to their home. I didn't stay very long at Moira because an uncle came to fetch me and took me to live at his home which was a public house in Great Bridge. Once again I was very confused as I had never seen this uncle and auntie before or their daughter, Audrey.

Why didn't my own mom come to fetch me? Time went by and I constantly asked my auntie 'when was I going home to my mother and sisters?' She would tell me that my mother would be coming soon with a new doll for me; this reassured me. We spent many nights in the air raid shelter and again, I would be frightened when the sirens sounded to let us know that the German aeroplanes were on their way. The devastation after the bombing was dreadful; houses blown to the ground, clothes strewn into the trees and people tired and exhausted after a sleepless night. As I got older I had to carry out many jobs in the home and also make journeys delivering bottles of beer to customer's homes.

One day when I was about ten years of age I was in a local shop when I overheard two neighbours say "What a shame that poor girl's family have been killed." I ran home and asked my auntie if what I had heard was true and her reply was "Yes". I fled to my bedroom and cried all night long; my auntie never came along to console me. I used to ask questions about my mother, father and two baby sisters but my auntie said that she had never met my mother or sisters and had not seen my father for many years so could tell me very little. There were so many things I wanted to know but to no avail! The loss of most of my family has affected me greatly over the years. It was quite a number of years before I met up with my two elder sisters and because we were brought up by different families we had never had the close bonding that sisters should have. I did so miss the love that I feel my own parents would have given me.

I was lucky though when I eventually met a wonderful young man who loved me and I loved deeply. He made up for so much that had been missing in my life. We had three wonderful children who have all done well with their careers. I was fortunate to have been sent to Matthew Boulton College for two years and was made a Domestic Services Manager at Sandwell District General Hospital. Quite a number of years after my parents death I found out that they were buried at Yardley Cemetery and once we were in a position to afford it my husband and I had a headstone placed upon their grave. This gave me wonderful peace of mind. Sadly, my beloved husband died in 2003 and my elder sister Florrie earlier this year. Both would have been so pleased to have seen the long awaited memorial for the 2,241 civilians who died in the last war and unveiled in Edgbaston Street, Birmingham on October 8th 2005.

Mary Reynolds nee Tudor

MY WEDDING

It was a bleak winter's morning, January 18th 1941, as I walked alone from my mother's house in Curzon Street to St. Michael's Church in Moor Street, Birmingham. My brothers and sisters were all evacuated and my mother had not got a decent coat to wear to come to church with me. My husband-to-be, John was waiting for me with his brother Ross and his sister-in-law Norah, who were to be our witnesses.

There was no Nuptial Mass, no photographs and no white dress – in fact, I was married in black. You needed coupons for clothes and I had none. So I asked a lady who owned a small shop if she could get me a coat without coupons and she came back with a black coat in what was called at that time 'Princess Marina' style after the then, Duchess of Kent. It had a flared hem, a black velvet collar and black velvet buttons. I also wore a black velvet 'pancake' hat. The ceremony was performed by Father Daley and, afterwards we went across the road to a pub called Paddy Murphy's – long since gone. I don't think I had ever tasted alcohol then so Norah and I had a juice and John and Ross, a pint of ale.

We then said goodbye to Ross and Norah and they went home and we caught the tram to the 'Piccadilly' Picture House on Stratford Road. I can't remember the name of the picture we saw. After the pictures we went home to 32, Albion Street, Greet. I had acquired this house from a private landlord, having been told about it by a friend. The lady who was leaving it had just heard that her husband had been killed in France. There was a snag though. She had had the electricity put into the house herself and had also just had a ton of coal delivered – this was before coal rationing – and had new lino laid on all the floors. She was, therefore, asking for £100. I also had to find what was then called 'Key Money'.

I pondered the problem and went to my boss and asked him to lend me the hundred pounds and stop it out of my wages at so much a week; and he very kindly did so. (By the way, I worked for that boss for thirty-nine and a half years.) So, our wedding day was nearly over but that night there was a bad air raid and we spent the night down an Air Raid shelter next door to us at the Watsonia Sidecar Factory. And so our married life began and lasted for forty five years until John died in 1986. Although it was a turbulent marriage, the words "not compatible" were never spoken!!

Doris Burke

I would like to mention my Grandfather Thomas Arnold who was night-watchman at HP Sauce for many years including the war. It was a very responsible job as he had to patrol the whole factory site and check on the horses stabled there. As part of his salary he was given miniature bottles of the different sauces each month so we grandchildren took it in turns to be given one. The factory had bomb damage. I trained as a nursery nurse in the day nurseries which were set up during the war and afterwards, they were for children aged 6 weeks up to 5 year olds. We wore uniforms as they were run like hospitals with a Matron, Sister, Staff nurses etc. I did a Saturday job at Woolworths to earn money to pay for shoes, stockings, hair dressing and personal hygiene because we had to be clean and tidy, and expected to wear coat, shoes, handbag, hat, gloves to match when attending oral examinations. I received 12s–6d each Saturday; part of my duties was to count the sweet coupons into bundles of a hundred, which were then sent to the Ministry of Food.

Another one was on the ice cream counter when the blocks of Neapolitan flavour came in Strawberry, chocolate and vanilla. We had a silver metal plate with sections marked on it to go over the blocks, and then we had to cut the sections up to form wafers. My father was a keen gardener and grew vegetables with a few flowers among them; he used to share them out to people in the street to help the rations. We had to go out with the bucket and shovel to get the horse manure up from the street for the compost. I also remember having to go with the wheelbarrow to Cuckoo Bridge to get coal and coke for the fire.

Dorothy Bradbury

THE BLITZ ON SALTLEY 1940-41

Air minded from the age of 12, the school holidays of early 1940 provided the ideal opportunity to sit entranced watching Alex Henshaw and his team testing newly built Spitfires being produced at Birmingham's Castle Bromwich factory, located directly across the road from the aerodrome. In the Blitz, and like a good many more of the population, by the end of 1940, the family had already become uprooted courtesy of the Luftwaffe, which in its wake, was to create a permanent loss to friendships made in the carefree days of pre-war. Saltley (Birmingham) my birthplace would see its share of devastation, but with "Backs to the wall", and the inspiring Winston Churchill, we carried on. Tactics previously employed by the Hun had allowed their bombers to penetrate the early warning system, thus, now keeping the civilian population in a constant state of alert. By October 1941 we had moved on 3 separate occasions out of which we were yet again bombed, this time at an address in Kings Heath. The same night saw the City Market Hall in the Bull Ring put out of action. Meanwhile the local Civil Defence team, gave immeasurable service to the region of Saltley, combating death and delayed action land mines etc.

One of several such highlighted cases was the parachuted land mine that settled on a house in Reginald Road Saltley. For obvious reasons of safety

Photo-D57 Saltley Civil Defence Team St Saviour's School 1943

the local people were evacuated well clear of the area. On closer inspection, Naval mine experts discovered the menace lodged on the landing of the property, with a stethoscope type of instrument the team quickly detected the timing device ticking away madly. **Only one solution (SCARPER)** Just moments later on that same day, and from an eye witness crossing Saltley Viaduct in the direction of Alum Rock Road Saltley, a gigantic explosion from the unexploded mine was seen to lift a whole area of masonry (Reginald Road) hundreds of feet into the air.

Amazingly, only minor injuries were suffered by a couple of the Naval Team. Others would not be so lucky, for on the night of 23rd of November 1940, a family of five, Mr. & Mrs. Smallwood and their three daughters, who lived in Gate Street Saltley, received a direct hit on their Anderson Shelter. The bomb blast devastated a huge area of Gate Street and the adjoining Clayton Road (my birthplace). In earlier raids 4 other roads, Wright Road, Wavell Road, Berry Road and Teal Road, were also severely damaged by an activated landmine. Berry Road was in fact obliterated!

John Cope a local newsagent, who lived at no 2 High Street Saltley, habitually used his cellar for protection during an air raid, but on the 17th May 1941, the local Post Office, next door, was hit sending hundreds of ten bob and 1 pound notes skyward. Floating down like a storm of snowflakes, Police and the local Civil Defence Volunteers gathered up the riches and returned them to their rightful place. Scattered over a wide area, blackened coinage, would require treatment by the Mint to enable them to become acceptable as legal tender.

In a line of now demolished buildings, sadly the High Explosive Bomb killed John Cope. On a lighter note John's pet dog was rescued alive from the rubble. On the opposite side of Saltley Viaduct, and what was certainly meant for the Gasworks in Nechells Place, a High Explosive Bomb wrecked the nearby Carlton Cinema, ending an era of what many cinema-goers, myself included, who rated the Carlton as always showing the best pictures! It would also end the ritual of cinema manager Mr. Bailey, who always inspected the hands of local urchins before allowing entrance to his "Picture Palace".

At last year's memorial service to the 2241 victims of the Blitz, at St Martins in The Bull Ring, I was able to meet in person the hero of my youth, the amazing Alex Henshaw, whose – aerobatics during the 40s ensured every young man of that era, wanted to be a 'Spitfire Pilot'. Like my Father, we both had at different periods, the privilege to serve in the Royal Air Force at home, North Africa and the Middle East, sadly though, not as pilots.

P.S. Special thanks to Fred Hancocks (Wartime Civil Defence Messenger)

Ed Grocott Member of Heartland's Local History and BARRA Associations

When war broke out I was 17 years old, we lived in Grant Street Birmingham. We listened to the radio on Sunday morning to hear Neville Chamberlain, the Prime Minister, announcing that we were at war with Germany. The first air raids were in 1940, we spent many nights in the air raid shelters, and we ate our dinner down there many times. On the 19th November 1940 we were eating dinner, Mother, Father, myself and two younger brothers. We heard the planes; Father went outside and told us to take cover we went under the dining room table, just as the doors and window frames were blown in, I don't remember anymore about that night. The following morning a young man came and asked Father to go with him. Later that day Father came home with the news that my eldest brother Joseph Beddowes had been killed while on fire watch. He had a wife and a six month old son also names Joseph, who were also bombed out of their house in Bell Barn Road, that night. It was a very sad time, we found out at a later date my youngest brother (Billy) witnessed Joseph's body being recovered. This must have been very traumatic as Billy was just 10 years old at the time. Even today while talking about it he is in tears.

I married Glenn an American soldier at Yardley old church in 1945. I left England to join him in America on Easter Sunday 1946, travelling onboard the Queen Mary Liner with other wives and children going to America. I have lived in Livonia Michigan USA ever since.

Elsie Isaacson 'nee' Beddowes

THE "BLITZ". BIRCHES GREEN 1940-1943

Our family lived at No 29 Bracken Road, on the Birches Green Estate. There was Dad, Mom, Harry, Joan, (Myself) Fred, Ellen, Amy and Sheila. It was a lovely estate, with its own School, and because it was built (in 1929) for families from inner city areas of Birmingham there were lots of children, to fill the School. As estates go, it was very small and all neighbours got on very well together. When the war started, I was working at Fort Dunlop, as office boy in the Traffic Office. I used to think at that time "Jerry" would never bomb "Brum" because it was too far from Germany, but I joined the Dunlop 165 Squadron of the Air Defence Corps, later to become the Air Training Corps, to train to become air crew in case the war lasted long enough for my services to be required. In early 1940, after work, my time was spent learning what I could about ARP, how to use Stirrup Pumps, how to put out Incendiary Bombs, and indeed to be as much help as I could in any emergency. Air Raid Shelters were delivered to every house, with sandbags, stirrup pumps, and ladders. Shelters were made as comfortable as possible, but as the floor was soil it invariably got very muddy, however later we made some duckboards from old pieces of wood, and later the Council concreted the floor and sides. "Be prepared" was the official slogan, and indeed we were. Air Raid warning sirens started during the first few months of 1940, with the Dunlop Hooter, known to locals as the "Dunlop Bull", doing its best to get people out of bed and down the shelters. Our Mom got Sheila, Amy, Ellen out of bed, wrapped them up as warm as possible, and took them down the shelter, sister Joan helped our Mom, and brother Harry and myself used to stop in bed. Dad was on permanent nights at Dunlop. Harry and myself used to worry our Mom to death, but as the months went by, we saw sense, and we used to get up as soon as the sirens sounded.

Up till August nothing happened, but about the middle of August sirens had sounded, Mom and my sisters were down the shelter, Dad was at work, Harry and myself were in the garden, when following the drone of Aircraft engines there were three loud explosions. This was our first Air Raid, with bombs dropping on Rookery Park, Wood End Road, and I think Lydford Grove. The following morning I went to Rookery Park to see what had happened, there was a crater about 4 yards in diameter and about 2 yards deep, lads were already there looking for shrapnel, this was the first bomb dropped on "Brum". Raids started to increase in frequency and length during 1940 (13 hour raids were common), and because of the Birches Green Estate's close proximity to Fort Dunlop, and the Castle Bromwich Aircraft Factory, and being situated on the north eastern side of Birmingham, there were not many nights when the sirens did not sound. Bombs started dropping on Birches Green during the latter part of 1940, one close to Birches Green School where my future sister-in-law lived, another in Kingsbury Road and Inland Road, houses were destroyed in all instances, and families were taken to the local Bus Repair Station until other accommodation could be found for them. At the start of 1941, most of the family's eldest sons, had either been called up for National Service or had volunteered. Sons in their teens such as myself were still at home, and most of the men folk were in the ARP Services, and others in the LDV. There were no uniforms, but tin hats were issued and arm bands with the letters LDV for Local Defence Volunteers, jokingly we used to call them the Look-Duck-and-Vanish Brigade, but what a wonderful job they all did, this later became the homeguard. In 1941 raids increased, and all bombs dropped caused more substantial damage, it got to the stage when during heavy raids sirens sounded at about 6.00pm and the all clear about 7.00am the next morning.

As the sirens sounded we looked at the sky and if the moon was visible used to say "it looks like a bombers moon we could be in for a 'Big Un' tonight" on most occasions we were right. On one such night, Harry and myself were on Fire Patrol, the raid was well under way Dunlop had been hit, Castle Bromwich Aircraft factory had been hit plus other surrounding areas, Pype Hayes and Erdington, when a sound which we had never heard before, like the rushing of an express train brought our first major incendiary bomb attack on the estate, hundreds of incendiaries were scattered over the estate. Wardens, neighbours, Fire Patrols seemed to appear from nowhere, and within a short space of time all visible incendiaries were covered with sandbags, some bombs went through the roofs of houses, but stirrup pump skills soon put them out also. Fire damage to houses was, unfortunately substantial.

This year was the worst, spirits of the local people was magnificent, and their humour despite all what was happening was brilliant, this humour showed itself, by the regular visit by an elderly woman neighbour who used to pass our house on her way to the local pub (The Norton). I don't know what she used to drink, but she always seemed to be lets say "slightly" inebriated. She always stopped to talk, and was always trying to get anyone around to join her in singing "Old faithful we roam the range together", everyone used to call her "Old Faithful". Before she left us to go to her home in Hartwell Road her last words were in typical Brum "Adolf ain gooin to keep me out of my bleedin bed". This sadly was soon to be her downfall. It was the 11th April 1941, the worst night I can remember, it was a cloudless night sirens had sounded early and bombers had started to arrive during the evening, the first of which dropped flares and incendiaries which fell on local factories, and other estates. Heavy "Ack Ack" guns opened up as each plane came over, with shells from the local battery sited on the edge of Spring Lane Playing Fields whistling above our heads, in effect "all hell was let loose", planes following up dropped their bombs, and it was obvious the main targets were Dunlop and the Spitfire Factory, the constant drone of the aircraft seemed endless. Mom, Ellen, Amy, and Sheila were in the shelter, I was in the back garden in front of the shelter with a mate of mine Jimmy Boot, sister Joan had left the shelter to go to the outside toilet. We were told that the one bomb to get you, you will not hear. I never heard this particular one, other than a sudden rushing of wind, and being lifted bodily in the air, I was in fact blown up.

I landed on top of my mate, and the only thing that saved us was our neighbour's shelter which was in direct line between us and the bomb. Mom, and my sisters were obviously in shock and Sister Joan who was in the toilet, had the ceiling of the toilet fall on top of her. Jimmy Boot and myself went to see exactly what had happened, our Mom and sister Joan despite being shocked got together with other neighbours and did what they could to comfort the Clarkes, Taylors and the Meades. The bomb had landed in the garden of 19 & 21 Bracken Road, the crater was at least 12 yards across and about 6 yards deep, lying by the back door of No.19 was Mr Clarke, who was being attended to by a warden, who said he was dead. In the garden of No.15 Mr Taylor was screaming with his leg hanging off and blood covering his face, a stretcher was not available, but the back gate of No.23 which had been blown of its hinges was used to carry him to the First Aid Centre at the bottom of Bracken Road, he was in a critical condition and lost his leg and an eye, Mrs Meades was in her kitchen at No.23 unconscious, we could not get her round, but our Mom said I'll go and get some of your Dad's "Brandy", he always kept a small bottle for emergencies.

A small spoonful of brandy soon brought her round, but after licking her lips, she quickly lapsed back into unconsciousness, a further spoonful brought her round again. Jimmy and myself then went up Summerlee Road as we were told Hartwell Road had been hit, four houses completely destroyed, including poor "Old Faithful's" she had lost her battle with Adolf. There was not much we could do, neighbours and wardens were digging amongst the rubble, five bodies were recovered, all had died. On our way down Summerlee Road we noticed a large hole in the side of one of the houses, which we pointed out to one of the Wardens. He investigated and found that a huge bomb had gone through the floorboards of the house, the tail fin of which could be seen deep into the ground, it was a delayed action. Immediate evacuation was ordered with the whole of Summerlee Road cordoned off. The following afternoon at about 5.00pm the bomb exploded, completely destroying four houses. Debris was scattered everywhere, some housebricks even landed on the green in Bracken Road. Houses in Ismere Road, Quorn Grove, Danby Grove, Spruce Grove also suffered damage as a result of these three bombs, the largest dropped on the Estate. On his return home on the 12th April, after his night duty at Fort Dunlop, our Dad said he had heard that Birches Green had been hit, and it worried him. He was shocked to see the damage in Bracken Road, including our own house, kitchen ceiling down, toilet ceiling down, every window broken, garden fences down, we were alright, that was the main thing.

On being told about Mr Clarke and Mr Taylor, he was of course saddened, but when our Mom told him about Mrs Meades, and the fact that she had given her some of his Brandy, his typical brand of Brummie humour came out "she only kept passing out all the time, so she could keep having my bleedin' brandy". Sadness and humour, what a contrast, but how could people have kept going without a mixture of both. There was no let up to the raids, and a further heavy one late in the year brought another incendiary attack, with hundreds scattered over the estate. The house next door No.31 Bracken Road had one through the roof and two houses in Elmwood Road also had an incendiary through each roof, the ones that fell into open spaces were quickly extinguished by sandbags, but where houses were on fire, neighbours using stirrup pumps, and the AFS dealt with these very efficiently, and no major fires occurred. At No.31 Bracken Road the bedroom was on fire and brother Harry and myself put our stirrup pump skills to the test, Harry used the nozzle, I used the pump and members of the Roberts family and ours kept us supplied with buckets of water. This team effort put the fire out, and made the bedroom safe in about twenty minutes. This sort of team effort was repeated more or less simultaneously at other houses with similar circumstances throughout the estate.

It was later learned that the incendiaries were of the "Anti-personnel" type, each one had an explosive charge on the end. The one in No.31 Bracken Road did actually explode, but fortunately we were shielded by the bedroom door. A school mate of mine was not so fortunate in attempting to extinguish one with a sandbag, it exploded, and blinded him. He was just sixteen. From the first bombs in 1940 to the end of raids in 1941, I have related what happened during the hours of darkness, but life during daylight was a constant worry. How our Mom coped I do not know, but of course all families were the same. Rationing was a major problem, our Mom always managed to sort something out for us, from the meagre allowances. The slogan "Dig for Victory" helped people to make the effort to help themselves. Our Dad had an allotment at the back of the "Forget-me-not" Club in Tyburn Road. I helped to plant and dig it, with the main vegetables being potatoes, "Late and Early" cabbage, sprouts, carrots, parsnips, peas, beans, and turnips. This certainly helped to supplement our rations. I used to love carrots, and I ate lots of them.

There were comments made over the radio that carrots can make you see better in the dark. Whether or not this was fact I do not know, but it didn't seem to make any difference to me, during Air Raids, it was still damn dark. Certain foods, our Mom just could not get eggs, tomatoes, bananas, oranges and many others. Our Dad always did what he could, and one day, I think it was late in 1940, he said "I'm goin' to get some hens". "Okay Dad" I said I'll make a pen. I got some old packing cases from the salvage department at Fort Dunlop, for a few shillings and made a pen and run. On completion me and our Dad went to the Bull Ring Market, and bought six hens. They soon got used to the pen, and within a few days our first eggs were laid. As we had hens we were allowed to purchase chicken meal, which our Mom mixed with old scraps and boiled potato peelings. The hens loved it, and to supplement their food we used to let them out into the garden. The supply of eggs increased, and from these six hens we used to average at least 2 dozen per week.

As time went on further hens were bought, and our average number then increased to ten from which we averaged 5 dozen eggs per week. I was in personal charge of the hens, and I made sure that as some got older, new ones were introduced. In one batch of new ones we had six Rhode Island Red Chickens; five were hens and one cockerel. This cockerel grew and grew, and indeed it used to keep all its family of hens in order, and they always looked very contented. He was so jealous of his family that the only two people who could get anywhere near them was me and our Mom, sisters Joan, Ellen and Amy could not go in the garden unless they had a broom or stick to protect themselves. Ellen and Amy bore the brunt of his attacks. It used to cause great amusement. The older hens, ones after their laying days ceased, gave our Mom the wonderful opportunity for making chicken stew. Not content with hen eggs our Dad suddenly decided he would like us to have some duck eggs, as these were supposed to be full of vitamins. He came home one Sunday after his regular weekly visit to the "Forget-me-not" Club, with a cardboard box in which were six Khaki Campbell day old Ducklings. These are for our duck eggs he said. They were looked after very well, and as the months rolled by, they got bigger and bigger, with our Dad saying, "should be some eggs soon". Oh, what a shock was in store for him, one of his friends came round to see him, and after seeing the six lovely ducks, as our Dad called them, he said "you ain't expecting any eggs off them are you Harry (our Dad), they're all bleedin' drakes". One by one they each in turn contributed to our Moms lovely beautiful roast duck dinner, followed a few days later with duck stew made from the bones.

Trying to feed their families was very difficult for the mothers of Birches Green, but in some way it brought them all much closer together. Certain items of food became available on occasions, if you were in the right place at the right time, and it became more or less a duty for mothers to inform each other when they did become available. It was a regular occurrence for our Mom to rush to the local greengrocer (Turners), after the word had been spread around that they had some tomatoes, or indeed fruit or other vegetables in short or scarce supply. Long queues were commonplace, but mothers did not seem to mind, it gave them the chance to talk to each other about their families. 1940-1941 saw our family following the general pattern of all others.

Harry had his medical, and went before a selection board in early 1940 and because of his qualified skill as a fitter with the LMS Railway; the panel suggested he should join the Royal Navy as an Engine Room Artificer. Shortly afterwards his calling up papers arrived, but as his work was considered to be a reserved occupation, he did not have to go. Ellen and Amy were evacuated to private homes in Ashby-De-La-Zouch, despite our Dad's protestations, that he wanted our family to remain together. However, their stay was only for a short period, they got so homesick that they had to come home. Joan was still doing what she could at work and helping our Mom at home, but she was always wishing she could join the Forces. I myself carried on my ATC Training, and also during this period I joined the Dunlop Fire Brigade Section of the National Fire Service. Mrs. Griffiths our next door neighbour at No.27, lost her son-in-law, killed in action (he was a Spitfire pilot). Mrs. Fletcher's son came home wounded from Dunkirk, and Bob my brother-in-law, husband of my eldest sister Lil also came home from Dunkirk, only to be sent abroad with the 8th Army again after his leave. Lil lived in the neighbouring estate of Pype Hayes with her young son. The testing of Spitfires by Alec Henshaw and his team of pilots over the estate was to me a joy to watch, climbing, diving, looping, rolling, every possible aerobatic was performed, one thing was certain, every Spitfire handed over to the RAF was in perfect condition. This also highlighted the skills of workers at the Castle Bromwich Aircraft Factory. 1940-1941 certainly proved to be very harrowing and eventful years. 1942 opened up, in similar pattern, but the use of further aids to protect factories did cause added problems and discomfort to local residents. Smoke screens were the worst. These were similar to dustbins, but with a chimney instead of a lid, each one was filled with diesel type oil. They were placed on pavements throughout the estate, and dependant on wind direction, they were set alight by soldiers, and within a short space of time thick black smoke came belching out of each one.

A pall of smoke soon covered the area. In addition mobile screens mounted on army lorries were also introduced, and when these were set alight, I should say the amount of smoke from each one, must have been a least fifty times more than the single screens. No doubt it did block out the factories from aerial view, but after their use, everyone had sore eyes, coughs, everything in the houses smelled of oil, and the clothes you wore stank for days afterwards. We hated this method of protection, probably because it was self imposed, and caused such distress. However, if it did help to detract bombers from their targets, then it served its purpose. I personally thought it didn't make any difference, smoke screens or not, bombs still continued to drop on Birches Green.

A balloon barrage operated from a unit sited in Rookery Park, which we used to call our own and got struck by lightning, and set on fire. The unit crew tried frantically to winch it in to prevent this huge ball of fire falling onto our houses. This they did quite successfully but it was quite frightening to see this ball of flame swishing to and fro across the estate. During one raid before the introduction of smoke screens it was a clear full moon night. Suddenly a bomber appeared in full view directly passing under the moon. Within seconds is seemed as though every "Ack Ack" gun in Birmingham opened up. We could actually see shells exploding around the plane, firstly by red dots of fire followed by puffs of smoke. For sometime afterwards shrapnel from shells fell onto houses and into gardens. I do not know what happened to the bomber, but if it was not brought down, the intense barrage must have put "the fear of God" up the crew. Our hens (kept fit by Karswood Poultry Spice) continued to do there bit for the war effort with a constant supply of eggs. Our Mom used to give our neighbours (Rose Griffiths and Elsie Roberts) the occasional one or two, and our record supply in one week was sixty two. We did eventually get some duck eggs. Our neighbour a Mr Cope at No.17 had a solitary Khaki Campbell duck. I felt really sorry for this duck it looked half starved and scruffy. He offered it to our Dad for a couple of bob, and then it was left to me to look after it.

Our duck soon got to look nice and healthy, and was laying an average of four eggs per week. The awkward part though was she kept laying some of them under a bush in Mrs Griffiths garden. We sorted this out by occasionally giving Mrs Griffiths one or two of them. The family took it in turns to have a duck egg (for extra vitamins) to keep our Dad happy. Our Joan volunteered for the Women's Royal Air Force, and in August I was told to report for my medical and appear before a selection board. I passed the medical A1, and was asked by the selection board which one of the Armed Forces I preferred. My answer the Royal Navy surprised them especially after my ATC training, but that was the service I chose. My ATC mates asked why, but to me the Battle of Britain had been won and my enthusiasm to be a pilot had waned, and after seeing the Navy in action on Newsreels I decided this was the service for me.

I just wanted to help to end the war, and as the war was spread throughout the world the Navy seemed to be the obvious service. Entertainment for the Estate centred on the local Cinema (The Apollo), it never closed and did matinees on Saturdays for the younger children. A large number of evening performances were disrupted by sirens and explosions of bombs, but the performance carried on and across the screens was flashed "There is an air raid in progress, if anyone wishes to leave, please do so as quietly as possible" not many people took advantage of this request. The nearest the Apollo got to being hit was when the "Constructors Factory" opposite the Norton Pub was set on fire. This was some fifty yards from the Cinema. People's attitude at this stage in the war was "If a bomb has got your name on it you'll get it wherever you are". 1943 started with the war being spread throughout the world. Air Raids seemed to be easing off, with more of the men folk being called up. The Yanks were more in evidence with everyone of them seeming to have a "Jeep" of their own. The kids were constantly chewing gum given to them by the Yanks after their requests of "Got any gum chum". Tinned meats such as "Spam" "Mor' 'Tang" to name but a few became more plentiful, easing some of the food problems of Mothers. Dried eggs also helped.

The Estate population had reduced to being just Moms, Dads, daughters and young children. During this period hardly a house on the Estate escaped damage of some sort, Complete Destruction – Heavy Structural Damage – Minor Structural Damage, (Tiles off Roofs), (Broken Windows), (Collapsed Ceilings), (Fire Damage), (Water Damage), (Burst Pipes) and (Shrapnel Damage).

If medals were given for Courage and Resilience, then each and everyone on the Estate deserved a sack full. This is as it was. Of the original intake of pupils at Birches Green School in 1930 at least 80% of boys had either volunteered or had been conscripted to the Armed Forces, and at least 20% of the girls had volunteered for the Women's Services, Nursing, Land Army, or other Civil Defence duties. Others worked in the local factories – Dunlop – Castle Bromwich Aircraft Factory – Schraders – Valor – AMAC being the main ones. To me these three years showed that whatever the adversity, community spirit, with the urge to help each other overcame any problems that arose. No one wanted the war but in some ways for all that happened, it made each and everyone more aware of the need for compassion and understanding. I was glad to have spent these three years within my family circle and amongst neighbours and friends. My eighteenth birthday was on March 11th and shortly afterwards I had my calling up papers for the Royal Navy. Except for a few days leave, and embarkation leave that was the last I saw of Birches Green until the end of my Demob leave in November 1946. However that is another story.

Fred Overton; Erdington, Birmingham
A 'Blitz' story of the Norton family who resided at 12 Osborn Road, Sparkbrook, Birmingham 11, during that period Ada and Fred, son George and his Uncle Walter.

A SCHOOLBOY'S STORY

As a 10 and a half year old at the start of WW2, we were all in anticipation of what and when the outcome would be. We had to wait until Thursday August 8th. 1940 before the first bombing raid on Birmingham, when four people were killed, and ten wounded. No warning was given, which meant that I slept through it.

Living very near to the BSA factory, it was obvious that we would be in a prime target area. The bulk of the seventy seven raids on Birmingham, coming in the following nine months. It would be difficult for me to recall every incident over that period, so here are some of my most outstanding memories, plus dates if known.

The night the house three doors away was burnt out by an incendiary bomb the occupants were away,with my Father remonstrating with a near neighbor screaming and shouting in the garden that we're all going to die. During a raid one night we were shaken by a tremendous thud, which shook the air-raid shelter violently, bringing cascades of earth down inside. My parents and I looked at each other silently waiting for an explosion that never came. It was caused by an unexploded bomb, which wasn't found until after the war. At this point I will add that I was never evacuated, as my Father wanted the three of us to be together. Plus his youngest brother, who lodged with us, and not forgetting Patsy the dog. As there was no regular schooling during this period, us school children would do the daily rounds of collecting shrapnel and bomb or shell cases or help friends that had been bombed-out try and retrieve anything from the rubble.

After breakfast one morning, following a raid, I noticed a gathering of people down the road. On investigation I was told by a bomb disposal soldier to keep clear as an unexploded bomb (UXB) had been found in the pantry of a house in a Croft nearby. Within seconds of his warning the bomb exploded scattering everybody in all directions as debris went flying through the air, sadly killing two bomb disposal men. Anytime I had a restless night in the shelter, and my parents had dozed off (we had 3 bunks and a box for the dog), I would slip out into the garden to see the 'action'. One such night it would have been possible to read a newspaper due to a local factory on fire. Suddenly, an aircraft came swooping very low over the rooftops firing their machine guns and killing some firemen. This disturbed my parents who roused to see me diving head first into the shelter. I was really in trouble, and had a good telling off. Very often, when there was a lull in a long raid (one lasted thirteen hours), and waiting for the next squadron of bombers, we would go into the house, usually to make fresh tea, my Father and myself went out into the road where we chatted with a local ARP Warden. It was a very moonlit night; we used to call it a bombers moon, when one of us noticed a parachute hovering above the roof tops. Our immediate reaction was that it was an aircrew member that had baled out, but a second look told us that it was a land mine. We stood there petrified, and rooted to the spot, as it passed over us and out of sight beyond the rooftops. The story goes that it travelled a considerable distance on the wind, and did not explode when it eventually landed.

I witnessed a most unusual incident on Thursday 21st November 1940. About midday while out shopping with my Mother in Sparkhill, on the corner of Stratford Road and Durham Road, I heard the familiar drone of a German aircraft, there about 2,000 feet directly above us was a Junkers Ju88. When I brought it to the attention of my Mother, her reply was, what, at this time of the day, it must be one of ours. No sooner had she uttered the words all the anti-aircraft guns in the area opened up. Everybody in the vicinity was ushered by a soldier into a nearby greengrocer's shop where we watched the shrapnel bouncing off the road and hitting the roofs. I gave myself ten out of ten for aircraft recognition. This particular aircraft was eventually shot down by a Hurricane of No.79 Squadron into the sea off Strumble Head, Fishguard. None of the four crewmen survived. Incidentally, the shrapnel was too hot to pick up at the time.

An amusing story regarding Ack-Ack Guns was during a brief lull one night we had popped into the house. We then heard, in the distance, the next wave of bombers approaching. Suddenly there was an ear shattering bang, Father shouted what on earth was that and shot out of the front door, with me in hot pursuit. A few yards from our house, on the crossroads, they had set up a mobile AA gun. My Father, who was rather displeased, requested that they take it somewhere else as it was bringing all the slates off the roof, and it was bad enough having to put up with the noise of the bombs. They moved it shortly afterwards, much to the relief of everybody in the vicinity.

A friend of mine and his parents had a very lucky escape one night. I went round to their house early one morning, although the fronts of the houses in Barrows Road looked alright, as I turned into their entry I was confronted by a mound of earth. Managing to climb through a small gap at the top, I was greeted by a scene of total devastation. A land mine had dropped on several air-raid shelters at the bottom of gardens between Barrows Road and Fallows Road, demolishing the rear of all properties in the area. There was not a soul to be seen, and it was very eerie. As I stood staring at the remains of my friend's mangled and twisted shelter, a voice called me from the remains of their house. It appears that they had just popped into the house, and sat down in the front room when the bomb landed. Somebody was certainly watching over them that night. The raids didn't vary in timing all that much. Usually starting just after tea, until varying times in the middle of the night. We had our own early warning system in Patsy the dog. She always detected the approach of aircraft before the sirens had sounded, and stood whimpering by the kitchen door. As soon as you opened the door she would dash off down the garden, and was always first in the shelter, where she would remain until the all clear sounded. She was totally confused one night when a direct hit on the BSA works set the all-clear siren off, and they weren't able to switch it off for several hours. My Father and Uncle both did their regular stints of fire-watching at their places of work, my Mother always worried on those nights, and she and I would always go into neighbours shelters.

She also worried if the sirens sounded before my Father came home from work, especially if the bombs started dropping before he arrived. My Uncle would never go in air-raid shelters, I think he was claustrophobic, although he was trapped in the cellar of a public house one night for several hours. As there was beer on tap, we didn't have any complaints from him. On another occasion he was travelling on a bus during a raid when the driver pulled up and asked all passengers to go to a nearby shelter. My Uncle decided to curl up on the rear seat on top deck for a doze.

Sometime after the driver and conductor came out to check their bus as a bomb had landed nearby. Although the bus was still standing upright, all the windows had been blown in. They discovered my Uncle still fast asleep, and covered in glass. He was awakened by one of them shouting, "Hey, there's a body up here". Imagine the shock they had when he sat up asking what was going on. My Mother went through the Blitz taking everything in her stride; I never saw her panic over anything. Her favourite comment was "what will be will be" and she always retained her sense of humour. Father was quieter and more thoughtful, and didn't admit until after the war that he was terrified throughout. Probably because he was wounded in the trenches in France in the First World War.

On the evening of Wednesday April 9th 1941, my Father was fire watching at his works and my Uncle went off for an evening with his pals, my Mother and myself went to stay the night with nearby friends, and the dog guarded the house. That particular nights raid commenced at 9.45pm until 2.05am on the 10th. The aircraft used were a mixture of Heinkel HE111 and Junkers Ju88, a total of two hundred and thirty seven in all, dropping two hundred and eighty five tonnes of High Explosive (HE) Bombs, and Forty thousand Incendiary Bombs.

When the sirens sounded we retired with our friends to their shelter, back at home my Uncle returned from his evening out about midnight, settled down on the settee in the living room, and the dog jumped up beside him. At approximately 12.30am the house received a direct hit from a HE Bomb. Had my Uncle not have spoken to a local Warden before going into the house, we would not have known that he was buried under the debris. My Mother and I were duly informed, and somebody got a message to my Father at his works. The rescue party eventually found out that Walter was still alive, erected a cover over the spot where they could hear him, and used a low powered light. They had to be careful, as there were still a lot of bombs dropping in the area, plus a lot of loose overhanging debris falling. They had to dig very carefully for several hours, and Walter remained conscious the whole time. The only time he got worried was when he heard somebody say they thought they could smell gas. Eventually the hole was big enough to retrieve Patsy the dog, who came out unharmed. My Uncle's rescue was rather more complicated as they had to saw through furniture, wooden joists and a staircase; he was also trapped by his legs. It took them about three hours to extricate him. Luckily, without injury, but covered in brick dust. He looked like a ghost. The rescuers, Senior Warden Charlie Rudge, Warden Charlie Bowker and Police Constable Geoffrey Canning, were all awarded the British Empire Medal (BEM) for their wonderful effort of saving my uncle's life, for which the family were eternally grateful. A report of the incident appeared in the London Gazette dated 20/6/1941.

The reason for Walter's miraculous escape was that the bomb hit the front of the house, pushing the staircase over the settee, on which he and the dog were lying. The staircase landed on, and was supported by, the iron-framed upright piano standing against the wall near my Uncle's head, forming a small alcove. The house (No.12) was totally destroyed, and numbers 10 and 14 lost their upper floors. After moving in temporary with nearby friends for a couple of weeks, somebody found us accommodation to rent in Hall Green. My parents and myself moved in with Patsy, but Walter found himself some lodgings a few doors from our old bombed house. One evening shortly after we had moved into our new house, the sirens sounded. Mother said "What are we going to do, we haven't got a shelter?" Father replied "Don't worry, they don't drop bombs in this area". Within minutes a stick of bombs straddled the area, one demolishing a house nearby. Mother was not amused, and Father was in the doghouse.

A memorable comment of my Mother's was when we were bombed the blast blew her 'nightie' into a tree outside. Her comment was "just think, it's a good thing I wasn't in it". We don't know how long it hung there. We gradually settled down to our new life, now virtually ignoring the sirens when they sounded as we hadn't got a shelter to dive in to, although the dog was confused at first, she eventually got used to it. The air-raids eased off eventually, as Adolf Hitler had other things on his mind. It was without a doubt a remarkable experience to live through, and looking back I was at the age not to feel the fear of older people. I'm sure I would see it all in a different light today, and feel lucky to be able to tell this story all these years after.

George Morton

Dawn broke on Sunday August 25th 1940 with blue skies and sunshine, although the smell of smoke and cordite was very pronounced. One could see the smoke rising from many buildings still burning in the City, after one of the heaviest air raids of the war over Birmingham. The people of the city awoke after very little sleep, to find widespread devastation in many parts of the town and surrounding areas, the casualty figures were high and countless people were now homeless. The sixth air raid of the war on Birmingham started at approximately 9.40pm the previous evening, when the sirens first sounded the alert; and the blitz continued until the early hours of Sunday, when eventually the 'all clear' was heard. Whilst the raid was in progress, my family and I had sheltered under the stairs of our house at number 101, Welwyndale Road, Sutton Coldfield. Many people took shelter in this way as most of us were still awaiting delivery of an Anderson or Morrison Shelter. After several hours of exploding bombs and Anti Aircraft Fire, which produced a continual horrendous noise, the sirens eventually sounded the 'all clear' and we retired to bed for what little remained of the night. During the course of this raid, my father had remarked that he thought he had heard at least two bombs fall in soft ground, probably in the fields at the rear of our house. He was convinced that they did not hit anything solid as there would have obviously been a completely different sound. Later that morning he was to be proved correct. Getting up after that dreadful night, he looked out of the bedroom window and immediately noticed in the field, about 200 yards away, two round holes of approximately 2 to 3 feet in diameter. Not a lot more was said at the time and the family had breakfast. After the meal, my father was still puzzled by these indentations in the field and could not understand what they were. Had they been small bombs, there would have been craters, but this was not in evidence here. These were two sharply cut holes in the grass. My father then decided to call across to our neighbour Cyril Allen, who had recently returned from ARP duties in the City, where he had been throughout the raid. He asked Cyril if he wanted to take a walk over the fields, to find out the answer to these mystery holes. The answer was 'Yes, I will come with you, but I must have a wash and shave first'. Meanwhile, during the time my father and Cyril had been talking the Home Guard and Royal Engineers had arrived and roped off the area around these holes. In no time at all, many of our neighbours had left their gardens and strolled across to the spot to find out what was going on.

Very quickly a crowd of people had gathered to watch the soldiers, who were by now digging at one of the holes, hoping to find what was in the ground. This really was becoming very interesting or so they thought. Eventually Cyril and his son Eric (my best friend) appeared and called over the hedge to say they were ready to go. So the four of us set off to join the others at the scene. My mother stayed at home with my younger brother and watched as we climbed through the hedge at the bottom of our garden and into the field. We had gone about fifty yards, when there was a tremendous explosion. The ground shuddered and the earth erupted to a height of at least a hundred feet.

Among the many tons of soil, one could clearly see the bodies of the military personnel and other on-lookers being thrown into the air like rag dolls. After the explosion and as the dust began to clear, there followed the incredible and inevitable deathly silence. Within seconds, my father and Cyril pushed us lads to the ground and ordered us to stay still and not move until told to do so. Having now realised that these holes contained Delayed Action Bombs, they were very worried that the one explosion might set off the second which was around thirty feet away from where we were in that field. The men then ran as fast as they could to the scene of utter carnage and devastation to try to do whatever they could in helping the victims. However, there was little that could be done. The Military and our neighbours had been standing directly over the 500lb Delayed Action Bomb and had no chance of survival whatsoever. There were several who had minor injuries but they had been either en route or walking back to their homes and were fortunate in not taking the full blast.

My father and Cyril did what they could for the survivors, but could do absolutely nothing for the other poor lads. In all 14 men lost their lives, including members of the Home Guard, Royal Engineers and residents of Welwyndale Road and also Berwood Farm Road. These DA bombs were among the first to be used over Birmingham by the Luftwaffe, and it appeared that the authorities did not have sufficient experience and knowledge of them to know how to defuse and render them safe. The second bomb did not explode until two days afterwards, but fortunately did not cause any casualties and damage to nearby properties was minimal. Needless to say, with another bomb waiting to explode, parts of Welwyndale Road had been closed off and many families including ourselves had been evacuated. Although, at the time I was only a young lad of seven years of age, this dreadful tragedy in that field at the back of Welwyndale Road, on Sunday 25th August 1940, imprinted an image in my memory that would never be erased. I still remember it so clearly, but obviously more detailed memories were passed on to me by my late parents. My friend Eric and I, now into our seventies are still big buddies and often talk about our experiences of the war years. We live relatively close to each other and are in regular contact. This was a typical occasion when curiosity caused needless death. Looking back on that dreadful day, even though it is now many years on, I cannot believe how fortunate the four of us all were. I was so lucky, very very lucky, as were my companions on that day. Simply, had it not been for Cyril asking us to wait for him to have a quick shave and a delay of a few minutes, and then this account of the tragedy would never have been written.

Graham Weaver

WARTIME

In 1940 I left school and joined the Post Office as a messenger boy delivering telegrams, in those days we were not welcome on the doorstep as mothers and wives all feared the worst for what message the telegram contained. I registered for national service in 1944 and by then Ernest Bevin, who was the Labour minister, had introduced a scheme, that the last digit of your national service number, for each call up period, was put in a hat and one number drawn out. All men with that number then were required to work in the coal mines, rather than the Services. I was unlucky enough to be caught this way and had to work in a coal mine at Rugeley, Staffordshire. The system was a disaster from the start, for several reasons;

1. The only check on you was that you didn't have a P45 so that you couldn't legally get a job elsewhere. But if your family could support you, then you didn't have to work in the coal mines.

2. All the conscripts that I knew hated the idea and consequently only worked the bare minimum amount possible. This, of course, had a bad effect upon those who had volunteered for the mines, rather than the armed services, because they quickly realized that what we could get away with, so could they. So absenteeism and poor production, increased.

3. It appeared to us that, although theoretically one out of ten of every call up period was to work down the mine, I never heard of any son of an influential person, MP, titled person etc. that was treated this way.

By the time that I was nineteen, the Government had realized their mistake, and we had to report to a tribunal and told "Either mend your ways, or you will be called up for the armed services". This is exactly what we wanted of course, so I started my national service all over again, but this time with the Royal Signals, and had a uniform to prove it.

MY TIME AS AN EVACUEE 1939-1941

On Friday the 1st of September I was taken to School about ten o'clock in the morning along with my brother, who was 5 years younger than me. I don't remember having a case for my clothes, but I suppose that I must have had one, but I do remember having my gas mask in its cardboard box, with some string arranged as a sling, so that I could carry it over my shoulder. There were several Midland Red Coaches lined up outside the School, and after a lot of tearful good-byes we were told which coach to get on, I never saw my brother again until many months later, because his coach had a different destination to mine. My mother had died two years previously, so I suppose that parting wasn't as painful for me as it was for my classmates, and the whole thing to me was just a big adventure. I can't recall what the journey was like to Herefordshire, so I suppose it must have felt like any other coach trip that I had been on, except that I didn't have any of my family with me, but it certainly didn't bother me. Our destination was to be a small village called Much Cowan which is situated just off the Bromyard – Hereford Road, about half way between the two towns. It was early evening when we arrived, and we were assembled in the village hall, where a whole lot of women were waiting for us. I don't know if it was pre-arranged as to whose house we were going to stay at, or whether it was, as it seemed to me, we were auctioned off in job lots. I was given to two ladies, along with Gerald, a lad who I knew quite well but who was not a particular friend of mine. We walked to a farmhouse, which was only a short distance from the hall, and were soon introduced to our new home, and the family we would be staying with. This was a farmer (who looked every bit the part), his wife and two daughters, Kathleen who was in her early twenties, and Freda who was about my age, and still at school; they had a brother, Percy, who would have been in his late teens. I was to meet the rest of the family, two men in their middle twenties, and another girl who would have been about sixteen, when they came home in a few days time.

It was soon bedtime and Gerald and I were ushered upstairs to a bedroom, which had one double bed. This did not bother me at all, as this was the practice in those days for boys to sleep in one bed. It had been a long and exhausting day and we were soon fast asleep. Next morning we were both up quite early, and sat down to a breakfast of bacon and egg. I must say that living on a farm was like staying at a holiday home to me. I was treated as a member of the family in every respect. I was given three good meals each day, bacon and egg for breakfast, meat and two veg for lunch, bread and jam plus home made cake for tea; then at supper time we could have one glass of cider or as many glasses of milk as we wished, along with some bread and cheese.

Remember that I had been used to being looked after by my father, assisted when he was working, by my thirteen-year-old sister. We weren't expected to do jobs on the farm but, being lads, we were quite keen to help when we could. I remember helping to round up the sheep, with the help of the two dogs, so that they could be inspected for lice, which gave the sheep nasty patches of raw flesh, and also ruined their fleece. They were treated with a lotion (there was no sheep dip on this farm), which was applied with a piece of rag. The sheep didn't like the treatment, but I feel sure they were much better off for it. I also helped to round up the cows for milking, along with the dogs again. I remember the one dog, an Alsatian cross called Ben who used to get over enthusiastic and would jump up and hang on the cows tail if they were not going quick enough, but this did get him a good scolding from the farmer. I did have a go at milking but, although I was shown by Percy how it was done, I never did get the hang of it. Each day some of the milk was kept for the family's use and the rest was put into a machine for separating the cream from the milk. Each day's cream was kept for several days, and then turned into butter by churning it. I did have a turn at working the separator; there was a handle that had to be turned fast enough to stop a small bell that gave a small ring until you had got up past a certain speed. The milk was put into a container at the top, and the cream came out of a small pipe at the bottom, with the separated milk coming out of another pipe. It was very hard work doing this and not a job I liked doing at all. Churning the cream to make butter was another tedious job. The churn was a small wooden barrel held on its side in a metal frame. There was a handle to turn it with, and you just kept turning the handle, with the cream sloshing about inside until it turned into butter and some residue milk, which was called buttermilk.

Another job we helped at was gathering apples for cider making. First of all the horse had to be fetched from the field over the road, he was then hitched up to a cart and away we went to the orchard. The apples weren't hand picked but they were shaken down using a long pole with a hook on the end. Once the apples were on the ground they had to be picked up and placed in sacks. These were then put on the cart and away we would go to the next tree. Some of the sacks of apples were kept for the farm's own cider making and the rest were put on one side to be collected and taken to Bulmers Cider factory in Hereford. When the job was completed, the horse was unhitched and I volunteered to take him back to the field where he had been grazing before Percy had caught him.

All his harness had been removed and a rope halter was placed round his neck for me to lead him to the field. I got to the field across the road ok, but when we got past the first gate, the horse spied his friends the other side of the hedge and he made off to join them. He knew the way to the other field ok, because he was off at a good gallop taking the halter with him. No way was I able to hold this huge Shire horse and stopping him going just wherever he wanted to go, so I just had to leave him, and return alone. On the Sunday morning I remember listening to Neville Chamberlain with the rest of the family, on a very ancient looking Radio. I remember hearing him say "Consequently we were now at war with Germany". I can't remember this bothering me at all; everyone had been expecting it anyway. That afternoon the two eldest sons came home, I understand they both had jobs in Hereford, and came home at weekends. They got some boxing gloves out after lunch, and had Gerald and me boxing each other, with two-minute rounds and rests in between. The gloves were so big it was impossible to hurt each other. Another thing that I did while I was living at this farm was to go 'Hop Picking', the Farmers wife, and Kathleen, had a crib at a neighbouring farm that grew hops.

The crib was made with wooden poles and had sacking draped around the poles. A vine was pulled down from the wires that supported it, and we all stood round and picked the hops into the crib. Periodically the owner would arrive on horseback with a bushel measure, which was a cane basket, about the size of a waste paper basket. The hops were scooped into the basket and then emptied into a large sack, a check was made of the number of full baskets (bushels) and entered on a card so that the person in charge of the crib could be paid for what had been picked. As this was the summer holidays, I never met any other evacuees or even any of the local school children, except for one girl Audrey, the local Postman's daughter, who was also Freda's friend. Sadly at the end of the School holidays, it was decided to re-group the Evacuees, and move us all about twenty miles or so, to the other side of Bromyard, where there were more evacuees and our Schoolmaster. By this time as no bombing had begun, lots of the evacuees had returned home, including Gerald. Life on the farm had been very good to me and I was sad to leave.

We were taken by coach once again, to a village just off the Worcester-Bromyard Road, called Whitbourne. I was billeted this time with a new boy, Freddie, who I had never met before; he wasn't a pupil at my school. The house we went to was on a large country estate and we were to stay with the head gardener and his wife Mr. & Mrs. Henderson. Once again I had been very lucky; the estate we lived on was called Gains, it had two private tree lined drives that were at least 400 yards long.

The garden where Mr. Henderson worked was very large and was on the banks of one of two lakes that were at least two hundred yards long. The lakes had lots of fish in them, which you could see when they basked in the sunlight. I was well looked after once again, and very well fed as this new foster Mother was an excellent cook and did her own baking as well. My favourite meal was rabbit pie and we were allowed more than one helping if we wanted. Mrs. Henderson was much younger than the farmer's wife which I had just left, and just had one daughter, a girl called Prudence, who would have been about three or four years old. One day I was told that it had been arranged for my brother to stay as an evacuee on the farm that was part of the estate where I was; I don't know who made the arrangements, whether it was the school, or my father, but I was told to go to the bus station at Hereford and bring him on the public transport back to Whitbourne, a distance of some 20 miles or so. I got to the bus station ok and to the spot where it had been arranged for us to meet.

I waited here for some minutes when I noticed this young lad; I had not seen my brother since leaving on the coach that day, and failed to recognize him. Anyway, seeing this boy obviously waiting, I approached him and said, "Are you Reg?" He said, "Yes, are you Jack?" That's how we met and I can't help thinking how different things were in 1940, to what they are to day. I can't imagine a young lad of eight, making his own way to a large busy bus station, to be met by his thirteen-year-old brother. The farm where he stayed was only a hundred yards or so from where I was, I actually used to fetch the milk from there each morning. As he was that much younger, and with different school friends, we didn't see a great deal of one another. It was time now to resume our schooling, and so we had to report to the local village school where we were reunited with our schoolmaster.

Our classroom was a large room that was divided by a curtain with the local village children the other side of the curtain. We got on very well with the local boys and were soon playing cricket with them on the field adjoining the school. I was even picked to play cricket with them against the next village. The chauffeur to the owner of the estate lived with his wife in another cottage on the estate and I knew them quite well; I was invited to go in the car with him when he went on errands in the car. He had a daughter who was a schoolteacher and she used to come and visit her mother and father most weekends. I got to know her quite well; her name was Nellie, which is what I called her.

After I left Gains, she applied for, and got, the position of headmistress at the local school that I had been attending. I don't suppose that I would still have been able to call her Nellie, if I had still been there. I did correspond with her from Birmingham and gave her some graphic descriptions of what it was like to live through an air raid. Each Sunday morning I was taken by car to the local doctors, where I was used by the doctor to demonstrate how to apply slings and bandages at his First Aid lessons. The women, because it was only women who attended the classes, also used me to practice their First Aid skills. Sunday was also the day for attending the local Church, and rather than sing in the choir, I volunteered to pump the church organ. I sat in a small room behind the organ, where a large wooden handle protruded from the wall; this handle worked the bellows that provided the air to work the organ. There were two brass strips attached to the wall and a small brass bob that hung by a cord between them. My job was to pump the organ so that the bob was kept between the two brass strips, the bottom indicating when the bellows were empty, and the top one when the bellows were full of air.

Life was once again very good; Mr. Henderson took me with him when he went rabbiting which I found quite exciting. Once finding the warren, nets were place over each hole and then a ferret was sent down, and the rabbits would come scurrying out, only to be caught by the nets. One day Mr. Henderson taught us how to make a catapult out of a forked twig, some rubber elastic, and a bit of shoe leather. So we went off in search of a twig that would do. This wasn't easy at all, and after showing our disappointment, Mr. Henderson went outside in the dark, returning a few minutes later with a perfect example; that's how kind our foster parents were to Freddie and I.

Friday night was bath night when we were with the Hendersons, and we had our baths in an adjoining outhouse, which they called the Bothy which is a Yorkshire term so I understand. This Bothy was used to store all the gardening tools, and upstairs the fruit was stored. The apples and pears were kept on racks, and each section had the name of the apple or pear. I had never seen so many different varieties of fruit, and we were allowed to help ourselves whenever we wanted. On the ground floor, where we had our bath, there was an open fireplace, which had a blazing fire of wooden logs on bath night. It became our job to saw up the logs for this fire on Fridays.

That winter was very cold indeed and the lakes were frozen solid, with ice thick enough to support many people, and on the weekend the man who owned the big house invited all his family down for ice-skating. He had several grandchildren and they hired a bus to bring all their classmates to the estate for an ice skating weekend and we were invited as well. Being as I could roller skate, one of the daughters loaned me a pair of skates that clipped onto my boots so that I could skate with them. There were enough people to make up two teams, and we had great fun playing ice hockey, using walking sticks for hockey sticks. As I was now old enough to leave school and find a job, I left my temporary family and came back to Birmingham and all the bombing. Not fully realizing what good people I had been lucky enough to live with I did write to the people for a while and, after a couple of years, I went back on a bicycle but nothing was the same. The farm had changed hands, and Gains was now made into flats, and the family that I had stayed with had gone.

MY TIME AS A BEVIN BOY

As I was approaching my eighteenth birthday I had to register for national service, and from then on I began to look forward to receiving my 'Call Up' papers. Then one Saturday morning, when I had slept late, my sister brought up an official looking envelope that was addressed to me. I got quite excited as I opened it, thinking that this would be the 'Call Up' papers that I was expecting. Upon reading the first sentence though, I began to get really worried. The letter started off by informing me the Minister of Labour in the government, Ernest Bevin, had passed a bill in Parliament, to the effect, that on each call up period, a number would be selected at random. If the last digit of your national service number was the same as this number, then instead of going into the services, you would be required to work underground, in the Coal Industry.

When I first registered for national service, I was, along with everyone else, offered the chance to volunteer for service in the coal industry rather than military service, but declined. I read the letter over and over again, hoping that I had made a mistake and read it wrong. You could appeal against the decision, and naturally I did this at the first opportunity, and was given a date for the hearing. It was all a waste of time though, I went with my union rep to the hearing, but all that I can remember, was the lady chairman saying, "How do you know that you won't like working in a coal mine?" So I found myself catching the train some weeks later, on my way to a training establishment at Kersley, Coventry. This camp was a set of Nissen Huts, where we were allocated a bed in one of the huts, and then issued with a safety helmet, and a pair of industrial boots, that had steel toecaps. The next day a coach took us to the mine at Kersley, where we were to be given two weeks training. This was a complete waste of time when I think back, because what I was shown was nothing like what I was to experience at a working coal mine. A guide took us underground, and I remember the eerie feeling that I got, as we entered the cage that was to take us down the mine. The metal doors slammed shut with a bang and the cage descended quite rapidly, much faster than a normal lift. I remember after a few seconds, getting the sensation that we had stopped going down, and started to go up again so I was quite surprised as we neared the bottom, and the cage slowed down, to see that we were actually still going down. I discovered later, that this was because, as our cage passed the one that was going up, the air pressure changed. The shaft that is used for hauling men and coal, is the intake for fresh air that has to be blown round the mine, the extracted air being sucked out at great pressure, via a separate shaft. The pit bottom where the cage had stopped, was beautiful, in comparison to what I was going to find at a working mine.

It was very well lit, and all the walls had been white washed. The height of the tunnels leading to the coalface was well above six feet, and walking was quite easy. This is about all that I can remember about my training period at Kersley. After spending a fortnight at this training camp, I was told to report to a hostel at Wimbleberry, near Cannock, Staffordshire. This was to be my home for the next eighteen months or so. From this hostel I had to catch a private bus that took miners from a neighbouring village to a colliery, in Brereton, Rugeley. This mine was very much different to the one at Kersley, and was a fully working mine. The first job that I was given was a surface job. What the job entailed, I can't remember now as all that I can recall was that it was very early in the morning and, being winter, it was very dark and cold. All the surface workers had large braziers burning coal, which, of course, was plentiful and free. I remember huddling round the fire, half asleep, and hating every minute.

The surface job lasted a week or so and then came the dreaded moment when I had to go underground. The mine at Brereton was what was known as a drift mine. That is to say there was no shaft with cages to take you down, it was just like a cave, which went sloping down to the bowels of the earth. I was issued with a metal token, which was exchanged for a lamp. The token was hung up on a board, so that it was known who was underground at any time. The lamps that we were given, were not the sort that fitted onto your helmet, oh no, these were big, heavy, cumbersome ones powered by lead acid batteries. They gave off a very good light and, if they could be hung up somewhere while you were working, were very efficient, but of course this was not very often. Most times they had to be carried and as they weighed several pounds, they were a curse. The road down to the pit bottom was used to haul coal, so there were narrow gauge railway lines, and an endless steel rope between the lines. A clamp could be attached to the rope so that it could be hooked onto a metal tub full of coal. The ground between the rails was very dusty and uneven which made the walk down not pleasant at all. This road was well lit and the ceiling quite high; you were not allowed to walk while coal was being hauled, so you had to be underground by a certain time.

My first job was a real nightmare. Coal, from the face, was brought to a loading point, by conveyor belt, where it spilled into waiting tubs. Tubs were what the miners called the small metal trucks that ran on the narrow gauge railway lines. One man controlled the amount of coal that was spilled into each tub, and my job was to feed empty tubs to this man. As I have mentioned earlier, there is a constant airflow round a coal mine, to keep it ventilated, and my position was down wind from the coal pouring off the conveyor. So you can imagine, the amount of dust that was being blown at me. At the end of the shift, I looked like one of the Black and White Minstrels, as I was covered with black coal dust. This one shift was enough for me doing this job, so I took the rest of the week off I had already paid my 25 shillings for board and lodgings at the hostel, and there was plenty of company, so I stayed the rest of the week. Meals were obtained by tickets, 3 per day, but at lunch and dinner there was always soup, to which you helped yourself.

Then, being as we were working in the coal industry, there was always cheese. So for the evening meal I had soup, bread and cheese, and a pudding for afters. To get your pudding, you had to exchange your dinner plate. So the trick was to sit with colleagues and offer to fetch their pudding for them. I would then take back two dinner plates, and collect three puddings. The kitchen staff never caught on to this dodge, or if they did, they never let on. Living this way in the hostel, brought home the fact of how unfair the system was as there was never any check on whether you were working or not. The only thing you couldn't do was get another job, or volunteer for the forces, which my colleagues and I tried to do about every three months or so. This explained to me why I never met any sons of influential people that had been conscripted to the job, as I had been. Also, if anyone wanted to dodge being called up for the army, all you had to do was volunteer for the coal mines. Provided that you had a family that could keep you, you need never go down the mine at all, because no check was ever made. Also the whole idea of conscripting men to work in a mine, was counter productive because all the conscripts couldn't care less about discipline or time keeping; they just felt hard done by, and acted accordingly. So when the volunteers saw what the conscripts were getting away with, they began to act in the same way. At one time I got a job doing casual work at an Electro plating firm in Birmingham. I didn't have any cards, and no references at all, I was just paid in cash for the hours I worked. One of the items for plating was the base for electric irons. They had been cast, and my job was to take off the rough edges using a grinding wheel. All went very well for the first two or three weeks, until one day I was careless, and caught my hand on the grind stone, which ground a nice groove on my right index finger, just below the nail. It bled of course and had to be bandaged. This frightened the management I think, and I had my marching orders that day. Going back to the mine to earn a few more pounds I found myself on the maintenance shift. The mine was worked so that in the morning, the loose coal was shovelled onto the conveyors, then tubs, to be taken to the surface.

Nothing was allowed to interfere with this because all the coal had to be cleared off the face before any other work could be started. The afternoon shift would then come on and start moving the conveyors three feet further on. Packs had to be built 12ft by 3ft, made of loose rock; to support the roof when the pit props were taken down that were supporting the roof all along the coalface. There were two packs, one each side of the road that carried the conveyor to the coalface. When 50 yards by 3ft deep is taken out of a 5ft seam, the weight above is so enormous that nothing can stop it coming down, the rock packs can only slow it down. The props are taken out from the face just cleared of coal, to relieve the pressure. A coal cutting machine then drags itself along the face cutting a 4 inch slot along the bottom of the seam, this is followed by a man drilling holes 3ft into the seam, ready to be packed with explosive.

The explosive needs a detonator to explode it. This is a very responsible job and is done by a Fireman, who is like a foreman. Each Fireman is allowed 40 detonators, which he keeps locked in a steel box when he carries then down the mine. The explosives are harmless on their own, and anyone is asked to carry a tin full of sticks down. My job on this shift was to drag two halves of the steel girders that have to hold the roof up on the road that is being extended each day. There were two of us to do this and it was about 50 yards to the coalface, and we had to do two trips. This was not as easy as it seems, because the roof is gradually descending all the time, and at points the road would only be about 2ft 6 high. With experience this could be done in about 2 to 3 hours and the rest of the shift would be spent lying on our backs keeping an eye out for the Overman, who was the real boss, being one rank above a Fireman. We knew when he was coming, because he had a bright lamp that fitted onto his helmet that shone a beam of light like a powerful torch would do. One day I had to go with a Fireman to recover a coal cutting machine from a disused part of the mine; it had to be dragged using block and tackle. A large ratchet type tool was used to move this very heavy machine an inch at a time. It was hard work for the man with me, but not for me as I was only there because no person is allowed to work on his own down a pit.

The road that we were dragging the cutter along had very little headroom, the steel girders that supported the roof were twisted into all sort of shapes as the weight above had pressed down. At one point we were sitting down resting and eating a sandwich. When the Fireman shouted at me to look out, as a few hundredweight of rocks came tumbling down from the roof, I don't know if it was something he heard, or whether it was his sixth sense that warned him, but it was only just in time. He got away with it, but as I sprang from a sitting position to move, my right arm went out in front of me, and my left arm went out behind me, just as a large piece rock, or coal, came down and caught my left hand a glancing blow. It gave me quite a deep cut, so I was made to make my way to the surface, and report to the office. From here the pit ambulance, a very old converted Rolls Royce, took me to Rugeley Hospital, where the cut was stitched. I still carry the blue scar on my hand to this day, along with my slightly disfigured finger, from my brush with the grinder.

The bus that took us from the hostel to the Colliery at Brereton had to go along a road, which went through Cannock Chase which is a beautiful part of the country, and it was very disheartening on a lovely afternoon when we knew where we were going. I can remember several occasions when a conscript would suddenly say that he had changed his mind about going to work and was going to catch the bus back to the hostel. Within minutes he was joined by several others, which meant the bus taking the morning shift back was really crowded.

Before being called up, I worked for the Post Office, and one day I received a letter from the Civil Service informing me that I was now a proper Civil

Servant, and therefore I would be paid when on sick leave. This seemed too good to be true to me, I quickly filled in the form that they sent me entering the days that I hadn't worked. The only snag was that I needed a note from the Post Office doctor. I actually had the cheek to go to the doctor when I was home that weekend, and asked him to sign the form for the days that I had been off work. It was a terrible mistake though, because the doctor bawled me out of his surgery shouting loud enough for all the people waiting in the waiting room to hear. I have never been more embarrassed in my life as I was that Saturday morning. However, I still had the odd week off sick, until I got another letter from the Post Office to the effect that I had now used up all the sick leave that I was entitled to, and all sorts of thing would happen to my career if I had any more. I just couldn't win.

After being at the hostel in Wimblebury for around 18 months, several of us conscripts were called into the manager's office and told that, if we didn't improve our timekeeping, then we would be liable to be called up to serve in the Army. He thought this would frighten us, but of course this was exactly what we wanted, and we took no time in telling him; he didn't like this at all, and accused us of being truculent. I hadn't ever heard of this word before, and it has stuck in my mind ever since.

Not long after this I received another set of 'Calling up papers', this time for the Army, along with a new 'Demob number'. I did 4 weeks basic training at Wrexham, learning how to be a soldier, and then six months training at Catterick. My time at Catterick camp in Yorkshire, was the only time in my days as a soldier that I didn't enjoy. Soon after I was posted to the Middle East and enjoyed two years of sunshine.

Jack Harding

WARTIME SMILES AND SMELLS

I was a schoolgirl, merely ten years old when the war began, with my only concern was sitting the '11-plus exam' and hopefully doing well enough to satisfy my headmaster's expectations (and my father's!). So it was that when war was finally declared and eventually the bombing began in Birmingham, I found myself without a classroom at my Moseley Rd Junior and Infant School, for it was a separate wooden building in the playground adjoining Highgate Park, and was reduced overnight to a pile of virtual matchsticks! The school still functioned for those who were not evacuated and our class were given work to do at home each day and then taken back to be marked the following morning and another lot collected. In September 1941, I moved to King Edward's Grammar School at Camp Hill (not at King's Heath, where it is now). Many of the girls were evacuated to Lichfield; those few of us who were left carried on with our lessons taught by teachers who dedicatedly travelled to and fro between Lichfield and Birmingham to keep up with our education. Needless to say, this school didn't escape without damage either, but we still managed to have gym sessions in the Hall with the apparatus strategically placed to avoid the buckets catching the rain dripping through holes in the roof caused by the shrapnel and incendiary bombs that dropped night after night together with much more deadly bombs. At lunchtime, determined to carry on as normal, we danced around those same buckets, faithfully accompanied by the efforts of my form-mate, Vera Nash staunchly playing the piano until her fingers ached! Our classroom looked out onto the railway lines which ran alongside the school, and frequently during lessons we rushed to the windows to wave as the troop trains went by, much to the quiet consternation of whichever mistress happened to be teaching us!

Finally such was the state of the building that we moved out to College Road, Sparkhill, where we were given the use of a classroom in the school there, and I had to take sandwiches for lunch for it was too far to get home and back in time for lessons. The sandwiches were always 'jam' made with as little sugar as possible and therefore quite runny, and to this day plum jam is my least favourite! At night, we were down in our shelter under the Smithfield Wholesale Fruit and Vegetable Market, which is now long since gone. It bordered St Martin's Lane, Jamaica Row, Moat Row and Moat Lane, (which is where we lived at The Markets and Fairs Department). The shelter was an old basement kitchen, which was made usable for us and was quite palatial in fact, for we had two rooms and we were comfortable. We had a double and single mattress down there; with another room, which was our escape route up into the street, should we ever be trapped.

This room however, was filled from floor to ceiling with sand for filling all the sand buckets placed throughout all the markets premises and which if we had ever needed to use our escape route we would most likely have suffocated in sand in the attempt! My dad never slept in our shelter throughout its use; in fact we only saw him on rare occasions for as an Air Raid Warden he was busy racing around the streets surrounding the market area or the actual market building extinguishing the never ending spate of incendiaries. Smithfield Market itself was a huge building and there was just my dad and two night watchmen to patrol this great place, rushing with the aforementioned sand buckets to quickly douse a fire before it took hold. One raid comes to mind when my dad came down into our shelter with blood pouring down his face from a cut at the corner of his eye. Apparently he and the Watchman, Mr. Rutter had been knocked over by the blast of a bomb dropping and Mr. Rutter's helmet had caught my dad's face as they both were knocked off their feet and blown under a porter's handtruck. There was a shocked gasp from my mother when she saw the blood, but a sigh of relief when she realised it looked more dreadful than it was although my dad had a nice black eye the next day. But what I couldn't understand was all the whispering that was going on between them and my mother's definite no's to whatever my dad was saying. Apparently, as they fell on top of each other under the truck, so Mr. Rutter who was a very portly gentleman lost all the buttons off his trouser flies and although my mother promptly supplied safety pins to help she firmly remained too embarrassed to pin them in place, and the two men were left to manage this delicate task.

We had to leave our shelter on a few occasions due to unexploded bombs in our area and the conditions that people endured nightly in these public shelters made us very grateful that we were provided with such comfortable conditions within our own shelter. The huge shelter beneath the St Martin's Market (the site of the present Rag Market) was appalling! It had been built but unused as an underground Car Park and then utilised as a public shelter. So many families in surrounding streets sheltered there and then as they were bombed out lived there night and day sectioning off their own spaces with sheets, blankets, old curtains and bedspreads slung on ropes or string from the girders to provide some semblance of privacy.

Only once were we forced to go to this shelter because there was an unexploded bomb too near to us for comfort and the police came checking shelters and directed us on into this dreadful place. One of the 'smells' that I can so easily recall was the stench of unwashed bodies, stale cooking smells, make shift toilets etc. that fouled the air so much that it met you as you walked down the long slope to the entrance. Only once more did I go willingly into this miserable place, and that was to follow Canon Guy Rogers and his choir in their pristine white robes as they conducted their 'Watchnight' Service there. Knowing that people would be too scared to venture out, en masse, to St. Martin's which had already suffered bomb damage, along with all the rest. However, thanks to the determination of the Canon they were not left to wonder, they were reassured as they joined in that age-old service that this was and always would be God's world and that right would triumph and peace would prevail. In spite of all the hardships that people underwent, times of bleakness and often sadness, spirits faltered but rarely failed completely to recover; for people were so willing to help each other overcome such obstacles that came their way. Times were hard and humour was a God given bonus to lighten many a bleak day or the darkest night. Shops with gaping holes for windows advertised that they were 'OPEN AS USUAL'. It became the norm to see a queue and automatically join it and then enquire what it was you were queuing for! (Sometimes, seeing people leaving certain queues with embarrassed looks on their faces if the queue was for pregnant women waiting for their ration of oranges!) And men queued just as avidly as women! Nowadays the scent of an orange being peeled is a reminder of the rarity of their existence in those days. Recently, the Bull Ring being modernised yet again, has recalled the lingering smell of brick dust and burning rubble that met you as you surfaced each morning from the shelter, gazing at the changed surroundings and wide open spaces. Often we were embarrassed to be seeing into the gaping remains of backrooms now in full view and never ceasing to be amazed at a solitary fragile article remaining unmoved and untouched in the midst of such chaos!

The aftermath of present day flooding disasters brings back the pungent stink and mess of filthy water dribbling off the ruins and flooding the gutters. Then too, the hot steaming smell of firemen's cloth coats as they hosed the blazing building and gratefully grabbed at a mug of hot cocoa but never failing to keep fighting the fires. Sadly, so often they were killed or injured by the blast of yet another bomb dropping as they fought the result of the ones already dropped. (Firemen have always been wonderful! And remember these were often volunteers, doing this after a full day's work at their normal jobs, as were all volunteer policemen, wardens, nurses, ambulance men and messengers etc!) Wartime was a time for pulling together, working with one aim in mind, to rid the world of the evil it had spawned, to regain the security we once knew and to bring all our loved ones safely home again. Sadly for some this would never be, but for many life would become more meaningful than they would ever have imagined and smiles gladly lit up our 'war weary' faces as peace reigned once more.

Jean C Frier

A VICTIM OF THE RAID ON THE BSA. NOV 19TH/ 20TH 1940.

My father, Ernest Edward Lord, was an employee of the BSA (Birmingham Small Arms) in Armoury Road, Small Heath. And at the time of the Air Raids on the city he was actually manning a machine gun on the factory roof as one of the factory firewatchers. Previously a man had fallen in the factory workshop and Dad dressed his injury telling him to have it checked at the First Aid Room. Consequently, my father was sent for and asked if he would transfer to the First Aid Unit. The night of the Air Raid on Nov 19th/20th when the BSA was badly hit, he was working in the Control Room when a man hurried in telling my father that women were fainting in the workshop due to the fires and chaos around.

The two men went into the building to bring some women out, and then my Dad went in for a third time but never came out. His body was recovered on Nov 21st and taken to a Funeral Parlour on Stratford Road without my mother being notified. Distressingly for her, she visited all Birmingham hospitals and mortuaries without any success. In spite of being sent to various places including an undertakers in Station Street (Wheatley's Funeral Directors) where she viewed 100 bodies she was still without any sign of my father's body.

The Council eventually informed my mother on Jan 4th that since the body had not been claimed he therefore had been interred in a communal grave at Brandwood End Cemetery, Kings Heath. She asked if she might have his remains reburied but was dissuaded from this, being told that this would prove distressing, as it was most unlikely that his body would be complete. Having already experienced the unpleasant task of identifying one of his shoes, which had been crushed flat sideways, my mother reluctantly agreed that he would remain undisturbed. One can only imagine the extent of the appalling injuries that had claimed his life, at the age of 38 years old. leaving my mother a young widow and myself, their only child, then aged twelve, to grow up fatherless. So Brandwood End Cemetery remains my Dad's final resting-place with many other victims of that dreadful time in history.

Jean Cox (née Lord)

Tuesday 19th November 1940, my father Ernest Edward Tucker age 36, left home in Yardley to go to the BSA (British Small Arms), leaving behind Mom Corrie 33, Jean 11, Evelyn 7, and Derek 20 months. During the evening, the sirens went and we joined our neighbours the 'Smarts' in their shelter, as we didn't have a shelter ourselves. Mr. Smart worked with Dad at the BSA. It wasn't long before the bombs were falling and soon Mr. Smart was at the shelter door telling us that the factory had been hit, and he had run all the way home to tell us. He had also added that we were "not to worry as Ernie was following". This was not to be. Morning came and still no Dad, what followed was five dreadful days and night of waiting. I remember friends and relations going to see if he was amongst the rescued but always the news was bad.

On Friday the 22nd another raid and again the factory was hit and all hope was lost, he was found Sunday 24th, at lunch time a policeman came to the door, Mom didn't need telling she just shouted "I knew it", yes he had been found, one of the fifty three people killed that terrible night. Neighbours took care of us till family arrived and we went to stay with Aunty May and Uncle Fred in Water Orton. Eventually we came home, we were very lucky to have a family who cared for us, pensions took a long time, Mom waited thirteen weeks. Mom had to find a job and this was cleaning at our school, which meant she went about six in the morning. I would get us ready for school pushing Derek in the pram and leaving him outside the headmaster's door. Mom would come off duty and take him home with her. In the afternoon she would come back on duty and we did it in reverse. I would get our tea and waited till she came home, we always had neighbours keeping an eye on us.

When Derek was able to go to school nursery she was able to get a better job which was at Thornley & Knights as a canteen manageress and was very well respected. She met her second husband there. We grew up like three sisters and she gave me away at my wedding, Derek well I think he had three moms to look after him.

Jean Tyler

THE DAY THE BUSES STOPPED

During the early part of the war I was stationed at RAF Henlow in Bedfordshire when an opportunity came for a visit to see my girlfriend (later to be my wife). I did not have any official leave but as a friend of mine had a car and sufficient petrol to get us to Warwick and back we decided to take a chance. After a pleasant weekend I got ready to return to camp and then the sirens sounded, I rushed around to the local bus stop only to be told that the buses had stopped running due to the bombing. I became really worried at the time about getting back and concerned about the consequences if I did not get back. I decided to start walking from Twickenham Road, Kingstanding to Snow Hill Station (about 5 miles) so I set off to walk despite the heavy bombing and shrapnel falling like rain. I had hoped to hitch a lift but there was very little traffic until an ARP car came along after I had walked about 2 miles, he said I could get in at my own risk. We finally arrived at Snow Hill Station about an hour later there were signs of devastation all around and a big crater outside the main entrance into which a coach had fallen. Fortunately although the station was completely blacked out some trains were still running. To my delight there was a train to Warwick almost ready to move out which I boarded, when I arrived at Warwick there was no sign of any bombings. I had arrived earlier than expected so I waited for my friend and some time later we arrived back at my RAF camp.

Jim Nicholls

It stands in all its glory with ivy round the door. Paper on a piece of string, and lino on the floor. Somewhere in which to meditate and you could hide there too.

It should go down in history, the old back yard loo.

So many children left their homes – with running water and flushing toilets, to escape from the bombing, in the cities. They had to get used to going to an outside toilet, when they stayed in a country cottage.

Joan Chell (nee Price)

WARTIME MEMORIES

September the third 1939 brings back so many memories and a time that changed all our lives irrevocably. Having just left school and worked for two months war came, not unexpectedly, but nonetheless with quite a shock. Preparations had been taking place over the last twelve months with the issue of gas-masks and air-raid shelters – organising blackout curtains and trying to put a few extra tins of food, sugar and tea etc into our larders to help to ease rationing when it came. Lights in the streets were dimmed as well as car and bus headlights. Gradual changes in the office were taking place when men were drafted into the services. At Church our choir men were called up and we formed a ladies choir at St Edmunds, Tyseley. I had been put into our sales department at work, taking over from the 'call up' men. In addition to working from 9am till 5pm, we had to work from 5.30 till 9pm two nights a week doing war work in the factory on machines. The awful air raids didn't commence till well into the first year and when they came they were long and frightening. My mother was a Hospital Sister at Dudley Road Hospital and many nights, on leaving duty at 8pm after a 12 hour shift, was confronted by a heavy raid in progress. There were no trams or buses but fire engines sprawling across the city fighting the many fires so there was no alternative but to walk home to Tyseley. She dodged bombs and craters, many times having to divert to a longer route. She'd arrive tired and scared on many occasions in the middle of the night to spend the rest of the night in the air raid shelter and be up and out by 7am to be back on duty for 8am to a ward of sixty odd patients. Whatever sort of night it had been we all went off to work next morning, wending our way past bomb damage and often having to take a round about route because roads would be closed owing to fires still burning. There were also a few occasions when we were disturbed at work with a daytime raid, and we all had to go to the air raid shelters that had been built on the firm's tennis courts. On one occasion a lone plane shot at the people walking to the shelters.

All over the country men and women were sent on National Service – Navy, Army, Air Force, Land Army, mines or as munition workers. A friend's mother, who lived in Acocks Green, had two Scottish ladies billeted on her; they were working on munitions at the Rover works. We all met up at my friend's home in Yardley Wood, and one of the ladies showed us a photo of her fiancé and family in Glasgow. Her future brother in law had just joined the Navy and Louie asked if I would be his pen friend. We were both eighteen. At nineteen I went into the RAF and Joe's mother began to write to me too. Sufficient to say, at this stage, that we eventually married at 26 but that is another story in itself. We've had 56 wonderful years, but to get back to the war....

I really enjoyed my service in the RAF, starting in September 1942 at RAF Insworth, Gloucester, then on to Morecambe for training and inoculations, long marches, with a gale blowing in from the shore, and then to Sheffield to train as a telephone operator. My first posting was to St Helen's in Lancashire where we worked underground on large switchboards. From there I had another short posting to Birmingham where I was on Balloon Command at Leyhill House in Northfield. Here I was back amongst the blitzes but, after a few months, I was sent to Derby, Newcastle on Tyne,

Burghfield Common and lastly RAF Kidlington, being demobbed in July 1945. Many friends were made along the way, some of whom I am still in touch with. One very funny incident took place whilst I was on duty at RAF Burghfield, actually on my first shift. A call came in asking for AC Ernie Wilson. Private calls were discouraged, for obvious reasons, but the caller explained that he needed to speak to him urgently regarding a broadcast. He told me he worked in the cookhouse so, as it was next door to the exchange; I decided I'd try to get him. On asking who was calling, I was told "This is Victor Sylvester here".

My quick retort was "Yes I'm Janet Gaynor". I found Ernie elbow deep in washing up and advised him to take the call in the Orderly Room. It was only when I went into the NAAFI at lunchtime I saw Ernie sitting at the piano and producing the true strains of Victor Sylvester. Ernie was his pianist. Whenever Victor Sylvester phoned after that he'd say "Ah, it's Janet Gaynor isn't it?" and kindly sent a ticket for one of his tea dances, but I never did get to meet him. Peace came at last but settling back to such a different world and three years older wasn't easy with new jobs, friends and so many changes.

Joan Terrace

CHILDHOOD MEMORIES – RALPH AND JOHN CORFIELD 1939-1943

I was just 4½ years old and my brother Ralph 10 years old at the outbreak of World War Two. Our memories of these times may prove to be patchy. But there are certain things that we think we can both recall quite well. This is possibly due to the impact on us both at the time. Our parents owned a sweets and tobacconist shop on Lozells Road, with living accommodation above the shop together with a small back garden.

We remember that day when Neville Chamberlain announced on the radio that Britain was at war with Germany. It was a Sunday morning and the family were just getting ready (after closing the shop) to go out for a trip in the family car. Mom and Dad who were teenagers during the First World War were very upset at the terrible news. To my brother and me, it did not mean very much at the time and went completely over our heads. Father at this time was working at the Austin Motor Co. Longbridge, which would later be switched to war work making aeroplanes and military vehicles. Mother ran the shop and looked after my brother and I, with a little help from my aunt and a young girl who had just left school. It must have been soon after war was declared, that our Dad and Uncle set to, digging a hole, and then constructing an Anderson Shelter in the garden. This was fitted out with four bunk beds, candles and matches, tinned food all contained in a box. A small Valour oil heater was also put in for those cold winter nights during the Blitz. Our family like others, were fitted out with gas masks, to be carried everywhere. Thank goodness, it never came to having to use them. I did not like using mine in the practices; it smelled of rubber, steamed up and made noises when breathing heavily. Gas masks from time to time, were subject to inspection during the war, to see if they were functioning properly. Mine would generally need maintenance, where I had damaged it, by hitting it up against something in its carrying case. Identity cards, ration books were issued to each and everyone. Windows at night time would have to be covered by blackout curtains.

Mother used an old pair of velvet curtains dyed black for this purpose. No light should be seen through them on the outside, was the rule, ARP wardens on patrol would soon tell you otherwise, if even a chink of light was shown. It was sometime in 1940 that father took us all out in the car to see where one of the first bombs had dropped on Birmingham. The damage was to some houses in the Erdington area and may have been quite close to the Tyburn Road. I think this was the start of the bombing over Birmingham.

It was shortly afterwards I remember, at the sound of the 'air raids siren' I would be scooped up out of my bed at night by my father and taken down the garden to the air raid shelter. Mother would be following up with my brother and we would stay in the shelter until the 'all clear siren' had sounded and my father had returned from fire watching. Our shop was close to two public houses one was the Lozells Inn, the other was the Bell Inn. Not far away was the Lozells picture house.

My brother and I would go to see films here until its destruction in 1942. We were living in an area which was surrounded by industry, which was all turning out war work, with a number of large factories which the German planes were trying to destroy. During the early part of the 1940s air raids over Birmingham were a fairly regular occurrence especially at night. Whilst we were in the air raid shelter on these occasions, we would hear noises of bombs exploding, anti aircraft guns firing, the rattling noise of incendiary bombs falling and machine guns firing. Sometimes after such raids, my brother would the next day go looking for parts of exploded bombs, shells (called shrapnel) or spent bullets on the ground. With me occasionally tagging on behind, not I must say with the grown ups approval. One morning after a raid, there was an unexploded landmine dropped a few streets away from where we lived. People had to be evacuated from their homes and we remember the bomb going off with a terrific bang, the smoke curling up into the sky. My infant school in Lozells Street was damaged at the same time, no school for me for a while. Father that day, was repairing the shop windows which had been blown out the night before by the blast. He was using wooden boards mainly, with just a small window to view through the middle. Our parents must have thought like others, it was time for their children to be evacuated into the countryside.

This was duly arranged and we both remember going with our parents to meet the people willing to take us in for the duration of the war, or until it was safer back home. This never came to anything, as our parents decided that we would all stay together as a family. When attending school, in those days I never remembered a shortage of children at school or in the streets to play with, so a lot of families must have thought the same as our parents. It was about 1941 that our father was transferred to Castle Bromwich factory, to help make Spitfires and Lancaster bombers. In the evenings after work, he would eventually volunteer to become a special Police constable at the local station on Lozells Road. This allowed him to use his car for transporting policemen around, during his duties in the evening. Most people during the wartime were expected to do extra duties outside of their day jobs e.g. ARP wardens, Homeguard etc. Like many families during those war days our parents were working hard by day and by night trying to help the war effort and so it went on for our family until July 1942.

Ralph Henry Corfield

It was on the morning of the 28th July, that tragedy struck the Corfield family, like many, many families in wartime. The 'air raid siren' sounded as usual father got us out of bed and escorted us all down to the shelter. Settled us in safely, and then went about fire watching as usual. Some cottages which were quite close to the back of our garden had caught fire from incendiary bombs. We were told afterwards that Father was trying to extinguish some of the fires, when a large bomb was dropped on the Lozells picture house, exploding and killing him and two other people. One was the cinema manager the other an ARP warden. When the 'all clear siren' sounded and Dad had not returned to our shelter. Mother went looking for him leaving us two boys in the shelter. Mother returned shortly afterwards, very concerned, saying she had been stopped from looking for Dad, and knew something had happened to him. In fact she had seen him under a pile of rubble and thought she had recognised his wrist watch.

Shortly after this, we were all taken into the Bell public house, and the owners were trying to console Mother, when the policeman came in with Dad's belongings, wallet, and wristwatch etc. confirming he had been killed. My brother and I do not think Mother ever got over that morning. She did find the necessary strength to carry on in the running of the business, and bring up two boys. Mother eventually remarried in 1948 and sold the shop in 1954 after an illness. Mother spent the next 30 years in retirement.

Ralph and John Corfield

JULY 1942

My parents, Alice and Len Roper, had lived in Brookvale Park Road, Erdington since 1938. They were profoundly deaf since losing their hearing from childhood illnesses, (my mother from Measles at the age of five and my father from Scarlet Fever at the age of three), and so they needed people to stay with them during the war, to tell them when the air raid sirens sounded. At the end of July 1942 my mother's father, Walter Berry, was staying with them along with my mother's sister Nellie, who was disabled due to having suffered from Rickets as a child. There was also another sister Edie, brother-in-law Steve and their child Geoffrey, staying in the house. My mother was pregnant with me at the time.

On this particular night, I now believe it to be 30th July, when the siren sounded my grandfather woke my mother and father and the others and told them to make their way to the Anderson shelter in the back garden. This they did with my grandfather carrying Nellie after everyone else had left.

As my grandfather and Nellie reached the doorway of the shelter, the bomb landed on the house destroying their house and the ones on either side. (The ones on either side of those had to be pulled down later as they were deemed to be unsafe.) My grandfather and Nellie took the full force of the blast, my grandfather was so badly injured that he died later that day in Highcroft Hospital and Nellie was so badly brain damaged that she was looked after in a hospital in Leamington Spa for the rest of her life. (She died in 1950.) They were buried in Lodge Hill Cemetery. The rest of the family was taken to Highcroft Hospital to have their wounds treated; they suffered shrapnel wounds and shock. They also had their heads shaved as they were infested with creepy crawlies from the blast.

A point of interest is that my dad had made my mother a wooden sewing worktable for her 21st birthday. It had a lift up lid and was lined with satin. When my dad went to see if he could salvage anything from the house a few days later, he found the worktable, minus its lid and with no satin lining left but the rest of it was OK. Some time later he made a new lid for it but he never re-lined it. We always said afterwards, that my Dad's carpentry was so good that even a German bomb could not destroy it.

After being discharged from hospital my Mom and Dad went to stay with relatives in Bridgnorth, Shropshire and I was born there in December 1942. After a while, Birmingham Council offered them a council house in Chingford Road, Kingstanding and while they were living there my brother John was born in June 1946. We stayed there until the house in Erdington had been rebuilt in 1947 and then moved back into our home.

Joyce Hall

The Post Office Factory was bombed on Tuesday, 19th November 1940 and Friday 22nd November 1940. An efficient communications system was essential to the war effort and it was the fact that the work undertaken at this factory contributed to this communications system that caused the Post Office Factory to become a target of enemy bombing. The factory occupied a twenty acre site to the west side of Fordrough Lane. On this site stood various buildings including 'D' Block, 'F' Block and 'J' Block. All these blocks received damage during the raids. The factory shops at Fordrough Lane produced coils, spring sets and relays: these parts were used in telephone exchanges. The factory also produced switchboards, which were used by operators to connect calls. Cables were also produced ready for use in both wireless and walkie-talkies used by the armed forces. Both my mother and father worked at the factory; my father in the Machine Shop and my mother in the Cable Shop. Many years later, my father spoke about being involved in the production of equipment, which had been developed at Bletchley Park.

The Post Office Factory, Bordesley Green

The hours worked were long and often followed by further hours on Home Guard duty. My mother has spoken of the extreme sadness felt, when she arrived for work the morning after a bomb raid, to find that workmates had been killed as a result of a direct hit on their own homes. However, it was

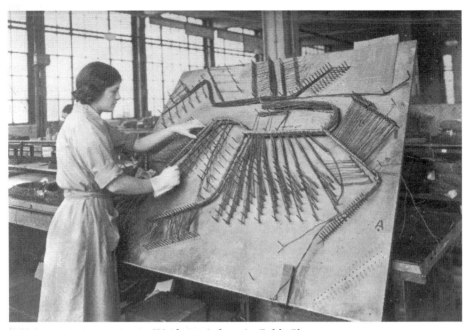

Work carried out in Cable Shop

Site after bombing raid 19th-20th and 22nd-23rd November

essential to continue working for the war effort – there was no time for counselling, as would be the case today in similar tragic situations. Birmingham suffered much bombing during the Second World War and, I think it possible that, the Post Office Factory could have been affected on dates other than those mentioned above, but these were the two main dates when damaged occurred.

Thank you to the Family of W Beckett for the story and photographs

CIVILIAN LIFE

I was eleven in the October, as war was declared in the September, I had just reached the stage at school when I had to transfer to the senior school. My parents were in dispute with the Education Dept. as they did not want me to go to Bierton Road School, they considered it too rough and too far to go. The school was some distance away and quite some distance to walk, as the bus service only ran morning and evenings mainly for the convenience of

Lucas workers. The school they chose was Yardley Senior School at the Yew Tree a much better class of school, also by walking to the top of our road I could catch the outer circle number 11, bus which would drop me at the gates of the school, but because I lived the wrong side of the boundary line it had to go before a committee to decide. So you see nothing has changed, we had the same problems then as you do today.

War being declared, did not mean much to kids, we did not really understand, all we knew was all the schools had been closed down and we were on what seemed a permanent holiday. While every thing was in chaos and every one was panicking we just ran wild. Our favourite pastime was to take some sandwiches and a bottle of lemonade and go up Spion Cop, this was a huge piece of land, which fronted Station Road where the Swimming baths are today, and rose steeply up to Old Yardley at the top with Manor Road running along the left hand side. The ground was cut away in cliff like terraces and was composed of sand and clay, there were miles of brambles on there from which we could pick our fill of blackberries and wild raspberries, hours were spent playing cowboys and Indians and numerous other games.

There was a call from the government for the children from cities to be evacuated to the country for safety, but mom and dad decided against it and we did not go, my best friend at school Rita Boston was evacuated to Cleobury Mortimer, I missed her very much. One day we had to go with mom to collect our gasmask, each one had to be fitted properly, I can still remember that horrible smell of rubber, the man fitting them told you to breath in and put a piece of card over the filter end to test it, at which it made a horrible sound, I just hoped I would never have to wear it. The next step was going with mother up to a church hall in Washwood Heath to collect our Ration books, for food was to be rationed, and horror of horrors so were sweets. Later on we had to go to the Council House Offices in Broad Street by the hall of memory to collect our Identity Cards, who's number I can still remember today, from then on the whole pattern of our lives changed. Finally it was decided to open up the schools again much to the disgust of us kids. The Education Committee informed my parents that I had to go to Bierton Road Girls School, the irony of this decision was that I spent every Monday the whole day at Church Road School, Yardley for cookery and laundry lessons. In the mean time while we had been absent, huge brick and concrete air raid shelters had mushroomed in all the playgrounds.

It was with much trepidation I arrived at Bierton Road, on my first day I was assigned to a wooden hut classroom in the boys' playground, see nothing changes! We were instructed that we must carry our gas mask at all times and a box containing emergence rations in case we were in the shelter for any length of time. It was suggested that the box should contain a piece of cheese some chocolate and raisins and any thing else we could squeeze in, mine contained a pack of Maltesers and some cheese triangles, I wonder why Maltesers don't taste like they did then! Mind you they had only just come out on sale then. Bierton Road School was a school split in two, boys in one half and girls in the other half and in theory never the twain should meet, but it did not quite work out like that as our temporary classroom was in the boys' playground, when the teacher's back was turned they would take every opportunity to chat us up.

The first time the siren sounded while at school was quite a surprise, we were all marched into the shelter where we sat and waited for what seemed like an eternity for the all clear to sound, and in the mean time most of us had eaten our emergency rations. Of course at that time none of us had experienced a real air raid and had no idea what was in store for us. Every house in the country with a garden had been issued with an Anderson Shelter an igloo type of shed made out of corrugated galvanised metal sheets and named after the man who invented it, ours was in the top half of the garden and buried deep down into the soil with a covering of soil over the top. In later years the site of the shelter was made into a fish pool. The first experience of an air raid, was really frightening, one minute you were in your nice warm comfortable bed, next you was being woken up out of a deep sleep to be urged to dress quickly and get down the shelter. You soon learnt to recognise what the siren meant, a wailing sound for an air raid and one long note for the all clear.

With the siren wailing full blast you hurried in the pitch darkness, down the yard under the rose arch into the garden, where you scrambled into the shelter, there you sat in the cold and damp, when you suddenly heard the drone of planes over head. Then all hell would break lose, the horrific noise of bombs falling and the explosions which followed that rocked the ground. Added to that din was the sound of the ACK, ACK guns firing on the Aeroplanes from the railway sidings, it was a most terrifying experience and everyone was very frightened. In the years ahead we were to experience this over and over again.

If anyone had told me that I would grow accustomed to this noise I would not have believed them, but some how you adjusted to it. After a while it was decided as we got deeper into winter to stop going down the shelter and to go into the butlers pantry under the stairs at least it was warm and we could have candle light. Every window in the house had wide bands of brown sticky tape criss crossed over them, this was in case of bomb blast to stop the glass from showering on you. All the windows had thick blackout material curtains, which was most depressing. You were not allowed to show a pinpoint of light. The Air Raid warden's precautions officer patrolled the road to make sure no lights were showing.

As the war progressed there was a shortage of food and we had to queue for nearly everything, even potatoes were rationed, they were very tough times. We were well into the nineteen fifties before rationing ended, no oranges, bananas, pineapples, grapefruits, only our own grown fruit and vegetables, yet we survived. Once we got into the 1940s the raids got really bad, the Bull Ring was bombed quite badly, and a great favourite of mine the market hall was bombed to the ground and with it a very special clock that was a focal point of the hall, it had figures which moved on the striking of the hour, that clock would have been worth a fortune today. No more the pet stall with tiers of cages from floor to ceiling containing all manner of cage birds of brilliant hues, the numerous cages containing kittens, puppies, rabbits, tortoises and ferrets.

The hall was also home to the fish market stalls selling all varieties of fish and shellfish, china stalls where stall owners entertained you by juggling plates and with the performance went the patter to convince you to buy their wares. A café where you could buy a mug of tea and a bacon sandwich, and numerous other stalls were you could buy almost anything. This place was much loved by Birmingham people and the bombing of the Bull Ring and the market hall made people very angry. The Bull Ring was a very special place with a special atmosphere of its own which was lost forever, outside the market hall used to be flat-topped barrows with Barrow Boys selling fruit and vegetables and day old chicks, at the bottom of the Bull Ring in front of the church we had people standing on soap boxes preaching on politics, religion, and all sorts of subjects, men parading around with sandwich boards advertising local shops and sometimes informing us the world was coming to an end. The escapologist who enclosed himself in a sack bound with chains which was then padlocked, the Salvation Army with their brass band recruiting people to their ranks, with the bombing that night we lost that entire special atmosphere never ever to return. When the raids were at their height we lost so many of our city buildings, the look of Birmingham would never look the same again, so many historical buildings lost forever. In one of the worst raids in September 1941 we got bombed out of our house in Frederick Road, a landmine fell on the railway lines, because of the embankment our house did not get the full blast, mom, gran, and my brothers were sheltering in the butlers pantry under the stairs, granddad and I lay on the floor in the hall, and dad in the kitchen, we could hear the bombs dropping all around us, then suddenly every thing went like black treacle and the air seemed to be sucked from the building, ceilings came down, the doors and windows blew in, the miracle was every one escaped unhurt except granddad who had his head cut open by falling plaster. The next day dad decided to go and check if his parents were all right, grandma and granddad Bessey, when dad returned he told us we would all be moving to Waddington Avenue, Great Barr, his brother and his wife's home till our house could be repaired, I don't know how we all fitted in because, besides us there was granddad and granny Bessey, aunty Poll, (granny Bessey's sister) and aunty Maggie my dad's eldest sister, 14 persons in all.

To complicate things my mother was pregnant with my sister, my mother was terrified of the raids and to get to the shelter we had to navigate a field of sprouts in the pitch black, very often mom would get into a blind panic. My sister was born while living at Great Barr on December 22nd 1941 the shortest day of the year. It was to be many months before any work could be carried out on our house and we were allowed to return home. That winter was a very bad one with very deep snow which froze over for weeks. Gran and I would make regular trip over to Stechford to check on the house, I can remember very vividly melting snow and boiling it on the stove to wash nappies because with so many people in the house it was impossible keep on top of the washing, all the water had been cut off at our house. What a relief when we were finally allowed back home and I had my own bedroom back to myself.

Many of my friends were killed in the air raids; the girl who always stays in my mind is Barbara Rodgers she lived in a council house almost opposite the YWCA in Richmond Road corner of Bordesley Green. Barbara was in my class at school, the only member of her family to survive was her mother who was left crippled, the house was just a heap of rubble and they had to dig them out, my friend Rita and I used to visit her grave to put flowers on. The night Bordesley Green got bombed was a very bad raid, when we came out from the shelters the following morning it was carnage up Bordesley Green, with dead bodies every where and so many properties badly damaged including the fever hospital now re-named the Heartlands. There was a huge crater in the grounds where a bomb had just missed hitting the hospital, I know of this because my sister had caught Hooping Cough off my brother, she was still only a young baby so was taken into the hospital there as it was an infectious disease in those days and she was very poorly with it.

The family when we came back from Great Barr had started using the public air raid shelter on the Station Road, it was a reinforced shelter under the butchers shop on the corner of Station Road and Lindon Road, as the raids were quite bad dad would not let us risk sheltering under the stairs again. The shelter was quite spacious with rows of bunk beds on which to rest as the raids sometimes went on for hours, soon after tea each evening the siren would wail out.

All important papers such as insurance policies, birth certificates, marriages lines, ration books and jewellery were always kept in a bag ready to take with us to the shelter in case the house was not standing when we returned from the shelter. I would wrap my patchwork quilt around me and a scarf wound around my head like a turban to keep me warm, there was no heating in the shelter, then hasten up the road as quickly as possible for it was not unknown for the planes to swoop down and machine gun you.

If it had not been for my family going to the shelter I would not have met my husband Leonard, his family had also been bombed out of their home in Morden Road and like us had to leave their property and were re-housed in near by Manor Road, so therefore used the same shelter. I never took much notice of him till one night when I had gone outside for a breath of fresh air he asked me for a date and I turned him down, then one night in a scramble to get out of the shelter with all our blankets and possessions, a gas mask got left behind and Leonard brought it to our house so we got talking and became friends so the war played a large part in the shaping of my life. I would often during a lull in the raids nip down home and make a jug of cocoa to take back to the shelter. One night there was a very heavy raid on Parkinson Stove Works and we all had to evacuate the shelter as the ARP considered it unsafe to remain in the shelter, often in the raids they would drop loads of incendiary

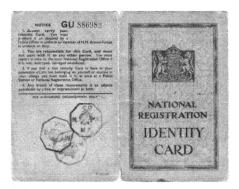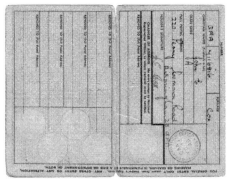

(Identity Card of John Cox member of BARRA)

bombs on us which would set fire to buildings, I myself have helped to put these out when they fell in the road outside the shelter.

Everyone during the war had to carry Identity cards, the police would swoop at regular intervals at public places and check everyone's card; they did manage to catch spies by doing this. All ethnic people had to register during the war and report to the police station every week. As the war went on and things got very tough, everyone was called upon to give up their railings and anything else made of metal such as saucepans etc. so they could melt them down to make war weapons. We have in our possession a teapot specially commissioned by Dyson & Horsfall Ltd. to commemorate the handing over of such items. We were also encouraged to keep poultry to help feed ourselves, we kept poultry at the bottom of our garden and to do this we had to give up part of our egg ration in exchange for coupons to buy feed for the poultry, all our vegetable scraps were boiled up including potato peelings and outer leaves of cabbages etc: and made into a mash with Karswood spices added, nothing was wasted, the job I hated was dusting hens with DDT powder to get rid of the mites, DDT is now banned as it is a dangerous substance. I worked during the war, first at Allen's a fashion shop on the corner of Carr's Lane and High Street in Birmingham city centre and though I was only 14 years old I had charge of the keys to the premises.

In case of damage to the property from air raids the police and wardens would call me out. In my job as a cashier it was me that had to take the takings to the night safe, on occasions the sirens would go and believe me Birmingham city centre was no place to be with a raid going on. I always had my dinner at the British Restaurant this was set up by the government where you could get a cooked meal without giving up any coupons, it meant one less meal for them to find at home from our very limited rations. Clothes, blankets, furniture in fact very little was not rationed. All the factories were busy making weapons, vehicles, munitions, uniforms and all kinds of merchandise and items for the troops, everyone who was not in the forces, fire service or an exempt job had to register for work, it was a very tough time, no dodging of work if you had been up nearly all night because of an air raid. I found a shop in Birmingham that sold cot blankets, these were exempt from coupons, I used them to make into short coats for friends and myself. Leonard's brother Sid was in the Paratroop Regiment and he brought me home a white silk Parachute and from this I made some underwear, sheer luxury! To buy stockings was very nearly impossible as they were made of silk (before Nylons were invented) so we used to paint our legs with gravy browning or sand and draw a seam down the back of the leg with a pencil. From typewriter fluid we made nail varnish, make up was like gold dust it was very hard to buy. I remember once when walking to the Ice rink down Spring Hill we found this small shop selling Brandy Snaps, we could not believe our luck, how they managed to obtain the ingredients I cannot guess for they made these on the premises and we did not have to give up any coupons, we became regular customers for quite a while.

RASC SERVICE, JUNO BEACH (D-DAY) AND LIFE IN WARTIME BIRMINGHAM

Army Life

I am the youngest male in a family of 16 siblings – 12 boys and four girls. I was just 15 and starting a new phase in my life at work when war was declared in 1939. World War Two – what was the impact and implications going to be on a teenager like me? I had no idea how much it would change my life. The first twelve months were reasonably quiet – they were mainly spent preparing for what was to come later, like issuing gas masks, conscription, civil defence (ARP) and black-out precautions. Corrugated-steel Anderson air raid shelters were delivered to all homes. I remember quite well helping my Dad dig a hole in the back garden to put the Anderson shelter in. The Air Raid Precaution Warden would come round every night to check that you had no lights showing; you were in trouble if there were.

Working for the MOD

My youngest sister was still at school, and my three older sisters were all doing essential jobs. As for me, I was working at the Co-op cycle factory in

Kings Road, Tyseley, assembling cycles for the MOD. The Government was to bring in very strict regulations about where you could and could not work. Some conscripts who did not want to serve in the forces were sent down the coal mines, and became known as Bevin Boys. The first air raids on Birmingham took place in November 1940 and became a regular occurrence with some being much worse than others. Because of them I was soon to become accustomed to death and a lot of destruction. Every morning when I went to work I saw houses destroyed, and rescue squads, police and firemen were digging at the rubble, sometimes with their bare hands to rescue people. This was something I was to experience on more than one occasion over the next couple of years. You have to remember that we didn't have bulldozers or mechanical diggers then – it was all pick and shovel work.

Watching for firebombs

You could be up all night with the air raids but still had to go to work in the morning. We didn't use our Anderson shelter because it was always full of water. Instead, my Mum, sisters and 85-year-old grandmother sat in the hallway, while my Dad and I would go outside to watch for any possible fire bombs that might be dropped. One fateful night in September 1941, a bomb dropped in the garden of the house opposite ours, but fortunately Dad and I had gone inside for a cup of tea when the bomb fell. It landed right up against the Anderson Shelter. Sadly the family inside didn't stand a chance – the blast from this bomb blew most of the front of our house in. Every window went, doors were blown off and all the ceilings came down on top of us. The furniture was badly damaged by shrapnel. Dad and I heard it coming so we threw ourselves on top of Mum, the girls and Gran. Incredibly, none of us were injured.

Underground shelter, Albert Road School

My Dad told me to take my Gran and sisters to the underground air raid shelters in the grounds of Albert Road School. We turned into Francis Road and to our amazement saw an unexploded bomb sticking up out of the pavement with its fins showing not 18 inches from a gas street lamp, but we got to the shelter OK. Mum and dad stopped behind to collect important documents and to turn off the gas and water. Next morning we were taken to the YWCA, on the corner of Bordesley Green East and Richmond Road, and we stayed there for a week, sleeping on the floor. We were very well looked after by the WVS. We were then temporarily allocated to a house in

Manor Road right by the railway station and sidings. Each time the sirens went I had to take my Mum and sisters to the underground shelters beneath the shops on Station Road, Stechford. We had to go down steps that went from Astons, the Butchers, and then under all the other shops. One of the shops had been turned into ARP premises, so I enrolled as a messenger.

Love at first sight

By this time I was working, learning the trade, at Payne's Boot and Shoe Repairers at their shop in Albert Road, and every day I watched a gorgeous young girl go past on her way to and from school. I was only 16 and good looking! I found out that she and her family also went to the same shelter as us. One morning after spending the night in the shelter, I went down to check it was clear and found she had left her gas mask. Fortunately her name and address was on it, so on a night when I thought she would be in I took it to her house and chatted her up. Her name was Irene, we became good friends and started to see each other.

Casualty

One night during a raid they tried to target the railway sidings, but instead they hit Parkinson's Stove factory the other side of the station bridge, doing a lot of damage. I looked across from the warden's post to see a man crouching against the side of the bridge, but he didn't seem to move at all, so I went over to see if he was OK, but he was obviously dead. Yet there was not a mark on him – he had been killed by the blast from one of the bombs that hit the roof. I think it was one of the last air raids I remember. By this time our house in Morden Road was now repaired so we moved back there. Irene who was now my girlfriend had left school and was working for the National Savings Committee.

Volunteering, 1942

We were now into 1942, and when I became 18 in October of that year I volunteered for the army. With eight brothers already serving, I don't think I could have done anything else. I didn't have to report for training until February 1943. In December of 1942 my last Christmas at home before going away, the family that lived next door somehow managed to get hold of two pigs and they put them in their Anderson Shelter. Knowing my dad used to be a slaughter man at the Birmingham slaughter house, they asked if he would kill them. He could keep one for us. So I helped him to do the job, but have you ever tried to stop a pig from squealing? It's impossible! Police Sergeant Hodges lived just a couple of doors away – if he had heard the pigs we would have ended up in prison as meat was very strictly rationed. However, we got away with it and a lot of people enjoyed pork for their Christmas dinner, so I think we can be forgiven. Having volunteered for the army you had the privilege to choose which branch you would like to serve in. Those that were conscripted had to go wherever they where sent. I elected to join the Royal Army Service Corps (RASC).

My brother Les, who was next to me in age, was also in the RASC but he was a regular serving soldier and was in France at the time of the fall of Dunkirk in 1940. He was one of the less fortunate ones that was taken prisoner by the Germans when he was just 19 years old. I had three other brothers who were also regular serving soldiers: Arthur, Warwickshire Yeomanry (Royal Armoured Corps) and Fred (REME), who had finished their full-time service when war broke out in 1939 so they were unable to leave and ended up doing another six years on active service in various areas. Sid was also a regular serving soldier. He had been with the RASC, Tank Corp, and finally with the Parachute Regiment serving with the 8th Airborne Division. My other four serving brothers were George, Royal Artillery, Jack, Royal Artillery, Joe, Army Fire Service and stepbrother Albert (RASC). We all saw active service in various regions. Brother Jack won a bravery citation at Monte Casino, but he was injured.

Norton Barracks, Worcester

On the 28 February 1943 I reported to Norton Barracks, Worcester, the headquarters of the Worcestershire Regiment, to do my 12 weeks of basic training with the General Service Corps. All the instructors and training staff were regular soldiers of the Worcestershire Regiment and what a tough lot they turned out to be – loudmouthed, offensive and very abusive, especially the drill sergeants. The training was very tough indeed – just as you would expect. There was a very good assault course, which I really enjoyed tackling at least twice a week, and we had P/T every morning, sometimes before breakfast. One of the P/T instructors was sergeant Roly Jenkins, who I believe played cricket for Worcester County. Very often we had to do a cross country run just before tea, and of course there were the dreaded route marches. You started off doing 5 miles, sometimes running a mile and walking a mile. The longest one we did I think was about 25 miles.

As I said at the beginning it was really tough but I enjoyed every minute of it, and it made a man of me and a proud man at that. I finished my basic training on 14 April and was sent home on 14 days leave. On return from leave, because my transfer had not come through, I was posted to the Worcestershire Regiment at Norton Barracks to continue my training, which was basically an extension of what I had been doing, except that I now had to do guard duty on the main gates. Each time I was picked for guard duty I won the very honoured title of 'Stick Man' – this was awarded to the best turned-out soldier on guard parade by the orderly officer of the day, and it meant that you did not have to do the two on four off duty, and you just wore your belt and bayonet. My transfer to the RASC came through, and although I tried to get it cancelled so that I could stay in the Worcesters my request was refused. I had really enjoyed my time at Norton Barracks.

Hadrian's Camp and 524 Coy

I was given a 48-hour pass home, and sadly while on this short leave Irene and I had a falling out and parted company. On return from this weekend pass I was posted to the RASC driving school at Hadrian's Camp, Carlisle. Here I was taught to drive a wide range of vehicles but mainly lorries. After six weeks of intensive training I passed my driving test with flying colours on 9th August 1943. On completion of my training at the RASC training school I was posted to 524 Coy (at least I think that was the number but I cannot be 100% sure), stationed at Codford in Wiltshire. We moved about the country for a while until just after December 1944 when we took over special Amphibious Vehicles and I think the company became 199GT Coy.

Terrapin, Buffalo and something like a Pontoon

We moved to the west coast of Wales and started to train and test out three different types of vehicles – the first of which was the Terrapin, a tank-like vehicle but with an open top and instead of tracks it had eight rubber tyre wheels and got its power from two Ford V8 engines. It was slow and very cumbersome both on the road and in the water, with leaver steering, which made it very difficult to handle. If one engine broke down while in the water you went around in circles with no way of getting back to shore other than by towing. The second vehicle was the Buffalo, again with a body like a tank, but it did have tracks on it with very deep cleats. It had a powerful seven-cylinder Wasp Radial engine. Because of the deep cleats on the tracks it did a lot of damage when driven on the roadway, on rough ground it was brilliant and it could climb very, very steep inclines. In the water, however, it was dreadful – it was very slow, it didn't ride the waves but just drove through them, and if the sea was even just a bit rough it took on a lot of water. You could not see where you were going most of the time – you just had to rely on your co-driver.

When driving off a landing craft the Buffalo was known to dive straight down in the water. More than one soldier lost his life training on this vehicle in just that way. They were, to say the very least, dangerous in the water. The third vehicle, was the American-built GMC-DUKW – the best way I can describe it would be to say it looked like a Pontoon with three rubber-tyre road wheels each side. It weighed 7.5 tons, unloaded, and was 31 feet long, with 270 cubic inch engine, six-cylinder petrol tank, and had a land speed 55 miles per hour, 6 miles per hour on water, with a payload of 2.5 tons or 25 soldiers and their equipment. It had 10 forward gears and two reverse. It had its own compressor by which you could inflate or deflate any tyre on the vehicle without stopping, and you could check its pressure just by moving a small leaver on the dashboard. It also had its own bilge pump for pumping out any water taken on board, which proved to be very important.

On the road the DUKW drove just the same as any road vehicle and when you wanted to drive off the beach into the water, you disengaged the road wheels and engaged its own propeller and reversed the operation coming out of the water. It rode the waves very well indeed and because of its very efficient bilge pumps you were able to get rid of any surplus water that you had taken on board.

The real advantage of these vehicles was of course that you could pick up your load from a ship well out to sea and deliver it straight to a supply dump several miles inland without having to stop, to me they were a fantastic piece of engineering.

Invasion imminent
It was now very apparent to us that an invasion was not too far away and we had been officially attached to the third Canadian Infantry Division. In May 1944, we moved to our port of departure, which was Southampton. To get there, I remember driving through the streets of London during the night with a very heavy Police and Military escort. The roads were blocked off and all traffic movement stopped until we had passed. We parked up in streets,

which had been sealed off around the dock areas of Southampton for over three weeks, and slept on our vehicles. We did actually load up onto the ships and started out to sea once (I think it was ten days before the actual invasion date), but we got called back after a couple of hours out to sea and had to unload again. The night of 3 June 1944 the activity was unbelievable, but for me personally it didn't turn out the way that I expected it to – instead of being loaded onto a landing craft as before, I was loaded onto the top deck of a large supply ship and off we went.

Juno Beach

About a mile or so from the French coast I (in a DUKW) was unceremoniously slung over the side of the supply ship and into the sea and had to drive that distance onto the beach to rendezvous with the rest of my platoon and to discharge the load of stretchers that I was carrying. This beach was to be known as Juno beach, and the name of the place where I landed was Benneries Sur Mer [sic]. I must point out at this time that all hell had broken out. The noise came from all types of gunfire, shells and bombs exploding everywhere.

What I was about to witness in the next few hours, and months no training or teaching in the world could prepare you for. Death and destruction was all around me, there were unbelievable scenes and ones that I will never EVER forget, but for all that I had a job to do and had to get on with it if I wanted to survive. We made our HQ in a small Chateau about a mile from the beach, and by midday the Canadian infantry had got about three to four miles inland and were able to set up a supply dump. This meant that we could start our work of getting supplies ashore from the supply ships as quickly as possible. We worked from dusk until dawn every day, seven days a week. Do you know what? I was sat in my DUKW at 4.30 in the morning, waiting to go down to the beach to start work when our Provo corporal climbed up the side of my vehicle and said, 'Caught you Smithy!' – I was smoking on a WD vehicle, and he put me on a charge.

I went before the CO the next morning and they stopped two weeks' pay. This was in the first week of the invasion – how's that for discipline. It didn't end there – two weeks later the very same Corporal Cleckner did me for being improperly dressed, not wearing my hat – that cost me another two weeks' pay, so in five weeks I lost four weeks pay, but what the hell, there was nowhere to spend it anyway.

Because the Germans had us bogged down we worked the beaches with our DUKWs for about five weeks until the fall of Caen, which I think was about the middle of July. We then changed the DUKWs for three-ton lorries, namely Ford Wat sixes. They turned out to be really good reliable workhorses.

Route through France and crossing the Rhine

As we moved forward we took the more northern route through France, Belgium, and Holland, and finally into Germany. However, before reaching Germany, there were a few very hard battles to be fought and won. It was our job to make sure that the lads up front were kept well supplied and I think we did just that. In so doing I was in a way involved in all those heavy battles, like Falaise, Brugges, Nymagen, Antwerp, Brussels and Arnhem. Having reached Arnhem I had no idea that my brother Sid was one of those that had dropped with the 8th Airborne Division. Unfortunately he was shot before he hit the ground and lay in a ditch for two days before being rescued. When we reached the River Rhine at a place I think was called Velo, we changed back to DUKWs for the crossing.

I remember very well indeed that when I entered the water the current was so strong that I thought I was not going to make it. I did of course, but nowhere near the place I was supposed to get out of the water. I was a mile or so further downriver than I should have been. The units that crossed in Buffaloes did so much more easily than I did. The terrain was just perfect for them to show their capabilities. Once across the Rhine, everything was so much easier – we just knew that it was the beginning of the end, although we did have a little skirmish at Munchen Glad Bach. We made our last HQ in Hamburg.

News of the surrender

I was on my way back to Calais in a small convoy when the news came through that Germany had surrendered. I celebrated VE day in Calais before driving back to Hamburg, which took us a couple of days longer than it should have done but nobody questioned it. I was then sent on detachment to a company of the Royal Engineers that were building an airstrip just outside Kiel. It was our job to ferry German prisoners of war from their prison camp to the airstrip to work. They really didn't like that – they would sometimes refuse to get out of the lorries but a couple of shots fired into the air soon changed their minds. The very tiny village that we camped in was on the edge of a very large wood, and I went shooting deer in there mainly on my own. I never shot more than two, so I gave one to the man in the village that dressed them for us and he shared it with the villagers. When my CO found out we had to send some of the meat back to our HQ in Hamburg, that way he let me have some more ammo.

Back to England then off to Egypt

In May 1945 the company was recalled to England. On arrival we had orders that the company was to be sent out to Egypt. As I had only about twelve months to do before my demob number came up, I was told that I would have to go to a holding camp for that duration. I didn't want to spend that time with a lot of strangers. I appealed to my CO to let me go to Egypt with them – after all we had seen a lot of action together. After some deliberation he agreed.

We were given 14 days of disembarkation leave. While on this leave brother Joe, now demobbed, had arranged a night out at the Birmingham Hippodrome to see a show and we agreed to meet outside. Imagine my surprise when I arrived there to find Irene, my ex-girlfriend, with my sister-in-law Hilda and Joe of course waiting for me.

It turned out that Irene had stayed good friends with Hilda, Sid's wife. Irene had been visiting Sid in Hospital at Burntwood while he was recovering from his injuries received when he dropped at Arnhem. I think it was the best show that I ever went to – why? – because, thanks to Joe, it brought Irene and I back together again. I think I saw her every day of that leave. I wonder if I would have still volunteered to go to Egypt if I had met her earlier. Irene and I decided to get engaged – we would get married when I got demobbed. On return from leave we set sail for Egypt in June 1946 and went to Cambria Camp, Abbasia Garrison, Cairo. I was sent home from there for demob on 19 May 1947 in a depot at York. And there endeth my military story.

Band of Brothers

The Birmingham Sunday Mercury, a local newspaper, published an article with the heading 'Band Of Brothers' on Sunday, 11 November 2001, relating to my eight brothers and I who all served in the army on active service at the same time between 1939-45. What I think is really incredible is the fact that we all returned home. Only brothers Sid and Jack sustained war injuries, from which they recovered quite well. I think this was a great achievement for just one family. Sadly there is only my brother Joe and myself still surviving.

Service records
BRUMMIE BAND OF BROTHERS

As my own service record is pretty well documented in my own story, this is a brief service history of my other EIGHT brothers that served in the Army between 1939-1945. There were NINE of us serving in the British Army 1939-45 but it never dawned on me until recently just how many of us had served at the same time until I became interested in writing my own story for BBC. WW2, and people reading it pointed out that it could be a record.

Some of us were regular soldiers and served pre-war as you will see from their records. Two were wounded and one taken prisoner. As a family we were very lucky as we all returned home at the end of the war.

JOE: Enlisted 1940 - RAOC. Served in UK and then India in the Army Fire Fighting Service (Later that unit was transferred to the Pioneer Corps) Max Rank attained = Sergeant.

GEORGE: Serving in the TA (Birmingham Artillery Unit) in the late 1930s. In 1939 called up for full time service. Served in the UK (Scapa Flow) unit then moved out to India where it was disbanded. George then transferred to the Royal Military Police. Max rank attained = QTR Master Sargeant.

JACK: Joined North Staffs Regiment - 1940. Transferred to Royal Artillery-served in North Africa (took part in Operation Torch with the U.S forces), and Italy-mentioned in despatches at Monte Casino. Max rank attained = believed to be Corporal.

FRED: Joined the Kings Royal Irish Hussars in 1933 - served in the UK, and Egypt discharged to the Reserves in 1939 - re-called up again in 1939 and joined the Royal Scots Greys, served in North Africa and possibly Italy. At sometime transferred to the REME. Max rank attained = TSM or CSM.

SID: Enlisted in 1939 into the RASC served in the BEF in France 1939/40.Transferred to the Royal Tank Corp. and was an instructor at sometime in the Westminster Dragoons. Promoted to Sergeant on a number of occasions and busted a number of times. Transferred to the Parachute Regiment and was seriously injured during the last assault on the Rhine crossing in March 1945. Max rank attained = Sergeant.

ARTHUR: Enlisted in the Royal Irish 8th Hussars in 1930 - served in the UK and Egypt. Discharged to the reserves in 1936. Called up again in 1939. Joined the Warwickshire Yeomanry. Served in the Middle East - North Africa (El-Alamein). Max rank attained = Remained Trooper throughout service.

LES: Enlisted 1939 - Joined the RASC served in the BEF in France 1939/1940. Taken prisoner. Then sent to prison camp in Germany. Max rank attained = Corporal.

ALBERT GEORGE: (Step Brother) Joined the RASC 1939 - certainly saw service in India in later part of war.

Sadly there is now only my brother Joe (91) and myself (80) this year still surviving. I would just like to point out that my older brother SAM served with the Royal Artillery and saw action in France during the FIRST world war (1914/1918).

Leonard J Smith

My story begins as a lad of eight, the youngest of twelve children born in Skinner Lane in 1932. Spending a lot of time with my older sister, Doris, who retold these stories to me throughout our childhood and adulthood until she passed away. I am now able to convey this story to you. When the heavy bombing of Birmingham (what became known as The Blitz) began, I lived on the corner of Bromsgrove Street and Gooch Street North. A lot of buildings sustained bomb damage during these raids.

Behind our house were Kent Street Baths, the basement of which contained an ARP post and a first aid post. During a very heavy raid, a bomb was dropped through a skylight which landed in the men's pool killing some ARP personnel. The casualties would have been greater but a senior officer had advised some of the staff to take shelter in the basement. On the 15th October 1940, a bomb landed in Bishop Street, destroying three houses and a small factory. A first aid post and incident headquarters were set up in Weathershields factory and various personnel attempted to reach people who were trapped. There was a terrible gas leak which hindered the rescue work so a request was made for heavy rescue squads led by Commander G Inwood to attend. Several attempts had already been made to rescue the people who were trapped but to no avail. Commander Inwood made his way into the ruined building and discovered that some people were trapped in a strengthened cellar that was filling up with gas. Commander Inwood rescued a man and the body of a young boy was also brought out. Inwood again, crawled into the ruins and the other men were rescued, by this time the gas was becoming unbearable but Inwood again went into the ruins. However, this time he was overcome by the gas fumes and he had to be rescued by other members of the rescue squad. Several attempts were made to revive him however he was pronounced dead shortly afterwards. During this time various other members of the rescue squad made heroic attempts to rescue the trapped people, but again the gas fumes overwhelmed them and they also had to be rescued and revived.

The rescue attempts continued to be carried out by the rescue squad but only dead bodies were retrieved. One of the men rescued was my Dad's brother (William Hill) the dead boy who was retrieved initially by Inwood was my cousin, David Hill aged nine. My aunt's body was found a week later in the water filled crater by workmen. There was a big funeral held for the victims of the air raid, however as my aunt's body had not been found she was not buried as part of this funeral. My cousin was buried in a mass grave, in Yardley Cemetery, on approximately 22 October 1940 and my aunt was buried ten rows away from her son on approximately 29th October 1940. I would imagine that Commander Inwood had a full military funeral, according to my father he was given a hero's funeral.

He was awarded the George Cross posthumously, becoming the first member of the Home Guard to receive this honour in Birmingham. This was presented to his wife and son and is now displayed in the Birmingham Museum and Art Gallery. Following these devastating bombings, my Uncle Bill told my father (James Ernest Hill) that when the sirens sounded at approximately 8:15pm on 15th October 1940, my Aunt Lucy had just started to make a pot of tea, my Uncle Bill and cousin David were in the living room and my Aunt Lucy had just gone to the head of the cellar to get the milk for the tea. Suddenly, there was a terrible bang and an explosion and he was trapped. The bomb had directly hit my uncle's house, landing in the cellar before exploding. During this time many other buildings were bombed, including Eddystone Radio Works, Jarrets & Rainsford, Hawkes, Southalls Bros and Barclays.

These were all in a square flanked by Bromsgrove Street, Gooch Street North, Kent Street and Lower Essex Street. The only building saved in this square was The Rose and Crown pub, home of the Imperial boxing club. This building is still standing today as is part of Jarrets & Rainsford. These are part of the few remaining bombed buildings in Birmingham.

In Birmingham Undaunted there is a photograph of the ruins of Eddystone radios and Hawkes and the other bombed buildings and on the right hand side of the picture is the house I lived in until 1952, 115 Bromsgrove Street. In later years, I attended school with Commander Inwood's son, George, and we were also members of the 19th Company Boys Brigade at The Friends Hall, Moseley Road, Highgate. It seems ironic that I grew up with the son of the man who saved my uncle's life and retrieved my cousin's body and also lost his own life in the process. The implementation of The Tree of Life, the memorial erected by Birmingham Air Raids Remembrance Association in memory of all the air raid victims in the Bull Ring is a lasting tribute to the work of Commander Inwood, the rescue squad and all of the victims of the bombings.

Les Hill

Postscript – When unveiled the tree of life memorial led to a flurry of contact to BARRA regarding names missing from the memorial. Amazingly, one of these was George Inwood. The compiled list was taken from the Commonwealth war graves Commission records for civilian casualties. George Inwood had been recorded as a "Service" casualty. This led to several other Home Guard casualties being identified. Other casualties missed from the memorial, were people injured in Birmingham, but taken to Hospital outside the City, who later died from their injuries. 2147 names were added to the memorial, a further 74 have now been added and 2 misspelt names corrected. Now on with the stories, the next is my Mother's.

Brian Wright

Henry Hicken killed 10th April 1941

LIL WRIGHT'S STORY (BORN LILLIAN MAY HICKEN)

I was born 8th January 1931, which meant that when the war broke out I was almost 9 years old. I was evacuated with my younger brother Ted, to Stanton under Barton Leicestershire. Our journey started at the railway station in Saltley, by the Metro Camel Works. A lasting memory was of a tram driver stopping his tram (a number 8 or 10) and hugging us all with tears in his eyes as we queued for the train. Miss Hall head mistress from Arden Road School, travelled with us she took pity on my brother and bought him some Wellington boots, he was ever so proud of them. On arrival at Stanton we were lined up in pairs at a school. My brother and I were the last to be picked, probably due to the state of our clothes, nobody would take us as a pair and we were split up.

Mr and Mrs Holmes that took me in were kind; my brother however was not so lucky. The Holmes family had two sons, Terry and a baby whose name I now forget. The trauma of being taken from Birmingham and my family, led to me starting to wet the bed, my mattress was put onto the floor to save the bed. After 4 weeks my Mom (another Lillian May) had got word about the conditions in which my brother was living in. Mom arranged for my eldest brother Jack to fetch Ted home. I stayed in Stanton for two more weeks, but my dad (Henry) told Jack to go back and fetch me as well. Dad said if we were going to die it might as well all be together.

So we were back in Birmingham 6 weeks after the start of the war, and before the bombing started. Dad worked as a timekeeper at Thomas Smith & Sons of Saltley, which was opposite to our house in Adderley Road, Saltley. He could not be called up because he had lost all but a thumb and forefinger of one hand in a drop forging accident. I know he loved me a great deal. I used to potter around after him trying to help him all the time, hence he used to call me "Pots". The Die shop of Thomas Smiths was in Hams Road; we would shelter there during raids because it was re enforced. In April 1941 I remember seeing a German plane flying over our house there was no alarm sounded, so no one would believe me. One week later April 10th, Dad was fire watching when the sirens did sound, Dad checked to see if we were all right in the shelter, he went to check if the dog "Spot" and "Mickey" the Canary were OK. That was the last we saw of him, there was a big bang, two houses were destroyed one of them was ours.

It was a direct hit and dad was killed out right. Dad's body was taken to George Arthur Road swimming baths, until his burial in a grave at Witton Cemetery. Mom said he was buried with a lot of kids killed during this big raid on Birmingham.

Lillian May Wright

THE LANDMINE IN REGINALD ROAD, SALTLEY

I was most interested to read in a recent Birmingham Air Raids Newsletter the account of the landmine in the house in Reginald Road, Saltley. I remember it well. We lived in Havelock Road, which meant that the back of our house faced Reginald Road. We had heard about the landmine and that morning my mother was preparing a luxury rabbit. I myself had gone into the back kitchen to wash my hands, although, we heard no explosion everything just went black. I dashed back to my mother who put her hands over my face and shocked me by saying "it's taken her nose off"! As she put her wet hands over my face, my mother felt my face in the darkness and thought it was blood. We staggered out to the front of the house where it just happened that our landlord had just been collecting rent. We leaned against his car to collect our thoughts. When he saw us he was fuming. How dare we lean on his beloved car! Afterwards we all saw the funny side of it. I do not know what happened to the rabbit!

M Sayfrites, daughter of Charles Barnard Killed April 1941

AMBULANCE DRIVER

My mother was an ambulance driver stationed at Court Road Sparkhill ARP depot No.16. She and her colleagues were sent to the Carlton Cinema incident.

When they entered the building her attendant collapsed when she saw the carnage. A relief ambulance attendant was brought in, riding pillion behind a despatch rider. When my mother returned from

*Clarice Summerhays –
Ambulance Driver
ARP 1940 (Civil Defence)*

duty the following morning, she burst into tears and then explained that she had entered the building, the only light came from the moon shining through the damaged roof. She could make out people sitting with their eyes open. It was only when she spoke to them that she realised that they had been killed by the blast. My mother was later involved in the devastating raid on Coventry. She was sent in a convoy of ARP personnel and firemen at the height of the raid and carried casualties to hospitals all over Warwickshire. I welcome the

ARP Depot. No. 16. Court Road, Sparkhill, Birmingham. Left to right: Arthur Moleston, Margaret Ball, Leslie Wakefield, Clarice Summerhays, Reggie McGee

memorial and hope that tribute is paid to the civil defence, fire service and police force that went out under fire to try and rescue people and tend to the injured.

Malcolm Summerhayes

WARTIME MEMORIES BY AGATHA'S GRANNY

I was born in summer 1929, so I was 10 years old when the Second World War started on Sunday September 3rd 1939. I was in the kitchen with my family of 6, preparing the Sunday lunch – we all had our jobs to do, mine was to prepare the rice pudding before laying the table with my younger sister. We had the radio on, it was a big wooden set, which had to have the accumulator battery charged every month, I think, for 1 shilling. At 11 o'clock there was to be an announcement, so we were all very quiet as we were told that we were at war with Germany. I did not understand, then, what that meant but the grown ups were very serious.

We went to the village school and were issued with gas masks in square cardboard boxes. We made cloth covers, with strings to carry them round our shoulders and practised putting them on and off – we must have looked very peculiar. We certainly sounded peculiar when we spoke. Babies had special Mickey Mouse cots with masks over the tops so they, like us, would not breathe any poisonous fumes if we had a gas attack. It was a ten minute walk from school to our house so, if the air raid warning sounded (a works hooter), we all went to nearby houses to shelter with friends until the all-clear siren sounded. If the warning came at night my family went down into the next door Anderson shelter built in their garden. We didn't have a shelter but used our garden to grow lots of vegetables for us to eat. My mother made most of our clothes, knitting and sewing every minute she could. MAKE DO AND MEND and DIG FOR VICTORY were slogans on the posters. My father also mended our shoes, buying sheets of leather and pounds of nails from the local shop.

I tried the 11+ scholarship exam (voluntarily) with a few friends in the Easter term and was lucky enough to get a place in the local County (Secondary) School. One brother went to the Technical and the other to the Boys County, so it must have cost my parents a lot of money to buy three school uniforms and bus fares to town at the beginning of the war. Autumn 1940 saw a lot of our big cities bombed – London, Coventry, Birmingham, Plymouth, Bristol and Swansea and a lot of damage caused. I well remember the barrage balloons which were such a hindrance to the German planes. There was one based in the field next to our house and, when a plane flew into it, it burst and the silk was used by the villagers to make blouses and underwear which saved having to use our precious coupons (which were more valuable than money) to buy clothes, food, milk and fuel. Sometimes Ration Books of clothes coupons were sold on the black market to people who could afford to pay the big families for the children's books but, if they were caught, they were fined! In 1947 I went to College, so my mother used the family coupons to kit me out with new clothes. One brother went to the Army so his brown pin-striped suit trousers were altered to a skirt and I wore his suit instead of school uniform which was passed on to my younger sister! Men who worked in the coal mines, the Bevin Boys, didn't have to join the forces – the Army, Navy or Air Force – but had extra cheese rations.

We had l/2d bottles of milk at school every day which we drank with a straw. The cardboard tops, with holes for the straws, we used to make raffia table mats and woollen pom-poms. When the air raids disturbed our sleep, we were allowed to go to school at 10 o'clock and finished at 3 o'clock with a short break at lunch time to eat our sandwiches. School uniform was compulsory and each item was marked with a name tape, we had inspections every Monday morning by prefects. Our school time-tables included lessons in: English Literature, English Language, Welsh, French, Latin, Greek, German, Spanish, Arithmetic, Algebra, Geometry, Trigonometry, Science, Physics, Biology, Botany, Chemistry, Zoology, Music, RE, Dancing, Hockey, PT, Tennis and Morning Assembly every day. Some of the teachers in the Boys' School went into the forces, so boys came to our school for some lessons and girls went to the Boys' School for other lessons, we had lots of homework too, we had conductors on the buses to take our fares and give us tickets.

Petrol was in very short supply so there weren't many buses and very few cars – we did a lot of walking if we missed the school bus. The girls came out earlier than the boys so the bus queues didn't get too long! We also queued at the shops – when there was any special food available, like bananas or oranges. The weekly rations were small amounts – 1 or 2 ounces each of butter, margarine, cheese, lard, and bacon, meat, sugar, tea, milk and eggs with 'points' for everything else – tins, packets, bread, jam, fruit, vegetables etc. We had London evacuees billeted in our village. They couldn't understand us and we couldn't understand them! Cockney and Welsh accents were very different. Paper and books, too, were very scarce, so we had to share school books, which had to be covered in brown paper to protect the utility soft covers. Furniture and clothes also had the utility marks on them which meant they were made in wartime of sub-standard or basic materials, which were not strong, so had to be protected. 1/2d stamps were used for letters.

Metal gates, railings, aluminium, tins, cans and saucepans were all collected for the war effort to make aeroplanes, guns and tanks and ships for the forces. We were encouraged to make woollen socks, gloves, mittens, scarves and balaclavas for the men at the 'Front' – the fighting troops, and to write letters to cheer them up when they were so far from home in France, Germany, Italy, North Africa and the Far East.

We all had identity cards with our own numbers – mine was XLKF 325-5, as I was fifth in my family. These had to be shown to anyone in authority and used in form filling. Some fathers were 'prisoners of war' in Europe or Japan and there were enemy prisoners over here. They were freed at the end of the war after VE day – Victory in Europe (May 1945) and VJ day – Victory in Japan (Aug 1945) when there were great celebrations with flags and bunting and parties in the streets, for PEACE at last. Dried eggs were introduced into our diets during the war. They were brought in from America, I think, as were nylon stockings.

Windows had strips of brown paper stuck across down and diagonally so that glass did not splinter and cause injury during raids. I think everybody in the village had coal fires. Ours had to be lit with paper, sticks, small lumps, cinders and then larger pieces of coal. Some of the paper was tied into knots and some rolled into balls so that they would burn longer. We had 10/-, £1 and £5 notes with 1/2d, 1d, 3d, 6d (tanner), 1s (bob), 2s (florin), 2s 6d (half a crown) coins, Farthings (f) l/4d had a wren on the obverse. 4f equalled ld, 12d equalled 1s, 20s equalled £1. A guinea was 21s still used for the sale of horses.

Mary Smith

THE DAY WAR BROKE OUT

The day war broke out I was eighteen months old. We lived in a cul-de-sac of eight houses and all but one house had children. My sister Audrey (6) and I with Mom and Dad lived at No 5. Next door were Joan (10) and Brian (1). My memories of this time are very few but Audrey tells me that most of the children, herself included, were sent off to Alfrick in Worcestershire in September 1939. Audrey was billeted with an old couple who argued and swore a lot and she was not happy. Mom went to see Mrs. Collins at Cheapside where Joan and Pat (11) (from No.3) were residing and asked if Audrey could move in with them, and it was agreed. They had quite a few adventures. Paddling in the local stream, Audrey went down into a hollow and nearly drowned. They were chased by a horse and Joan picked Audrey up and literally threw her over the hedge as the horse was almost upon them. Only having candles in the bedroom, the girls lit up and then went out, the candle was too near the curtains and they set on fire – they were in deep trouble. Mrs. Collins gave them so many jam sandwiches that Audrey has never eaten any since! One of the children from their school was killed when darting out from behind a farm cart into the path of a car.

I only remember one visit with Mom and, as we walked along a sunny country lane, there nestling against a wire fence was this huge black pig. My two year old self was so upset to see a BLACK pig (they were all pink in my story books). I promptly burst into floods of tears. Nine months on and Joan had passed the entrance exam to King Edward's and was to start in the September so Joan and Audrey came back in June. One week later the bombs began to fall. A few years ago Audrey went back to Alfrick and she did meet a man who remembered "the evacuees". "One of your lot stayed with us and when my Mom served runner beans with the dinner she said, 'I'm not eating grass!'" Talking to my sister about all this, I mentioned Mom told me that our relatives in Canada had begged her to send Audrey over there to them. "I never knew that" she said. "Did you have to stay there over Christmas?" "No, Joan's uncle fetched us in his car".

THE AIR-RAIDS

Oh what terrible nights we had. I remember going to school one morning and the teacher said, "You can all put your heads down on the desk and have a little nap". So this must have been when I was around 6 or 7 years of age as when we were in the Infant class and we all had a little bed to sleep on in the afternoon. I hated that. Even before I started school I didn't like having to have an afternoon nap. Many a time my mother would try to get me to have a nap with her on the sofa (Mothers always had afternoon naps in those days or so it seemed). There was always a pot of fresh tea on the table as we came in from school and settled down to listen to "Mrs. Dale's Diary".

Our air-raid shelter was in the front garden as was the Pridmores and Doughtys at Nos 6 & 2 and I think the Minetts at No 3. The Davises at No.7 shared with the Pridmores and the Nurrishes at No 8 just sat under the stairs, as did the Wards at No.5. I always wished we were in the Pridmores' shelter with them because they seemed to have such fun. We could hear them chanting "Old Brown's Cow went BOOMPS" against the wall. The Boomp coinciding with the next exploding bomb so that little Brian would not be frightened. They had lots of home comforts down there too, unlike ours which were very basic. Horrid(!) spiders and anything else you could imagine. One night after the "All Clear", Mom took me to the gate and lifted me up to see the red glow in the sky.

"That is Coventry on fire" she said. That was the night Coventry really got a lambasting. A few streets away they had a landmine right on the communal shelter where lots of people were sheltering. We never lost any friends in school although there were many raids and houses were blitzed round about.

There was a railway line at the bottom of our back garden. One night there was an awful raid and Mom could hear the man in the signal box uttering oaths; she asked him what was wrong and he wouldn't answer. Next morning she called up to him "What was all that about George?" "I'll tell you now" he said, "There were truckloads of ammunition standing stationary right here and I thought if ever we got a hit we would all go up".

When raids happened night after night, Mom and Dad decided on this particular night they were not rushing down to the shelter. We all got into their bed and stayed there, Mom shaking like a leaf. We used to play in the shelters sometimes and I do remember Brian, Margaret and Clifford going into Brian's shelter and starting a fire and it was only the fact that Brian's Dad noticed the smoke curling round the door that they were rescued. I wasn't playing with them for some reason.

I remember jumping into our shelter and landing on a plank with a rusty nail sticking up out of it, so I should have had a tetanus injection but we didn't have any transport of any kind to get me to the doctor's or hospital and no one phoned for an ambulance. So I never did get one, as there were no men about during the day who might have done something. Mrs. Pridmore, who seemed to be the First Aid attendant for anything like that, cleaned me up and that was that; it was very painful to walk for a while.

Meryl Cowley

I REMEMBER

I was born on 22nd March 1940 at 29 Pineapple Road Stirchley, my older brother Andrew was evacuated so I have no memory of him until after the war. I can remember hearing the air raid sirens going off, but do not know whether for a raid or the all clear. I do remember barrage balloons on Highbury Park also going into Uffculme Road with my Mom on our way to shopping in Kings Heath we saw a bombed out house. My aunt and uncle lived in Pineapple Grove they were both ARP wardens as was their daughter. I remember my aunt taking me into the air raid shelter on Pineapple Green, what a dark, damp and musty smell that was.

I remember the VE day party in the road red white and blue ribbon in my hair (I still have the ribbon) and Union Jacks hanging from windows. I remember after the war, Mom taking me at night into the city centre (what was left of it) to see the lights switched on again. What a lovely sight to a child who had never seen shops or roads lit up before.

Nadine Beddowes 'nee' Mason

WARTIME MEMORIES

My war memories are mainly concerned with learning and training as the war years coincided with my teen years; this was to be expected. 1940 saw me on farm work, helping with the harvesting and, in particular, hand weeding a 15 acre field of carrots near to Stourbridge. 1941 saw me at college where they had an Army cadet Unit, wearing breeches, brasses and puttees etc. Training was alongside the Home Guard, mostly 1918 staff – Morse code with flags and arms drill with single shot rifles salvaged from the Boer war! As a senior NCO, I stood in, with others, to maintain the smoke screen in Solihull Road and Sharmans Cross Road, whilst the Home Guard went off for training camp.

As I was more interested in flying, I joined the Air Training Corps (492 Squadron in the Beacon Building, Hall Green) and, because of my previous cadet experience, soon became a senior NCO studying Air Navigation, Bomb Aiming and Gunnery. By 1943 I was old enough to volunteer for the RAF and was sent to Scarborough for assessment, obtaining grade of PNB (Pilot, Navigator, Bomb Aimer).

In the winter I went on a Sunday morning gliding course and passed out solo in 6-8 weeks. Unfortunately for me I received a letter from the RAF saying that they had over budgeted for air-crew as we were winning the war, giving me the chance that, if I still wanted to fly, it would have to be as a rear gunner or, failing that, how about the RAF Regiment? As I did not fancy flying backwards or playing soldiers in RAF uniform I chose to join the army proper in the hope that my gliding experience would help. Thus 1944-1945 meant more training with oil, petrol, fire and steam pumps and pipes etc. Then VE Day came with a change of accent including jungle training and survival and then VJ Day. I got a lot of help with my geography, seeing France, Italy, Egypt, Aden, Bombay, Barrackpore, Calcutta, Rangoon, Bangkok and Singapore.

In Singapore I ended up in a white sailor suit and small boats in the harbour and around the islands. So, if any of the above named and unused skills are ever needed, I'm your man.

Memories of 1945

The year kicked off very cold, so cold that, when I lifted my kit bag to my shoulder, I knocked myself off my feet. Not for me Street parties and the like; I arrived home on 8 May at breakfast time at the start of 14 days embarkation leave! Only three things were on my mind – a hot bath, soft civilian clothes and my girl friend! Having completed two items and about to proceed on the third, my mother said "You're not going out like that, put your uniform on". I slept in over 35 different places, in hammocks, in the open air and the orangery of a stately home and other places.

I visited, or stayed in, ten countries and learned how to get by in three different languages. I taught myself to drive in a morning and became a driving examiner in the afternoon! I didn't have much opportunity to sample foreign foods but lived mainly on fruit, eggs and bananas, previously sadly missed, V J Day, or shortly after, is more vivid in my recollections. The formal surrender of the Japanese in Thailand was to be a hand over of symbolic swords by the senior Japanese commander at a sports ground in Bangkok. A British ceremonial guard was required; the quickest way was to get two volunteers from every unit in Siam on the 'you and you' basis. There was no rehearsal, straight in, berets, fore and aft caps, jungle hats, glengarries, bush hats turned up, bush hats turned down, flat hats and dress caps, khaki drill shirts, jungle green, camouflage and cream, short trousers, battle dress bottoms and kilt in all the above colours.

None of us had drilled for some time and, all together, not at all. With an assortment of short rifles, long rifles, short and long bayonets and the odd

Sten or similar, the column ambled on. The look on the Japanese faces was not inscrutable! Do the Japanese not have a word for souvenir?

Nevill Smith

CHILDHOOD WAR MEMORIES

War started for me the day I saw my first barrage balloon. Up till then I never knew much about it, as I was only five years of age. I feel sure it was a Sunday afternoon. I was walking along Yardley Wood Road by the canal bridge. I remember rushing home to my mum to find out about what it was. She said "We're at war now with the Germans, but don't worry if they come here, your Dad and I won't let them get you and John. We will put our heads in the gas oven". I don't know if she thought this would be a comfort to us, but I know I never really worried about it. I'm quite sure, to all us kids, it was a big adventure.

My dad worked nights. He used to ride to work on his bike because of getting home at 2 o'clock in the morning. He painted his light on his bike so only the bottom half shone down the road. His torch was powered by carbide, which he mixed with water.

We used to shut him outside when he did this, as the smell was terrible, like rotten eggs. Dad worked all through the war in Barford Street which was right in the thick of the bombing and, although he finished his night shift at 2.00am, he would quite often not return home until mid morning if the bombing was very bad. He would be out with the police and ARP rescuing people from out of the rubble.

There were times when he would come home very upset with what he had seen and had to do and, although he never told mum in front of us, we knew that war wasn't as we thought of it, just a big adventure. Later, at every bus depot they had a group of men who were in the Home Brigade. My father was one of them.

His uniform always smelt of mothballs, I think this was because he never really had much chance to wear it other than for parades. The one very sad part of the war for me was when my godmother's eldest son, Leslie, was reported missing. He was a rear gunner in the Air Force and was shot down over Germany. He never did return; this affected us all very much as we were a very close community.

Norma Taylor

WARTIME MEMORIES. BLITZ NIGHT, TUESDAY NOV 19TH 1940

Dad, my brother Alan and I were all sitting in the living room of our house at 190 Ash Road, Saltley; Mom was up at Grandad's house, no 180 (Mom's Dad) who had just been discharged from Queen Elizabeth Hospital following an operation and still had tubes and things from his wound and was sleeping downstairs. Up until now it had been a usual sort of evening – I can't remember if the Air Raid sirens had sounded but even if they had we were not usually worried at this time and didn't go to the shelter unless we heard the German bombers more or less overhead.

I can remember not being too worried; a couple of nights before we had stood on the top of our Anderson shelter and watched Coventry being bombed in the distance and seeing the glow of fires and shells exploding in the air, although I suppose this was 18-20 miles away. Suddenly as we sat there having noticed some 'plane noises' a different sort of noise, a clattering sound quite loud and very nearby made Dad jump up and tell us to get out to the shelter as quickly as we could. What we were hearing were incendiary bombs falling all round and the clattering was the sound of them hitting the slated roofs of the houses. Dad had recognized them because he was in the A F S (Auxiliary Fire Service – later the N F S National Fire Service) and he was away sick at this time, he had very bad stomach ulcers which, much to his regret had kept him out of the services. As we opened the back door, we had already put out the lights for blackout purposes; we were confronted by a terrific white light. This was the magnesium bombs burning all around, also by now anti-aircraft guns were shooting off and also some bombs were falling but not that close at this time.

Dad took one look and told us to put cushions off the settee on our heads and dash with him up the garden to the Air Raid shelter (about 50 yards up hill). As we came out of the backyard and into the garden proper we saw a bomb burning furiously about half way up. This was a terrific white magnesium fire and crackling and smoking quite frighteningly to us 9 and 10 year olds, but also very exciting I suppose. Dad told us to get behind him and he grabbed a shovel and dug up a large shovelful of soil and threw it onto the bomb. Whether this bomb happened to be of the new explosive type or whether the wet soil caused it, but there was a tremendous explosion and white hot chunks flew everywhere, one severing the clothes line and the prop nearly fell on our heads (this really must have impressed me more than anything because I can remember it most vividly). What we didn't know then was Dad had taken most of the blast and shrapnel in his chest and legs etc. We reached the shelter and more or less fell inside – there was no light inside and very little else except two candles in upturned flower pots that we kept inside to help keep down condensation. As I said before we didn't really use our shelter always before going into the neighbours (the Robinsons at No 184) because usually, when there was a raid, Dad was on duty and Mom and Mrs. Robinson, whose husband worked nights at Saltley Gas Works, used to share and keep bed clothes etc in their shelter. Also it had electric light, being only about 10 feet from the house just inside their garden.

Dad left us in the shelter while he went to find Mom, the raid had by now begun in earnest and we were becoming quite frightened, more because we had been left alone, than because of the raid. Meanwhile a drama in its own right was going on with Granddad. Mom and my Auntie Floss, who lived with and looked after him, had decided that he must be moved into a shelter; he hadn't got one himself and the nearest was the Robinson's I've mentioned before. So they, with the help of Mrs. Robinson and her son, probably about 15 or 17 years old, tried to carry him, bed and all to the shelter – a practically impossible task even in daylight and calm conditions, let alone in what was now becoming a massive raid. Somehow they managed it, with Dad's help, and got him into the shelter but his tubes and dressings etc were all disturbed and he was not in a very good state, I don't think, by the time he was inside. By now, the wounds that Dad had received were obviously much more severe than we kids knew and he was bleeding heavily. Mrs. Robinson and Mom wrapped him up as best they could with towels and Mom came with him to find us.

We couldn't stay where we were, so went next door (at No.192 lived a widow, Mrs. Beard, my Great Aunt Lizzie and, sharing their shelter, another widow Mrs. Clarke from the end house, No 194). Their shelter was quite comfortable since I think they slept in there every night in case anything happened (and it had). Dad got them to open the door which was bolted inside and asked us to take us kids in – it was at this point that I saw Dad's chest – his shirt was ripped and bloodstained and the towel wrapped round him was all red I could see this because the ladies' shelter was quite well lit with candles and possibly an oil lamp. Anyway, they took us in and Dad said he would go to the ARP dressing station in the public baths in George Arthur Road (he may have gone to the other entrance in Adderley Road). Mom was obviously very upset and distressed and went off again the see Granddad. Meanwhile the bombing was becoming more and more intense. As you will appreciate we lived right adjacent to the Morris Commercial Car and Lorry Works and very close to Adderley Park station and marshalling yards, Saltley railway sheds, Saltley Gas Works etc and only about three miles from the city centre and one mile from the BSA and all the other great factories engaged on war work. Although the whole night had now become one continuous whistling of bombs there were a couple that we thought were going to hit us. I should mention that Mrs. Clarke was quite a religious lady and spent the whole time praying out loud and imploring us to join her in her prayers. The bombs I remember above were so close, the screaming whistle became so loud and the explosion, when it came, so terrific, it threw us all off the beds and benches and the blast blew open the shelter door and all the lights went out. It had fallen in Arden Road about 25 yards away and hit the back of the houses and demolished two completely and destroyed the back kitchen and outhouse of two others.

While the door was open from this incident and before we could gather our wits and close the door and light the candles I saw outside every where was glowing red from fires all round and I could see men on the roof of the Morris Commercial offices in Bordesley Green Road trying to fight the fire that was shooting up through the roof. I remember Mom coming up to see if we were OK and this in itself must have taken some courage to leave her Dad, in his state, in the shelter and come along the yard and up the garden to us in this terrible fire storm and bombing going on outside. We seemed to have just got ourselves together, Alan and I kept trying to keep our heads under the few blankets that we had but, as can be imagined, it was quite crowded in the shelter, when there was another terrific whistling of a bomb and a tremendous bang – this much bigger one had fallen in the middle of Ash Road and a bit further down outside No's 120-150 (just above St. Saviors' Churchyard).

This bomb had destroyed houses on both sides of the road and fractured the gas main which caught fire and burned for most of the next day. Although I didn't know it at the time, one of the houses (148) badly damaged, subsequently rebuilt and repaired some years later, was the house of the Morgan family whose daughter Sheila some fifteen years later became my wife, Mrs. Jackson, but that's another story. Eventually, it seemed like years but I suppose it was only three hours or so later, the raid itself was over, Mom came to get us from the shelter and we made our way back to the house. We were lucky that it was still there although we crunched our way over piles of broken glass and when we removed the blackout shutters, big wooden frames covered with roofing felt Dad had made, all the glass came down with them, filling the living room floor with broken glass – most of the front windows were also smashed by blast too. When it became light the extent of the damage could be seen – the first thing I noticed and remember was that everywhere was white with plaster dust; all the hedges and paths along Ash Road were covered and in the roadway was a large crater burning all over from the leaking gas – up along Bordesley Green Road.

The front of the offices to Morris Commercial Cars had been demolished and rubble etc was all over, blocking the road. Fires were still smouldering in the buildings themselves. A direct hit had been made on the main railway line at Adderley Park station and further down Arden Road, on the corner of Hams Road, ARP wardens were still digging in the rubble of houses looking for the occupiers – sadly they were all killed, including two children who went to school with us (I think their name was Bucknell or something like it). Meanwhile, what had happened to Dad? Nothing had been heard or seen of him since he went off to the emergency dressing station at Saltley Baths, Mom was pretty frantic, as you could imagine. She had managed to get Granddad back into his bed with the help of neighbours, but couldn't get a doctor or medical help due to the situation all over the city. She was convinced that Dad had been killed by the bomb which had fallen in Ash Road, which could have happened had he been returning, having had his injuries dealt with.

Dad's brother Ted, who lived at 174 had been to the First Aid station but said that there was utter chaos due to the number of injured and they themselves hadn't escaped but had been quite badly damaged by nearby bombs. He was also told that there had been many injuries and some deaths in the Ash Road bomb but nobody could give him any details of who these people were. By afternoon things were getting quite desperate and the only information that they could get was that a list of casualties and deaths would be posted on notice boards in St Philip's Church in town. There were, of course, no buses or trams running or, even if there were they couldn't get into the city centre because of the damage. They also found that Lewis's building was being used as a temporary hospital and mortuary and, if they wanted to, they could go to search the bodies all laid out up the stair-cases there and, if necessary, identify anyone from the bodies. You can imagine that this didn't do a great deal to satisfy their fear for Dad I think, in fact, Mom did manage to get into town because I remember waiting with Alan at the bottom of our entry watching the dark clouds becoming lower and darker over town and thinking that, when they became so low as to touch the factory chimneys down towards Landor Street somewhere, that we would go in.

This must have been and this time she did get into town but returned both tearful and optimistic because I remember her telling Auntie Floss, who was looking after us, that there were now much longer lists and Dad was not on them, at least not among the deaths. It was then decided that we would go to stay at my Auntie's house in Sheldon because we would be safer there should there be any further heavy raids and, after all, Sheldon was nearer the country. I suppose trolley buses or buses must have been running again to get us there. So off we went – this was not really a good move because on Friday night there was another massive raid and this time the Germans concentrated on the South East side I think the BSA was bombed on this night but also the Elmdon aerodrome and the various 'shadow' factories at Kitts Green etc were targeted. Once again some of the windows were blown in and we all sheltered under an upturned settee because, as I said, Sheldon was considered safe so I don't think they had been given air raid shelters like in inner city areas. There was a happy ending to this night as Mom returned to Sheldon having walked from town or Saltley; I don't know which, through the raid. She told me of seeing the trolley bus wires all over the road and sparking because they were still live. She had spent the day in town at the General Hospital and eventually had been back to St Philip's Churchyard when another long list of injured persons had been posted and found Dad's name amongst those injured, evacuated to Evesham Hospital.

Dad's brother, Ted, obtained a car on Saturday and borrowed some petrol (I don't know if he could drive officially there probably wasn't a test anyway) and took Mom to Evesham and brought Dad back – still full of little bits of shrapnel which he had until he died. Sometimes little bits worked their way out over the years and he kept them in a matchbox for some time. Dad was extremely worried himself because, as he had made his way down Ash Road, he had seen and spoken to a number of men who were trying to extinguish incendiary bombs which had set fire to their roofs and bedrooms. He had offered to help but, when they realized that he was injured, they had declined his offer and he had gone on his way. These people in the houses were amongst those who were later killed when the high explosive bomb fell in the road. I don't know their names but Dad knew them and was most upset when he eventually heard of their deaths. Then later in the night or early morning, when it was decided to evacuate all the walking wounded, Dad had tried to come home but had to be restrained and told he was wasting his time anyway since the whole top end of Ash Road was destroyed with many deaths and injured. They weren't telling lies as there had been a very large bomb in the centre of the road at the top, above St. Savior's Church, and many people had been killed, so Dad had been put on a lorry and taken off he knew not where to.

He didn't know where he was and believed that possibly most of, if not all, his family had been killed. By chance I was looking through an old wallet of Dad's recently (Jan 1997) and found, tucked down the back, his discharge papers from Evesham Hospital dated 23 November 1940. When Granddad was returned to his bed under the window on the ground floor at the rear of No 180, the bed was covered with glass from the window blown in by blast. In the corner of the room, near to the front room and the under-stair pantry, there was a hole about 6 inches square in the ceiling through which daylight was visible right through the roof and in the downstairs room was a similar hole punched quite cleanly through the floor boards. Within the void under the floor was a black granite 4 inch cube road set which must have been blown to a great height in order to fall straight through the house and punch a clean hole through slate, lathe and plaster bedroom ceiling, bedroom floorboards, lathe and plaster living room ceiling and then through floorboards to the void underneath. Fortunately there was no-one in the room or directly beneath when this happened. Granddad really never recovered and went to live with another Aunty (Nell) in Kings Heath and died in 1941.

Peter Jackson

SAVING THE SAFE

My Grandfather's company, Charles Osborn (Hardware) was, like many others, set over to making shells and other ordnance for the war effort.

Father, William Eric Douglas Osborn signed up early on, but my grandfather Ernest Harry Douglas Osborn, was too old having been commissioned in the First World War. He therefore stayed behind to organise production. The story is that my father came home on leave (he was a Squadron Leader with the RAF at the war's end) on 2nd April 1941, having

heard about the bombing of the works the previous day (April 1st! – some joke!) so changed into his boiler suit to come down and look at the damage – with a view toward cleaning up.

Naturally the RAF style was to have his picture taken first – leaning against a heating pipe that had dropped through the floors! To be fair to them it would be a better photograph than a shot of them very dirty as they became quite quickly. All the effort of clearing up, which involved tens of thousands of people after the bombing, is a feature that seems to have little reference in the history of the time. Perhaps because that was the most boring job of the war! In the rear of the factory, which was in Edgbaston street, amidst all the mess, was my disconsolate grandfather trying to open the safe that had fallen through the floor (we still have it today complete with damage!) When seeing my father picking his way through the wreckage caused by EA (Enemy action, or the Hermann Goering regeneration company as we call it now, after all the damage caused to the City in the 1960s) Grandfather swore at him "Why don't you b****r off and win the war! We're quite capable of dealing with this ourselves".

It sounds far worse than it did at the time (according to my Dad). No doubt there were references to a wish that he should have shot down the bombers or given the "Jerries" hell in return, which was the normal reaction among civilians at the time – this being because the RAF was considered the miracle organisation, having just won the Battle of Britain! However the Boulton Paul "Defiant" the superb night fighter was not yet fully developed in quantity, because so many of them had been shot down during the daytime by the ME 109s who learned to attack it head on where it was at its weakest. It did however destroy more Nazi planes in the first part of the battle of France than any other, which is not a well known fact. And, to be fair to the general public, they had to wait for over two years, until the RAF scored their great success with 617 squadron in the "Dams raid" of May 1943. So things were a bit on the back foot regarding aerial warfare except in the Western Desert – but that was far away. However the safe was opened in the end, and the staff were paid for a day's worth of tidying up. Work was resumed with the roof in pieces. As the weather was quite mild that spring, and as most of the machinery survived, the levels of production were back within the week. Father and friends still managed to sweep all the rubbish of burned wood and asbestos sheets – just imagine the Health and Safety officers with their regulations today – into a giant pile at the entrance.

The following night the Luftwaffe returned and an HE (high explosive) landed right in the middle of the pile, so they had to do the same work again! I understand it was more frustrating the second time. The RAF kept the bombers off the cities during the daytime, but there seemed only the Ack Ack to defend them during the night. Luckily all members of staff survived the war, and there is a picture of the side entrance with Percy Greenwood, my father's business partner, who was on the dangerous "fire watch" in the City centre each night after work, and he ended up as the volunteer City Chief Fire officer after the end of the conflagrations. However both their hearts went out to the civilian casualties and friends who stayed in the central areas and were reported euphemistically as "missing" in the Birmingham Post (or Aris's Gazette, founded 16th. November 1741 which was proudly displayed on the mast head – I wonder what the first readers would have made of this war?) Today we realise the suffering that went on, but must admire the stoicism with which the previous generation to ours refused to give up, under an onslaught that could never have been imagined, and fought through as civilians with their military colleagues to beat the forces of evil.

Peter Douglas Osborn

THE NIGHT WE WERE BOMBED OUT

It was the night of April the 9th 1941. We were just getting ready to go to bed, when the air raid sirens went off. We didn't immediately go to the air raid shelter, because air raids had now become regular and a normal thing. My dad who was an air raid warden went out to his post to patrol the area. But he wasn't out long before he was back saying "come on you are going to the Prince, because it's going to be a bad un".

He realised that because the area had been saturated with incendiary bombs which would be followed by heavy bombing. We would normally go to the Anderson shelter at the top of the garden. But dad in his wisdom decided that we would be better off at the Prince, the local pub where the cellar had been reinforced and made in to a communal shelter. So off we went my mom and my 2 year old baby brother, my Gran and my aunt who lived next door. When we got into the street the sky was aglow with fires, the skyline in the distance was towards the Washwood Heath Road. It was about a mile away and you wouldn't normally see it, even in daylight. Because it seemed that every other roof top was burning, you could clearly see the whole length of the road. When we got to the shelter it was quite full about 20-30 women and children, all neighbours or people we knew. It was our first time there and we thought it was great as we settled down with the other kids for the night. We'd got used to the air raid sirens going off. But had not experienced bombing close at hand, but it all changed that night. The bumps, bangs and rumblings seemed to go on forever we kids did not know what was going on but the Mothers were getting messages in and the news wasn't good. We came out of the shelter at daybreak, it was a shock, there was devastation everywhere, the street was covered with broken glass, debris and thick dust, the air was filled with smoke. My dad met us with the news that our house had been hit. My mom broke down sobbing when she had realised that we had lost our home and all of our possessions. The bomb had landed in our garden between the house and the Anderson shelter. If it had hit the houses or the road it would have been ten times worse. As it was it had blown the roofs off a dozen houses and demolished the backs of six of them and left a massive crater thirty yards in diameter. The Anderson shelter that we had always used had disappeared, so we had something to be thankful for. The row of eight houses had all had long gardens and the bombs had more or less landed in the middle of the open space. My Dad then told us that they had rescued my Granddad. He had refused to go to the shelter and gone to bed. Fortunately he was in the front bedroom if he had been in the back he would have been killed. When they cleared the debris and got to him not knowing whether he was dead or alive, they could hear him mumbling. They thought he was trying to tell them where he was hurt, but what he was repeating was "My money is in a box under the bed". When my Dad retrieved his life savings later the box contained £14 10s. We did not put it on his epitaph but Dad always joked about Granddad and his money in a box under the bed.

Ron Peters

EXTRACT FROM BROMSGROVE MESSENGER FEBRUARY 20TH 1943

The death of a Home Guard convoy driver, following an early morning crash at Rubery on Sunday, February 7th was the subject of an inquest held by Dr W.H. Davison; (Birmingham Coroner) on Friday. The inquiry related to William Charles Hawkins (22), 218 Monica Road, Small Heath, a driver taking part in a Sham attack on Worcester, Hawkins lorry crashed through a hedge on Whetty Hill about 5 am and he broke his back. He was not found until some three hours later and first taken to Bromsgrove Cottage Hospital and later to Selly Oak Infirmary where he died early the following morning. Elsie Hawkins, Deceased's mother, said he was the main support of the family, which included an aged father and two younger children. Her son had been discharged from the Navy on a disability pension.

He periodically attended for medical treatment, but otherwise was in perfect health. On Sunday morning, February 7th, she was informed by the police that William was injured, and she had been to see him at Bromsgrove Cottage Hospital. He told her that his lorry had rolled over twice and she gathered that it had left the road. Bert Thomas Robbins, director of Robbins Transport Ltd, Bordesley, deceased's employer, said Hawkins was a competent man and a teetotaller. The lorry he was driving was in good condition and the deceased had never made any complaints. Witness gave authority for the lorry to be used on Home Guard exercises. Dennis Charles Makepeace, Home Guard transport officer, said Hawkins' lorry was the fifth in a convoy of six. It would be passing through Rubery about 4.35am. Herbert Deakin, 20 Cobnall Road, Catshill described finding deceased near an overturned lorry in a field alongside the main road on the Whetty Hill, he said about 7.45am.

He was cycling up the hill when he noticed that the hedge had been broken down over a considerable distance about 150 yards below the Waterworks Cottage. Thinking that there had been an accident, he dismounted and took a look. On the offside of the road facing Bromsgrove there was a steep decline, and peering down witness saw the lorry and the prostrate figure of a man. He heard a faint cry, and scrambled down the bank. The injured man asked him for water. Later witness contacted the police. Police constable Summers stated that wheel marks showed that lorry ran diagonally across the road for 40 feet and then its offside wheel mounted the footpath. About 50ft farther on the nearside wheel came over the kerb and for some 70ft the lorry ran with both wheels on the path. Then it broke through the hedge and fell down a 15ft drop. It overturned three times and came to rest 32ft inside the field. Dr Phillippa Mary Ludlam, Medical Officer, at Selly Oak Hospital, said deceased was admitted at 4.30pm on February 7th, after being transferred from Bromsgrove. He told her that the lorry had left the road. Not wishing to disturb him, she did not ask for any more particulars. He had a fractured spine, complete paralysis of both legs, and loss of all sensation. He died at three am on February 8th. Returning a verdict of "Accidental death" the coroner said it would be presumed that whilst driving the lorry Watkins had dozed and did not realise that he was nearing the precipice.

In Loving Memory of my Brother William Charles Hawkins.

Rose Gillett BARRA Member

AN AIR RAID

The 8th November 1940 was my eighth birthday and eleven days later, on the 19th, Birmingham experienced the heaviest raid of the war. Ash Road, Saltley was where we were living, in the house where I, and my father before me, were born. He had known no other home. The sirens sounded and my Mum, Dad and myself hurried to the bottom of the garden to bed down in the Anderson Shelter. We realized straightaway how heavy the raid was and seemed to be immediately overhead. The explosions were deafening and the ground shook.

My father ventured out at regular intervals and reported that things were grim. The road was ablaze as the gas mains were on fire and the flames were higher than the rooftops. We came out of the shelter, after thirteen hours, to tearful women and shaken, but stiff upper lipped men comforting one another. The houses from number 146 were flattened; our house at 148, which was next door, was still standing but with all the windows and doors blasted out. The grapevine network came into operation as we found out that people known to us didn't survive the raid. So and so didn't make it, whole families gone, children I went to Cherrywood Road School with, gone. The wardens on duty forbade us from going back into our house to retrieve some clothes and a few essentials etc, as the building was considered too dangerous.

The three of us then walked from Ash Road, Saltley to Chetwyn Road, Ward End, by the Fox and Goose amongst a lot of mayhem of hoses, firemen, ARP and people trying to recover their possessions and get back to some sort of normality. We arrived at my Auntie Gladys's (Dad's sister's) house and she was able to accommodate us. Dad and Uncle Will went back to Ash Road the following day to see what the situation was. Once again they were not allowed into the house. The front of the building was well guarded by wardens but not the back and people gained access from St Saviour's Road, as their gardens backed onto ours, and carpets and treasured possessions were taken, LOOTERS WILL BE SHOT was one of the many wartime posters, but it seems you had to catch them first. My mother vowed that she would never be house-proud again.

Sheila Jackson

1939-1945 WORLD WAR 2

On the 3rd September my mother, brothers and I were evacuated to Gloucester, my mother was not prepared to stay and hated the toilet at the end of the garden. We only stayed a week and my uncle came to fetch us back. My father reinforced our dining room with sandbags and wood putting in bunk beds and a top shelf which contained tinned food of all sorts. The bombs started falling soon after but we were OK until a bomb fell in the next road at which time I had chicken pox. Fortunately the other side of the road were evacuated to the rest shelters, but we were told to stay in the back of our houses.

Very lucky as we would have had to walk the streets and as I was infectious could not go into the shelter. About a month later a landmine dropped opposite George Dixon School and blew out the front. At this time the junior children (that was me) were evacuated to South Wales. The infants did not go so my brother stayed at home. I had a wonderful time for nearly two years with about 200 other children. How the village managed with the sudden influx I can't imagine.

We all managed to get into the village school. George Dixon children were in two classes back to backing the hall with our two teachers. After a few months it was decide to split us up with the village children in the class rooms. This all meant that we did not learn much and when the time was drawing near for the 11 plus exams. The war was not as bad as it was; we all came back to Birmingham. None of us passed the 11 plus in September, but after a term of hard work, homework and extra tuition we all passed in the February. We all started in George Dixon Grammar School in the next September. Coal and coke were in very short supply the main school was heated up to 50 degrees. There was no fuel for the outside classrooms where I was. We thought it was great fun as every hour we put on our coats in the winter term and ran round the playing field to keep our circulation working. We were told to wear two pairs of knickers and a pair of woollen socks as well as thick stockings. When the end of term arrived (Easter) we found out that no one in the class had been absent. It had never happened before, it was too cold for the bugs to live! By this time I had gone up from Brownies to Girl Guides and although the war was still on no bombs had fallen for sometime. It was decided that it would be safe for the guides to go to camp at Chaddesley Corbett.

Unknown to us while we were there another raid came to Birmingham with several bombs dropped in our area of Birmingham. You can imagine how worried our parents were about us sleeping in tents in a field on a farm. We did not know anything about it, no sirens or anything. By this time it was summer 1943. Not much seemed to happen apart from food rationing until the end of the war in 1945. Food seemed to come from somewhere for a wonderful street party, when we all wore red, white and blue clothes to celebrate the end of the war. Throughout the war everybody helped each other and was very friendly.

Sylvia a seven year old when war started

In 1942, things seemed to be easing up a little on the home front. I had just returned from two years in a hamlet in Staffordshire where, if it hadn't been for the newspapers, we wouldn't have known there was a war on, what a come down for me. My story is about some of the characters that I had to deal with in my short working life before I went into the forces. As most of the people who are reading this know there was a control of labour in force you just couldn't walk out of one job into another, especially at my age, fourteen, because of being conscripted, so the only jobs open were places like a milkman, or, as in my case a baker-boy, (Oh, Ma-Ma Get that man for me) remember that song? Despite of, or in spite of all the trials and tribulations we suffered, the war threw up quite a lot of characters and my characters were the different horses that I worked with, and what characters, talk about contrary.

The first one was Leek, thought he was a shire horse, it didn't matter whether you put the brake and the chain on, he would still run off, the best was when we finished early one day, and my gaffer felt like a pint. It was that nice summer of 1944 so we made a slight diversion to the "Country Girl" at the top end of Parkfield Road, Alum Rock, Bordesley Green. Jack got me lemonade (how times have changed); I put the nose bag on Leek, and settled down. All at once, there was such a clatter that roused me from a slight slumber, and fetched the inmates of the hostelry running out, Leek had also dropped off to sleep, and fell over. What a commotion, we managed to get Leek out of his traces and on his feet; he didn't seem any the worse for it that was one horse I had fun with.

I forgot to say that I worked out of Great Brook Street, Ashted Row, for the Co-op bread and some of the stables were in little Francis Street and some in Belmont Row (I wonder how many of you are saying 'I remember that'). The next one was Murdoch, he hated everyone and anyone, talk about light the blue touch-paper, he would go to any lengths to get a bite of someone, it you forgot and walked along the deck while Murdoch was in the shafts, watch your ankles, he'd have you. If I had to fetch him from the stables I would ride him, it was safer, although even then he'd try and have a nip. Now Lucy was a lady, it was her way or no-way, she thought she knew best and it was a question of whose will was strongest, or should I say arms, she knew exactly where to go, to get her apples, biscuits, carrots and water, it didn't matter that your round didn't go that way, that was Lucy's way, if you left her too long, you'd find her about three streets away.

Best of all was Zena, a big black mare, snow, wind, rain never bothered her, nothing bothered her and try as we might, we could never get a gallop out of her, not even a trot. All the coaxing in the world and all the cajoling did nothing for her. Till one day, yes, ONE DAY. My mate asked me if I would like a cigarette (I should have said no) which I accepted, and he gave me his box of matches, that I shook to make sure that I had a light, WHOOSH, Zena had gone like a bullet out of a gun, at last we had found her weak spot, and ever after to get her moving, just shake a box of matches. Another horse that always surprised me was Sloan; he had been on this particular round (Sparkhill Greet) for over ten years and he knew every stop, even the sequence of traffic lights. We would cross the Coventry Road at the Watery Lane junction and he knew exactly when to move or not, it was uncanny.

Terry Pardoe

I was 11 years old when the war came in September 1939. I remember listening to the announcement on the radio. I ran into the road expecting the soldiers to come marching down the street! Mother was very worried about the war; she had grown up with her next door neighbours' seven sons. They all went to the First World War, but only one came back with shell shock. These deaths made a deep impression. I vividly remember the first air raid on Birmingham. My mother was taking 2 cascara (opening medicine) when then the sirens went. She ran upstairs to fetch John who was five, wrapped him in a blanket and proceeded downstairs. I followed her and she thought she was at the bottom of the stairs but she wasn't and I fell on top of her. Then we proceeded to the air raid shelter in the garden. Again we both fell in as we didn't have any steps. At the end of the night Mother still had the cascara tablets in her hand, but I don't think she needed them anymore! After that night we made the air raid shelter fit to sleep in.

I remember Mother scooping out the water many nights from the shelter. Another night we came out of the house to find the sky ablaze with flames. We were frightened to death. It seems, one of the barrage balloons in Handsworth Park had come adrift and burst into flames. The war went on and the bombing got worse in 1940. Every night it seemed to me that we went down the shelter. If you explained to the youngsters that nearly every night whatever the weather, rain, cold, snow you went down through the darkness of the garden to this hole (the shelter), they would think you were mad! This is what we endured night after night. The raids got worse – incendiaries, delayed action bombs, etc. If there was a delayed action bomb, people had to go to the baths on Grove Lane, which had been turned into a shelter, whilst you waited for the bomb either to go off or to be defused.

It must have been very difficult for the adult population, they not only had a day job but hundreds of people worked voluntary at night, ARP, Civil Defence, Auxiliary Fire Service, Specials in the police, WRVS and many more. They must have been worn out but still went to work next morning to produce munitions; Spitfires etc.

Birmingham was a city of a thousand trades – munitions, Spitfires, guns, vehicles etc. and a prime target for the German bombers. On December 11th 1940 we were all settled down in the shelter when Mrs. Murphy knocked on the shelter door saying she had a jug of cocoa for us. We opened the door and a mighty explosion occurred. I could hear screaming from the other shelters, but I expect we were screaming too. The next thing I knew I had slivers of glass down my back. It seemed that the windows had landed on top of the ventilation pipe and hence down my back. At the end of all this Mrs.

Murphy still had the cocoa in her hand! It had been very quiet before the explosion and we all intended to go to the toilet – good job we did not because the whole of the back of the house had collapsed and the toilet had vanished beneath the rubble. It seems that four land mines had drifted down by parachute that night bringing their silent message of death. Our landmine landed on the air raid shelters between Albert Road and Douglas Road, Handsworth. Many people were killed and injured. Two ARP wardens ran towards the parachutes as they were drifting down, thinking I suppose, they were the Germans. Both of them were badly injured. Our lives changed forever that night. Our house was condemned the next morning and we were not allowed to go in. The whole of the back of the house caved in and there was not much of the front either. I don't remember what happened next but we lost many friends and neighbours that night. Thus ended my happy days in Handsworth.

Thelma Banks

WARTIME MEMORIES OF BIRMINGHAM

War was declared on 3rd September 1939. The Prime Minister, Neville Chamberlain, said on the radio that he had not received a reply to his ultimatum to Hitler for him to withdraw German forces from attacking Poland. Therefore a state of war was declared! Neville Chamberlain had some weeks before met Hitler in Germany and had come back waving a letter and saying 'Peace in our time'; so much for the word of Herr Hitler. With the declaration of war, arrangements were made for the evacuation of children away from military targets. Birmingham was one such target as there were many factories making munitions for the forces. Most of the children were evacuated, but some of us stayed behind. My father said that he thought it would be best to stay together, as he had seen the chaos in France and Belgium during the 1914-18 war, and the state of the refugees on the roads: the refugees had been bombed and machine-gunned on the roads whilst fleeing the fighting. As the war progressed things became more organised, but the air raids which were expected did not materialize, and quite a number of children came back home, but it was only the lull before the storm. The air raids began sometime after Dunkirk, the raids of 1940-1941 being the most destructive. Many homes and factories were destroyed and people killed, some very brave people gave their lives to rescue people trapped in the rubble of their homes. One such man was Commander George Inwood, who gave his life and was awarded the George Cross, there were many such acts of bravery during the Blitz. Some events stand out in my mind more than others. We lived just down the hill from the Bull Ring and when the Market Hall was on fire, the animals were let loose and were running around the area of the Bull Ring: there were dogs, cats, birds – it was like the world had gone mad! Other events often come to mind such as the sight of large sheets of plywood, which were on fire and were floating over the roof tops: it was reminiscent of a scene from the Arabian Nights. There was the night that the barrage balloon came down on fire, it was quite a sight in the night sky. On one night more than sixty separate fires were counted down Macdonald Street alone!

The landmines used to come floating down on parachutes, one landing in Ashley Street: there is no Ashley Street Birmingham 5 today, as the landmine blew it away!

On the night that Coventry was raided, the planes passed over Birmingham. There were four hundred German planes passing overhead. My friend and I tried to go to Coventry to see what damage had been done, but all the roads were closed by the police: no one could get into Coventry because of the utter chaos. We lived quite close to the Fisher Ludlow factory and all through the night we would listen to the thud of the presses as they produced equipment which was used towards the war effort. The factory manufactured pressed steel, but I don't know what they actually used the pressed steel for? As the schools had been closed due to the wartime situation, we spent some of our time collecting shrapnel, cones and dud incendiary bombs. As the war progressed and things became more organized the children that remained were grouped together for their schooling. The school that I attended was St David's where the ages of the children ranged from five to twelve years. There were about twenty of us: the education program consisted of games and listening to gramophone records. As the bombing intensified the school was struck by a high explosive bomb and was damaged; I remember that all the school animals were destroyed: rabbits and guinea pigs. After the bombing at St David's, we were moved to Rea Street School: here again all ages were grouped together for their lessons. Part of this school was damaged by the bombing and so off we went to another school: Hope Street, a very fitting name, well it must have been third time lucky as I left there after completing my education in April 1943 – receiving a first class degree in 'kidology'. After leaving school I went to work for a gunsmith and joined the killing machine. There was the constant fear that the Germans would cross the Channel and land in England, but Hitler attacked Russia and the very heavy air raids became less frequent. One of life's ironies was that after the war I was posted to Germany and stationed just outside Hamburg, which today is twinned with Birmingham. I was astounded by the destruction that this city had suffered. 'They sowed the wind and reaped the whirl wind'. On reflection will we ever learn?

Tim Keatley

In 1939, at the age of 9 yrs, I was evacuated from Stratford Road School, Sparkbrook to Gloucester. We travelled by train on a Saturday, taking with us a small suitcase, gas mask, and a brown paper carrier-bag (issued to us) containing food items. On arrival I was allocated to a family but cannot remember their name.

Sister (Valerie), Dad (William aka Bill), Mom (Vidah) and me (also Vidah)

On Sunday morning, September 3, we heard on the wireless (radio) the Prime Minister, Mr. Neville Chamberlain saying that war had been declared on Germany. I did not stay long because the expected bombing of Birmingham did not take place. Many children returned home, later, having moved from Spark-brook to Moseley where I attended the Church of England School. Incendiary bombs were dropped in our area, two landing in our garden, so my parents decided to take my sister, Valerie aged 4 and me to our maternal Grandparents in Shropshire. The village we had moved to had only one school, which we attended. It was full to overflowing as evacuees from London, Wallasey and Liverpool had also come to Maesbury for refuge from the bombing. In October 1940 we received dreadful news; our parents had been killed in the bombing of the Carlton Cinema. My Grandfather and my Aunty had to go round the morgues to identify the bodies. Since being an adult I have thought many times how awful that must have been for my Aunty, who was only 20 years old. We stayed in Shropshire until the end of the war in 1945 returning to live with our paternal Grandparents. I had attended Oswestry Technical College, so as Sparkhill Commercial School taught similar subjects I was able to fit in there while my sister went to Conway Road School. When I left school I went to work at The Post Office Supplies Dept., Bordesley Green where I was employed in the Typing Duty. I was also taught to use a Teleprinter and I stayed there for nine years leaving to have my daughter Jacqueline. I would just like to conclude by saying how very lucky my sister and I were to have Grandparents willing to look after us otherwise we would have gone into an orphanage. On the site of the Carlton Cinema, Taunton Road, an organisation called Groundwork, has made a 'Peace Garden'. There are paths and trees and a Memorial created by sculptor, Michael Schevermann. There are also nineteen plain blue stones across the front of the area depicting the people killed there.

Vidah Pearce (nee Bayley)

CHILDHOOD MEMORIES OF THE SECOND WORLD WAR

I was 6 years of age when the Second World War broke out on the 3rd September 1939. I did not know what it meant, but I knew something terrible had happened because all the neighbours in Artillery Street were outside talking over the garden fences. I sat crying, curled up on Grandad Baker's chair in the living room near to the window.

Prior to the war being declared, my mother, together with the four children, had been evacuated for a short period of time to Umberslade Hall at Hockley Heath. This was a mansion house in its own grounds with a herd of deer and a huge pool, but we had returned back home to Bordesley before the war started. There were other families evacuated there at the same time.

The heaviest bombing raids on Birmingham were from early August 1940 until the end of April 1943, with only an occasional raid afterwards. But it seemed to me, as then a seven-year-old, that they went on forever. I was terrified every time the sirens sounded. Some of the raids were in the daytime and I can clearly remember being in Garrison Lane Park with other children when a German plane dived down and machine-gunned us. We saw and heard it approaching and ran to take cover down the steps into the entrance of the public air raid shelter. None of us were hurt.

My most vivid memories are of the whistling sound the bombs made as they were falling, the noise of the bombs exploding when they landed, as well as the noise of the ack-ack guns shooting at the German planes. On top of this you also had the awful smell of smouldering and of burning buildings.

Every night my mother took my two younger sisters, my elder brother and myself down the air-raid shelter in Garrison Lane Park. We went down at dusk, whether or not the sirens had sounded, and came back up in the morning providing the 'All Clear' had sounded. The children slept on benches if the noise of the falling bombs did not keep them awake.

On Saturday morning, 17th May 1941, we came up from the shelter to find that my father had been killed by the blast of a 'Land Mine', which had fallen on the house next door. My father and Grandad Baker were on their way to the Fire Watching Post at the top of the road when the bomb fell. Grandad Baker was dug out alive, as was our dog "Gyp". Both lived for a number of years afterwards. I can remember Mom and the children being taken to a mobile tea wagon in Artillery Street, near to where our house used to be, and it was here I heard a voice say, "Give this woman a cup of tea, she has just lost her husband". Our house and all the houses around it had been flattened. My father, John Eastlake, was just 33 years of age. My mother Ellen was 31 years, a widow with four children, whose ages were 4, 6, 8 and 10 years. We only had the clothes we stood up in and the only item salvaged

Two months before the bomb fell, we went to Jerome's for a photograph to be taken of us all, because we were expecting Dad to go into the forces. It is the only photograph of the family taken all together. It shows Leslie (aged 10), John (33), June (8), Ellen (31), and on the front row Brenda (6), and Barbara (4)

from the house was the 'diddy tin' in which mom kept the birth certificates, insurance policies and receipts, etc. I still have that tin today. Because we did not have anywhere to go, we went to live with my grandfather Charlie Elliman and his son Ted, Mom's youngest brother, in the maisonettes on Coventry Road, just below the Kingston Cinema.

This same bomb also killed three members of the family who lived next door but one: Mrs. Alison Anderson aged 60 years, daughter Annie 22 years and grandchild Pamela Jordon aged 5 months. Pamela's mother survived. My mother said there was also another unknown man's body found, but he was never identified.

My mother did remarry later and had two lovely boys, John and Barry.

June Eastlake. BARRA Member 2005

At the Annual Service of Remembrance a new poem is written and read by Jean Frier these are reproduced below together with pictures from the blitz – Brian

Great Western Arcade bomb damage

'REMEMBRANCE'

We're gathered in remembrance
And our thoughts are tinged with pride
Of loved ones whom both young and old
Their lives span were denied
For those dark days of wartime years
That claimed so heavy a price
May seem of little worth to some,
    nor heed their sacrifice
The horrors of those 'blitz-filled' nights,
    the siren's sickening call
The scurrying to the shelters as the bombs
    began to fall.
Such anxious sleepless nights were spent
And as each day dawned fresh
'Twas witnessed with a prayerful sigh –
    or grief filled bitterness
For loss of family and friends as streets in ruins lay
And citizens in thousands died whilst
    our buildings blazed away.
But our spirits stayed unbroken,
    fighting weariness each morn
And from the smouldering ashes
    our city was reborn.
So, we're gathered in remembrance
And many here this day
Hold special thoughts within their hearts
Of dear ones snatched away
For God's gifts are the memories
That we keep bright, still yet
Too precious to be cast aside, too beloved to forget

Jean C Frier © October 2003

Edgbaston Street Bomb Damage

'REMEMBERING'

Why have we gathered? Why are we here?
Why do we remember as year succeeds year?
As we delve into memories recalling the cost
The horrors of wartime – loved ones that were lost
We fondly remember and with pride we retell
Of courage – and heartaches as bombs like rain fell.
For we are the privileged, the ones who survived
To inherit their future which man's evil denied.
So yes, we're here gathered, so grateful to be
Paying them homage, respectful that we
Owe so very much to those, never to greet
This city that's grown from the bomb-spattered streets
Where they lay in thousands 'neath rubble and flame
'Loved ones' to many – to some just a name,
But we've never forgotten the price that they paid
While on our memory's pages their names are displayed.
For wars do not end when the battle is done
And the cost to so many is only begun,
So that's why we gather as years take their toll
And peace throughout earth ever strives for its goal,
And we should remember, it's our duty to see
That their history lives on, – in you and in me

Jean C Frier © October 2nd 2004

Gooch Street 30th July 1942

'THE TREE OF LIFE'

From land, which gave the seed its birth
A 'Tree' grows firmly set in Earth
Securely rooted, strong it stands
It's 'Branches' the Creator's hands,
Holding the 'Globe' in gentle palm
Whilst shielding to keep it safe from harm,
This 'World' in which we live and love
Enriched by blessings from above.

This 'Tree of Life' now set on stone
In memory to each name alone
Depicts a message, strong and sure
That tells of suffering all endured
When heedless of man's right to dwell
War's darkness came to cast its spell,
And 'evil' triumphed for a while
As misery reigned within this isle.

Midst bomb scarred streets, their dwellings lost
'Twas such as these who paid the cost.
Our loved ones gave their lives, that we
Should in this land live peacefully,
And we here gather, in assurance
A living proof of Love's endurance
While we remember still, their claim
That history writes each treasured name.

Name upon name is now displayed
This now, their finest accolade
Though long we've shed our bitter tears
That war denied their span of years
In hearts while safe, we memories keep
They never died, they merely sleep,
'Life tree' stands tall for all to see
Our witness, our 'Humanity'.

Jean C Frier © 2005

'INGRATITUDE'

In gratitude we gather today, that we at last do see
'Life's Tree' now standing tall and proud, a lasting memory,
As witness to the sacrifice, when in war's darkest hours
So many lives were taken, mown down like fairest flowers.
Young and old, all paid the cost as this country battled on
While certain that right would prevail, and peace at last be won.
And old and young, those who survived, all laid their grief aside,
One people working with one will, in this city that we pride,

While wartime days stretched into months, then grimly into years,
We made the guns, the tanks, the planes, though oft with hidden fears.
Defying bombs and blast we laboured, yet with dust-grimed faces smiled
For we were so determined that this land be not defiled.
And when at last peace was restored, we who were left then vowed
For such lilting recognition of which all could be proud,

On which our dead, whose lives were lost, would bear at last their names,
A tribute to their courage as our city blazed, but rose from out the flames.

With bricks and rubble swept away, as peaceful years ensued
'Til slowly battle scars were lost as buildings were renewed
Then from the 'old into the new' this city spritely stepped,
But its toll paid during war years, still a secret closely kept.
While those who grieved, determined that their loss be not in vain
Still struggled for their rightful place in history to attain,
And long, long years we waited for their story to be told
And a worthy edifice be raised and their sacrifice consoled.

Though, we may carry still our grief as these our loved ones sleep,
Long years at rest they slumber on, while we their memory keep
Still yet, men pray for peace to reign, for the world to live as one,
So 'Life's Tree' tells all future youth of those lives before us gone,
For they and we all owe a debt to those, whose names we bear,
Whose toil and love all helped rebuild this city that we share.
When as they scan the names displayed... and maybe find their own,
They'll know at last, the cost thus paid, while this country stood... alone.

Jean C Frier © September 2006

'STEP FORTH'

Our King in the year of '39 looked out with deepest dread,
For he knew what this, his country dear, would face as it was led
Into a warring battle greater than ever before,
But would fight unto the bitter end defending its rugged shore.
And as he so prepared his words to his dominions, far and wide
His message he read with voice sincere and his peoples, he inspired.

Together as one, so we stepped forth, into the dark unknown,
Though came a time we faltered, while our country stood alone
Through those years of loss and hardship, still firmly we set our sight
On the light of 'Hope' still burning like a candle in the night

We sacrificed homes and loved ones, but fought on for the right to be
Living without oppression in a world once more set free.

This day, we again light a candle in remembrance of all we hold dear
While long in our hearts ever keeping memories, bittersweet and clear,
For we still need to tell out their stories and of many brave deeds that were
     done
Paid in lives snatched away in a second, as their homes and possessions
     were gone.
Such as these were our country's back-bone, day by day, facing dangers
     anew
While other loved ones fought on land, seas and skies, paying their
     dreadful sacrifice too.

So dear are the ones we remember, though so long is the passing of years
And these stories of daily survival, unimportant may seem to some ears
But our youth should be told of the darkness that fell on this land years ago
So that they might inherit a future that we fought for their right to know
And again, we recall that firm message that was said in the year '39
As still we 'step forth' ever onward in this land we hold dear, yours and
     mine.

And the candle still glows with a fervour, for the world has dark places to
     light
Where greed for an other's possessions ever man any chance for man's
     right
To live, side by side with his neighbour, in a world as God meant it to be
That a child, no more, cries out in terror of the bombs that haunt our
     memory;
For our act of remembrance is sacred and our thoughts ever special we
     frame
in the silence of prayer, still we hold them – and in love ever whisper their
     name.

Jean C Frier © September 2007

'IN MEMORY'

Across the way, 'Life's Tree' stands proud,
Firm ensign to the passing crowd
Cast in bronze and set on stone
As homage to the past we own.
Its leaves long fallen, never fade
'In Memory' of the price once paid
By all those named and many more
Their sacrifice – the price of war.

Friends and family, kith and kin
In hearts and thoughts kept close within,
Fond images stored in ageing minds
Of we, the survivors left behind
Each man and woman, girl and boy
Etched in witness to passers-by.
Some spot a name, so like their own
It's possible they might have known.

Then careful thought they just should give
To those that died that they might live.
Infant, parent, lover, friend
In ruined streets such lives did end
While mothers hushed the whimpered cry
Of their child, afraid as bombs dropped nigh
As this city blazed, and our buildings fell
Brave firemen fought the 'fires of hell'.

All people rallied with one will
Determined to live in freedom still
Thus our country battled and the war was won
But not before great harm was done
Across the way 'Life's Tree' stands tall
Our story there displayed to all
Witness to those held 'In Memory' near
As year succeeds each passing year.

When strolling past, pray understand
The cost thus paid for this 'Our Land'
And maybe pause to give some thought
To all whose lives, such freedom bought.
While still great nations fail to find
Solutions fit for all mankind
To live and work and love as one
And see on earth, God's Kingdom come.

Jean C Frier © September 2008

'SEVENTY YEARS ON'

I watched my city, as a child, fall to the bomber's aims,
My 'Bull Ring' lost forever, consumed by fire and flames.
The Market Hall, beloved by all for the magic of its stalls
Reduced to roofless ruin within its blackened walls.
This very church did not escape but 'shell-shocked' carried on,
A 'haven' midst destruction whilst we daily struggled on.

Yes, Seventy years have passed on by, since war came to this land
Bringing destruction and despair that few yet understand,
Our city now rebuilt again that once in ruins lay,
Where ancient buildings proudly stood, now glass and steel hold sway.
But still a greater price was paid that nothing can replace
As some sit here recalling a dear familiar face.

For human life will ever be the true cost of all wars
While battles rage to right a wrong for some misguided cause,
And names writ on memorials record the endless stream,
Until the world can learn to live according to God's dream,
That men might meet and brothers be, to clasp each others hand,
Then peace will reign secure for all in each and every land.

Yes, Seventy years have passed on by, and we recall each face
Keeping a vigil in our hearts for those that no one could replace.
Our 'Tree of Life' stands rooted in the names now listed there;
The Earth secure in hands clasped firm and reaching up in prayer,
While we vow our remembrance still of the price they dearly paid
With their names a silent whisper as our poppy wreaths are laid.

Jean C Frier © September 2009

New Street and High Street

'MEMORIES STAY'

Our 'Tree of Life' stands yet serene midst busy thoroughfare
Firm rooted in the names displayed that many here still bear
Its sap that rises sweet to feed is nourished by each soul
So sacrificed when wartime reigned, destruction its grim toll.
Years roll on by but memories stay of those thus honoured here
No bombs or wars could e'er erase the 'heartbeats' we still hear
Of loved ones ever with us when we do so recall

The daily round, of work or play, familiar to us all.
The vibrancy of laughter, firm handshakes, hug and kisses,
The cheery wave, the 'daily moan' these are the things one misses.
For 'Life' in its abundance was the price they dearly paid
Finally acknowledged in names, beneath the 'Tree' displayed.

While chaos and destruction rained down from skies above.
Marring towns and cities in this land we know and love
As death in all its darkness came to strike and snatch away
We struggled, toiled, fought, yet survived to live another day.
Our broken cities to re-build, and tyranny's hold repel
So then in peace and freedom we once again could dwell.
Remembrance ever still the goal sought for each life so lost,
For human lives in any war will always be the cost.
We struggled on for many years to bring them due acclaim
Triumphantly, we see at last name writ upon each name.
We honour our memorial and the names thus thereupon,
For we left still remember parent, daughter, friend or son,
And while our wreaths in memory are laid upon this day
May future years hold peace for all, we earnestly do pray.

Jean C Frier © September 2010

Medlicott Road Sparkhill

'TRUE COST'

The years roll by and gathered here,
Are those who still recall
Those dark, dark days and sleep torn nights,
When our country was at war.
This city formed our frontline as we rallied to the cause,
Making the planes, the tanks, the guns
To help defend our shores.
Through those long years of bombing,
We never claimed defeat,
Though battered stood our buildings
And rubble marred our streets;
Fires and flames raged wantonly
And so many lives were lost,
Forever the grim reminder of every war's true cost
We still live in a troubled world
While greed for power holds sway,
The peace we fought so hard for then,
Seems still a dream away
Memorials stand throughout the land,
A 'Tree Of Life' we claim
And this day, lay our poppy wreaths
In honour to each name,
Death, without fear or favour,
Both young and old did reap,
So to them in love filled memory
We silent vigil keep.
As we stand beneath the hands that hold
This world we claim to share,
'Let not them all have died in vain' –
Forever be our prayer.

Jean C Frier © September 2011

'MEDALS'

This year of the Olympics
Rejoicing's been our aim,
As athletes from all countries strived
To win honours for their game.
With strength and skill to prove their best
At sports of their own choosing
We've witnessed both the triumphs
Or despair when Oh! So near – but losing!
Yet though the Games are over
The 'Eternal Flame' burns on,
Reflected in the brightness
Of the medals that were won.
This day, some here remember
When greater flames did rage.
And tyranny's evil shadow
Marked those years on history's page.
We fought for our survival, together as if one,
Not resting from our struggles
Until the peace was won.
And as in each and every war,
In countries torn and tossed
The costly true price always paid
Is in the lives so lost
Throughout our land, memorials stand
To recognise their giving,
To realise their dying meant
For us the gift of living
So many unsung heroes, no glories did they claim.
A name on a Memorial, their lasting right to fame.
As golden leaves on Life's Tree un-withered, they live on
In memories long cherished – No medals harder won.

Jean C Frier © September 2012

Overturned tram at Aston Parish Church

'CANDLEGLOW'

Memory is God's given gift
That we can make our own,
For as we gather memories
Of all we've loved and known,
Our thoughts are lit like candles
And each flame lights up the past
Recalling times – some bittersweet
Of friendships made to last,
The laughs, the tears, the comradeship –
Burn brightly year by year.
Like 'Candleglow' within our hearts
Are times and people still held dear
Who in those grim, dark, days of war

For freedom's sake were tossed
Into such bitter turmoil and
In which so many lives were lost.
The pain of loss, so tragic then
Has eased, down years long gone,
But still treasured are those memories
As we're gathered here as one,
Today within our silence
As we ponder on each name
The 'Candleglow' unites to burn
– in one Eternal Flame.

Jean C Frier © September 2013

The Poem 'Candleglow' was also dedicated at this year's memorial service to the memory of June Eastlake who sadly passed away after many sterling years of work as the BARRA archivist.

* * * * *

We have now come to the end of our stories. I would like to take this opportunity to thank those that have contributed to this book, for the support of the Chairperson Barbara, committee and members of BARRA. Thank you to my wife Anne for her support and help whilst working on the compilation and to Professor Carl Chinn for his continued support and inspiration.

Special thanks also to Paul Green whose generosity made the "Tree of Life" memorial possible.

Finally this book is dedicated to all the casualties of the Birmingham Blitz. A list of those that lost their lives now follows.

Brian Wright

Union Street Bomb Damage

Tree of Life Memorial in Edgbaston Street

Desolation surrounds St Martin's church April 1941

List of Casualties

1	Abbot	Alfred	Age 36
2	Abrahams	Hyman	Age 38
3	Adams	William Edward	Age 62
4	Adams	Thomas	Age 84
5	Adams	Doris	Age 28
6	Addicott	Alan John	Age 15
7	Addicott	Cecelia Ann	Age 48
8	Alderton	Lizzie	Age 60
9	Alderton	Esme	Age 28
10	Aldington	Howard Burnaby	Age 55
11	Aldridge	Elton Edwin	Age 45
12	Allen	Percy Frank	Age 39
13	Allen	Arthur Abraham	Age 18
14	Allen	Clara	Age 55
15	Allen	William	Age 63
16	Allen	Edith: See Edith Mills	
17	Allsopp	Arthur Edward	Age 16
18	Allum	John	Age 54
19	Allwood	Elsie Elizabeth	Age 48
20	Amos	Vera	Age 56
21	Amphlett	George Henry	Age 65
22	Amphlett	Jamesina Mary Robinson	Age 64
23	Anderson	Annie	Age 22
24	Anderson	Lily	Age 60
25	Anderson	Henry	Age 33
26	Andrews	Leonard Cecil	Age 38
27	Ansell	Peter Benson	Age 23
28	Anslow	Alice Annie Elizabeth	Age 37
29	Anslow	Gertrude Annie	Age 69
30	Anslow	Albert William	Age 66
31	Appleton	Edith Jane	Age 51
32	Arkell	Horace	Age 41
33	Armson	Herbert	Age 68
34	Armson	Lily	Age 45
35	Armstrong	Elizabeth	Age 50
36	Armstrong	Eva	Age 20
37	Armstrong	Eva	Aged 3 mths
38	Arnold	Alfred Edward	Age 46
39	Ashford	Walter	Age 58
40	Ashford	Daisy Elizabeth	Age 40
41	Ashford	Emma Eliza	Age 82
42	Ashford	Edith Mary	Age 51
43	Ashmead	Sara Annie	Age 70
44	Ashmead	Betsy	Age 36
45	Ashmore	Ellen	Age 69
46	Ashmore	Ada	Age 62
47	Ashmore	Jean Mary	Age 1
48	Ashmore	Lucy	Age 29
49	Ashmore	Raymond Albert	Age 5
50	Ashmore	Sylvia	Age 7
51	Ashmore	Violet	Age 32
52	Ashmore	Walter	Age 38
53	Ashurst	Margaret	Age 27
54	Astle	Leah	Age 36
55	Astle	David	Age 7
56	Astle	George	Age 10
57	Astle	Horace	Age 9
58	Astle	Maureen	Age 2
59	Astle	Raymond	Age 8
60	Astle	Susannah	Age 62
61	Astle	Thomas	Age 10
62	Astley	Maud Mary Elizabeth	Age 27
63	Aston	George Edward	Age 51
64	Atkins	Henry	Age 56
65	Atkins	Frederick Kenneth	Age 17
66	Austin	Annie Maud	Age 28
67	Austin	George Alfred	Age 64
68	Austra	Christina	Age 24
69	Avery	Frederick Charles	Age 25
70	Bach	Cecil Arthur	Age 53
71	Backman	Samuel	Age 23
72	Badger	Eva Gertrude	Age 26
73	Bagshaw	Ernest	Age 57
74	Bahauddin	Tunku	Age 21
75	Bailey	Joseph	Age 76
76	Bailey	Jane Elizabeth	Age 50
77	Bailey	John	Age 44
78	Bailey	Agnes Genevieve	Age 32
79	Bailey	Agnes Margaret	Age 2
80	Bailey	John Thomas	Age 65
81	Bailey	Elizabeth	Age 67
82	Bailey	George Edwin	Age 49
83	Bailey	Arthur Alec	Age 38
84	Bailey	Harry Ernest	Age 31
85	Baker	Joseph	Age 17
86	Baker	Christine Mary	Age 10
87	Baker	Jean Iris	Age 14
88	Baker	Frederick Herbert	Age 20
89	Baker	Leo	Age 52
90	Baker	Albert Henry	Age 17
91	Baldock	Frances Mary Mallaber	Age 21
92	Baldock	Albert	Age ?
93	Ball	Ada Emma	Age 77
94	Ball	Eileen Mary Marguerite	Age 35
95	Ball	Florence Elizabeth	Age 50
96	Ball	Joan	Age 22
97	Ball	Edith May	Age 36
98	Ball	Elsie Elizabeth	Age 52
99	Banks	Annie Elizabeth	Age 65
100	Banks	Florence	Age 32
101	Banks	Helena Rose	Age 9
102	Banks	Selina Rose	Age 66
103	Banner	William	Age 69
104	Banner	Dorcas	Age 39

105	Banner	Dorcas Annie	Age 72
106	Banner	Hilda	Age 35
107	Banner	Catherine	Age 27
108	Barber	Ernest Joseph	Age 51
109	Barley	Sidney	Age 37
110	Barnard	Charles Henry	Age 49
111	Barnes	William	Age 48
112	Barnsley	Rose	Age 62
113	Barratt	William Henry	Age 37
114	Barrett	James	Age 64
115	Barrett	Patrick	Age 27
116	Barrett	William Oswald	Age 48
117	Barrier	Rose Ann	Age 59
118	Barrier	John	Age 63
119	Barrier	Joan	Age 16
120	Barrow	Harold	Age 28
121	Barsby	Harriet Anne Lloyd	Age 52
122	Barsby	Nina	Age 17
123	Barsby	Ruth	Age 12
124	Bartlett	Leslie Harold	Age 19
125	Bassett	Jane Maria	Age 86
126	Bastianelli	Anthony	Age 66
127	Bastianelli	Carolina	Age 67
128	Bastianelli	Laura	Age 29
129	Batchelor	Ada	Age 38
130	Batchelor	Barbara	Age 6
131	Batchelor	George	Age 47
132	Bates	Francis Arthur William	Age 26
133	Bates	Maurice Edwin	Age 31
134	Bates	John Joseph	Age 32
135	Battista	Bertam Olaf	Age 37
136	Bauer	Pauline	Age 75
137	Baum	Harry	Age 66
138	Baxter	Joseph	Age 46
139	Baxter	Laura	Age 46
140	Baxter	Sylvia Gladys	Age 15
141	Bayley	Vidah Blanche	Age 31
142	Bayley	William Henry Smyth	Age 32
143	Bayliss	Walter Howard	Age 58
144	Bayliss	George	Age 38
145	Baynham	John Henry	Age 34
146	Baynham	Alfred	Age 75
147	Beach	Ann Elizabeth	Age 31
148	Beale	Tanley William	Age 20
149	Bean	Annie	Age 54
150	Bean	Norman	Age 52
151	Beard	Doris	Age 36
152	Beasley	Albert	Age 16
153	Beddowes	Joseph	Age 32
154	Beech	Oliver Samuel	Age 56
155	Beet	Robert George	Age 20
156	Bell	Annie Elizabeth	Age 35
157	Bell	Gladys June	Age 6
158	Bell	Iris Jean	Age 11
159	Bell	Pauline Elsie	Age 4
160	Bell	Lily Minnie	Age 44
161	Bellamy	Edwin Walter Thomas	Age 30
162	Bellamy	Lily Prudence	Age 29
163	Bembridge	Francis Edgar Ernest	Age 52
164	Bennett	Margaret Augusta	Age 53
165	Benson	Ellen Louisa	Age 63
166	Benson	Joseph Henry	Age 69
167	Berry	Walter	Age 74
168	Best	Phyllis Margaret	Age 28
169	Best	Beatrice May	Age 24
170	Best	John	Age 54
171	Betham	Samuel	Age 58
172	Bethel	Joseph	Age 58
173	Bevan	Alfred	Age 46
174	Bibb	William Ernest	Age 50
175	Bibbey	Constance Mary	Age 5
176	Bibbey	Doris Adelaide	Age 31
177	Biddle	Allen Frederick	Aged 19 mths
178	Biddle	Elsie Valerie	Age 8
179	Birch	Annie Selina	Age 62
180	Bird	Clara	Age 67
181	Bird	Albert Montague	Age 61
182	Bird	Sarah Elizabeth	Age 78
183	Bird	Albert Burton	Age 54
184	Bishton	Ada	Age 62
185	Bishton	Charles Henry	Age 67
186	Bishton	Margery Ada	Age 17
187	Black	Kate Hinsley	Age 86
188	Blake	Charles Harold	Age 20
189	Blake	Thomas	Age 49
190	Blakemore	Albert	Age 24
191	Blakemore	Ethel Irene	Age 23
192	Blakemore	Kitty	Age 35
193	Blum	Robert	Age 53
194	Blunt	William	Age 66
195	Boddington	Samuel Joseph	Age 49
196	Bodenham	Charlotte	Age 61
197	Bodenham	Charles William	Age 62
198	Bohemia	Elizabeth	Age 49
199	Bond	Martha Bella	Age 73
200	Bond	Joseph	Age 32
201	Bond	Mary Jane	Age 58
202	Bond	Richard	Age 38
203	Bonelle	Ada Jane	Age 50
204	Booth	Daniel	Age 59
205	Booton	William Frederick	Age 54
206	Bott	Joan Kathleen	Age 16
207	Bott	Nellie	Age 5
208	Bott	Phyllis Marjorie	Age 19
209	Bott	Harry	Age 57
210	Bourne	George Albert	Age 44
211	Bowen	Margaret Alice	Age 31
212	Bowen	Lilian	Age 21
213	Bower	Sarah Kate	Age 42
214	Bowerman	Maude Blanche	Age 55
215	Bowyer	Ellen	Age 72
216	Bowyer	Stanley	Age 16
217	Bowyer	John William	Age 78
218	Boyd	Elizabeth Hatch	Age 23

219	Boyd	Elsie Mabel	Age 42
220	Bradley	Peter John	Age 3
221	Bradley	Doris Corbett	Age 50
222	Bradley	Ethel Florence	Age 60
223	Bradnock	Elsie Heath	Age 18
224	Bradshaw	Mary	Age 56
225	Bragg	George	Age 60
226	Bragg	George	Age 37
227	Bramham	Eleanor	Age 50
228	Bramham	Joan	Age 20
229	Bramham	Charles	Age 60
230	Bramwell	Elsie	Age 40
231	Bramwell	Henry Howard	Age 42
232	Bramwell	John Alfred David	Age 14
233	Bramwell	James Henry Howard	Age 17
234	Bramwell	Reginald Arthur	Age 15
235	Branaghan	Thomas Jeremiah	Age 59
236	Brant	Stanley Charles	Age 20
237	Brazier	Arthur Victor	Age 39
238	Brennan	Mary	Age 16
239	Brennan	Michael John	Age 18
240	Bretherick	George	Age 72
241	Bridgland	Emma	Age 63
242	Bridgwater	John Thomas Charles	Age 48
243	Briggs	Maud	Age 48
244	Brittain	Thomas Lambert William	Age 26
245	Britton	William Edward	Age 78
246	Broadhurst	Florence	Age 29
247	Broadhurst	Arthur Lewis	Age 25
248	Bromhead	Nellie	Age 60
249	Brookes	Alfred	Age 43
250	Brookes	Alfred John	Age 15
251	Brookes	Joseph Victor	Age 19
252	Brookes	Marjorie Ivy Irene	Age 37
253	Brooks	Leslie	Age 49
254	Brooks	Georgina Elizabeth	Age 54
255	Broome	John	Age 60
256	Brotherton	Emma Matilda	Age 74
257	Brown	Frances	Age 52
258	Brown	Ivy	Age 20
259	Brown	Bernard	Age 9
260	Brown	Frank	Age 22
261	Brown	James	Age 70
262	Brown	Wilfred Stanley	Age 22
263	Bruce	Andrew	Age 42
264	Brunner	John Frederick	Age 12
265	Brunner	Winifred Florence	Age 39
266	Bryan	Albert Ernest	Age 29
267	Bryan	Ernest	Age 52
268	Bryan	Bertie Leonard	Age 38
269	Bryant	Clara	Age 60
270	Bryant	Henry Charles	Age 72
271	Bryant	Marion	Age 26
272	Buck	Robert	Age 53
273	Buckland	Philip Sidney	Age 31
274	Buckley	Kathline	Age 16
275	Budd	Doreen	Aged 22 mths
276	Budd	Barbara	Age 7
277	Budd	Dennis	Age 4
278	Budd	Ethel	Age 32
279	Budd	Ronald Sidney	Age 11
280	Budd	Minnie	Age 46
281	Budd	Alfred Sidney	Age 37
282	Buffery	Henry	Age 37
283	Bull	William	Age 21
284	Bull	Mary Irene	Age 32
285	Bull	William Albert	Age 25
286	Bull	Vera	Age 20
287	Bullock	Hilda Muriel	Age 31
288	Bullock	Charles	Age 65
289	Bullock	Mary	Age 65
290	Bullock	Olive Nancy	Age 34
291	Bunch	John Thomas	Age 48
292	Bundy	George Edward	Age 51
293	Bunford	Caroline	Age 67
294	Bunford	John	Age 36
295	Burdett	Thomas Twine	Age 42
296	Burdett	William Charles	Age 52
297	Burford	Albert Edward	Age 37
298	Burford	John	Age 17
299	Burford	Dorothy May	Age 37
300	Burford	Ellen Ann	Age 59
301	Burnett	Mavis	Age ?
302	Burnett	Rose Elizabeth	Age ?
303	Burrows	Raymond Arthur	Age 26
304	Burrows	Joseph Henry	Age 52
305	Burton	Harold Charles	Age 41
306	Bushell	Charles Bennett	Age 76
307	Bushell	Ethel Blanche	Age 74
308	Butler	Beatrice Florence	Age 16
309	Butler	Emma	Age 40
310	Butler	Albert	Age 39
311	Byram	Mary Emma	Age 81
312	Byrne	Edward	Age 15
313	Caine	William	Age 59
314	Caine	Albert	Age 16
315	Caines	Clara	Age 26
316	Callaghan	Frederick	Age 41
317	Canter	Walter	Age 50
318	Capewell	Ernest Stanley	Age 16
319	Carey	Frederick	Age 24
320	Carey	Raymond	Age 17
321	Carey	Joyce	Age 10
322	Carless	Edward	Age 31
323	Carlin	Reginald Davis	Age 39
324	Carroll	Florence	Age 46
325	Cartwright	John Simmonds	Age 55
326	Casey	Eric	Age 34
327	Cash	John	Age 38
328	Caterer	Edwin William	Age 66
329	Cerrone	Dennis	Age 17
330	Chadney	Bessie Matilda	Age 30
331	Chancellor	George Frederick Raymond	Age 24
332	Chapman	William	Age 64

333	Chapman	Louisa	Age 65
334	Chare	Beryl	Age 42
335	Charley	Augustus	Age 44
336	Charley	Bertha	Age 42
337	Cheslin	Harriett	Age 66
338	Chick	Mary Ann	Age 84
339	Church	Frederick	Age 17
340	Clark	Albert	Age 27
341	Clarke	Thomas William	Age 11
342	Clarke	George Samuel	Age 39
343	Clarke	Stephen	Age 86
344	Clarke	Doris Joan	Age 17
345	Clarke	Teresa	Age 12
346	Clarke	Albert Edward	Age 29
347	Clarke	Howard	Age 50
348	Clarke	Charles Herbert Wreford	Age 39
349	Claytor	Hilda	Age 36
350	Claytor	Audrey Hilda	Age 3
351	Claytor	David Arthur	Age 6
352	Claytor	Kathleen Margaret	Age 10
353	Clews	Victor Leonard	Age 48
354	Clifford	Leah Elizabeth	Age 18
355	Clifford	Delia	Age 19
356	Clifford	Dennis	Age 22
357	Clifford	John Peter	Age 26
358	Clifford	Louisa	Age 56
359	Clifford	Walter	Age 58
360	Clifton	Doris Harriet	Age 38
361	Clifton	Emily	
362	Clive	George Ralph	Age 33
363	Clover	Joseph Albert	Age 17
364	Coates	Philip Francis	Age 16
365	Coates	Raymond Walter	Age 20
366	Coen	Franciscus	Age 45
367	Coen	Pauline Matilda Julia	Age 40
368	Cogin	Doris	Age 33
369	Colder	Selina	Age 68
370	Cole	Margaret Ellen	Age 18
371	Coleman	John William	Age 52
372	Coleman	Laurence William	Age 5
373	Coleman	Alfred	Age 91
374	Coleman	Esther	Age 80
375	Coles	Margaret Jane	Age 61
376	Coley	Doris Winifred	Age 44
377	Coley	Frederick Dennis Rhys	Age 45
378	Colley	Edith	Age 36
379	Collins	William Joseph	Age 45
380	Collins	Jane	Age 61
381	Collins	Jessie May	Age 31
382	Collins	Lily	Age 34
383	Collins	George	Age 38
384	Collins	Frank	Age 31
385	Constant	Francis Charles	Age 58
386	Cook	Frank James	Age 29
387	Cook	Geoffrey Frederick	Aged 3 Days
388	Cook	Mabel Esther	Age 26
389	Cooke	Maud Ivy	Age 36
390	Cooke	Ethel Emily	Age 49
391	Cooke	Joseph	Age 50
392	Cooke	Frederick	Age 20
393	Cooke	Kate Cissy	Age 39
394	Cooke	Arthur Ernest	Age 58
395	Coombes	Alan	Age 5
396	Coombes	Alice	Age 41
397	Coombes	Albert William	Age 59
398	Coombes	Barbara	Age 10
399	Coombes	Alice	Age 59
400	Coombs	Harry	Age 72
401	Cooper	Mary Ann	Age 49
402	Cooper	William James	Age 65
403	Cope	John Alfred	Age 60
404	Cope	John	Age 18
405	Cope	Alfred	Age 51
406	Cope	Mary Theresa	Age 60
407	Cope	Stanley	Age 18
408	Corbett	Nellie	Age 58
409	Corbett	Elsie	Age 32
410	Corfield	Annie	Age 80
411	Corfield	Ralph Henry	Age 41
412	Cotton	John	Age 30
413	Cotton	Charles	Age 38
414	Cotton	Hilda	Age 36
415	Cotton	Jane	Age 61
416	Court	Mildred	Age 19
417	Courtnell	Ernest	Age 39
418	Courtnell	Minnie	Age 38
419	Courtney	Christina	Age 19
420	Cox	Stephen George Gladstone	Age 40
421	Cox	Harry	Age 38
422	Craddock	Albert Edward	Age 18
423	Cragg	Emily	Age 36
424	Cragg	Frederick	Age 9
425	Cragg	Frederick Harold	Age 37
426	Crebbin	James	Age 31
427	Crichton	John Kennedy	Age 35
428	Cridge	Frank William	Age 13
429	Crisp	Thomas	Age 80
430	Crockett	Lily Rose	Age 39
431	Crockett	Sidney	Age 29
432	Crompton	Ronald Michael	Age 16
433	Cross	James	Age 25
434	Crowther	John	Age 66
435	Crozier	Millie	Age 41
436	Crozier	John Phillip	Age 42
437	Cumbey	Mary Anne	Age 25
438	Curley	Margaret	Age 53
439	Curley	Nellie	Age 21
440	Curley	Thomas	Age 24
441	Curran	William	Age 81
442	Curry	Eric Victor	Age 27
443	Daeman	Petrus	Age 61
444	Dale	Constance Mary	Age 18
445	Dalgetty	William	Age 47
446	Dandy	James Leslie	Age 28

447	Dandy	Albert	Age 54
448	Daniels	Thomas	Age 38
449	Daniels	Frances Magdalene	Age 40
450	Danks	Florence	Age 57
451	Darby	Olive Violet	Age 32
452	Darby	Alfred John	Age 26
453	Darbyshire	Harry	Age 74
454	Darlison	Alfred Frank	Age 3
455	Darlison	Chrystabel Irene	Age 38
456	David	Doris May	Age 32
457	David	Heman Llewellyn	Age 36
458	David	Thomas Charles	Age 45
459	Davies	Fred	Age 30
460	Davies	Mildred Lilian	Age 27
461	Davies	Sarah Hannah	Age 75
462	Davies	Joyce	Age 21
463	Davies	Dorothy	Age 45
464	Davies	George Richard	Age 47
465	Davies	Stanley Job	Age 20
466	Davies	Stanley Charles	Age 18
467	Davies	Charles	Age 33
468	Davies	Arthur John Thomas	Age 34
469	Davies	William Ernest	Age 61
470	Davies	Pearl Sylvia	Age 23
471	Davies	Gilbert	Age ?
472	Davis	Harriet Matilda	Age 82
473	Davis	Maud	Age 79
474	Davis	Frank Latham	Age 66
475	Davis	Elizabeth	Age 57
476	Davis	Sarah	Age 44
477	Davis	William Charles	Age 14
478	Davis	Laura Helen	Age 76
479	Davis	Reuben	Age 34
480	Dawes	Ronald Frank	Age 17
481	Dawes	Charles Edward	Age 28
482	Dawkes	Rose Annie	Age 53
483	Deakin	Ann Court	Age 84
484	Dean	Ivor	Age 24
485	Deane (Otherwise Watkins)		
		George	Age 54
486	Dearn	George Edward	Age 50
487	Deebank	Brenda	Age 3
488	Deebank	Elizabeth	Age 28
489	Denning	Joseph	Age 35
490	Denny	Bertie Alfred	Age 25
491	Dent	Annie	Age 69
492	Derry	Frank Charles	Age 65
493	Dickens	Charles Reginald	Age 25
494	Dillon	Edward	Age 70
495	Dillon	Matilda	Age 72
496	Dix	Stephen	Age 33
497	Dixon	Albert	Age 59
498	Dobbins	William George	Age 36
499	Dodsley	Frederick	Age 39
500	Donnelly	Dennis	Age 45
501	Dooling	Ada	Age 60
502	Dooling	Patrick	Age 74
503	Dorey	Ernest George	Age 40
504	Dorney	Amelia	Age 82
505	Doughty	Harriet	Age 65
506	Doughty	Muriel	Age 41
507	Douglas	William	Age 44
508	Dowman	Albert Edward	Age 34
509	Downes	Arthur	Age 19
510	Downes	Leonard	Age 15
511	Downes	Samuel Albert	Age 55
512	Downes	Mary	Age 14
513	Downes	Norman	Age 18
514	Dowse	Sarah	Age 53
515	Dowse	Thomas James	Age 59
516	Dowson	Minnie Evelyn	Age 52
517	Drakeley	Alfred	Age 46
518	Draper	Alfred John	Age 17
519	Drew	Ernest William	Age 37
520	Dudley	Arthur Robert	Age 36
521	Duggan	Robert Evan	Age 44
522	Dunn	Ada	Age 30
523	Dutton	Arthur Augustus	Age 63
524	Dutton	Laura Ellen	Age 60
525	Dwyer	Dennis	Age 17
526	Dyer	William	Age 50
527	Eagle	William	Age 28
528	Eastlake	John	Age 33
529	Eaton	James Harry	Age 30
530	Eddleston	Jannete Ann	Aged 7 mths
531	Edge	Marjorie	Age 19
532	Edgerton	Grace	Age 19
533	Edgerton	Charles Henry	Age 67
534	Edwards	Brian John	Age 6
535	Edwards	David William	Age 8
536	Edwards	Matilda Ellen	Age 35
537	Edwards	Matilda Grace	Age 4
538	Edwards	Sydney Thomas	Age 1
539	Edwards	John William	Age 55
540	Edwards	Louisa	Age 30
541	Eeles	Helen Gertrude	Age 39
542	Elder	Clara	Age 71
543	Ellerker	Isaac Sydney	Age 35
544	Ellgood	Annie	Age 40
545	Ellgood	Frank Augusta	Age 41
546	Elliott	Florence Emma	Age 63
547	Elms	Montague Bertie	Age 41
548	Elvins	Walter Edward	Age 33
549	Endean	William	Age 56
550	Essex	John	Age 59
551	Estill	Beatrice	Age 48
552	Evans	Annie Ada	Age 39
553	Evans	Harry Stanley	Age 42
554	Evans	Patricia Anne	Age 11
555	Evans	John Rowland	Age 69
556	Evans	Marjorie	Age 19
557	Evans	William Everett	Age 58
558	Evans	David John	Injured 3 Dec 1940

559	Evans (Otherwise Clifton)		
		Emily	Age 72
560	Everitt	William Ernest	Age 42
561	Everton	Albert	Age 51
562	Eyre	Dorothy Lilian	Age 32
563	Eyre	Roland David	Age 7
564	Eyre	Elsie Elizabeth	Age 42
565	Eyre	George Henry	Age 48
566	Eyre	Jack	Age 16
567	Eyre	Patricia May	Age 10
568	Facer	John	Age 9
569	Facer	Robert	Age 6
570	Facer	Sidney Joseph	Age 45
571	Fahy	Joseph	Age 52
572	Farrell	James	Age 19
573	Farrell	John Thomas	Age 65
574	Farrell	Sarah	Age 25
575	Faulkner	George Richard	Age 66
576	Faux	Alice Mary	Age 62
577	Felix	Mary Dorothy	Age 20
578	Fenner	Agnes	Age 71
579	Fenner	Walter	Age 73
580	Fenton	John	Age 84
581	Fenton	Sarah Ann	Age 72
582	Ferguson	Violet Beatrice	Age 26
583	Fern	Gladys	Age 25
584	Fidoe	Norman Edward	Age 36
585	Field	William Joseph	Age 29
586	Fieldhouse	Charles	Age 65
587	Finch	Bryan	Age 5
588	Finch	William James	Age 30
589	Finch	Leslie Harold	Age 30
590	Finch	Nellie	Age 33
591	Findlay	James	Age 39
592	Finnegan	William	Age 47
593	Firth	Annie	Age 26
594	Firth	John Alfred	Age 28
595	Firth	Sheila	Aged 7 mths
596	Firth (Otherwise Hall)		
		Lilian Mary Edith	Age 32
597	Fisher	Ivy	Age 16
598	Fisher	Charles Redgrave	Age 55
599	Fisher	Frederick William	Age 74
600	Fisher	Lottie	Age 45
601	Fisher	Sarah Ann	Age 67
602	Fisher	Harold Hubert Edward James	Age 50
603	Fitter	Alan John	Age 6
604	Fitter	Norma Olive	Age 2
605	Fitter	Winifred Olive	Age 30
606	Fitzpatrick	Philip	Age 26
607	Fitzpatrick	William	Age 38
608	Fletcher	Ida Summerfield	Age 59
609	Fletcher	John Charles	Age 59
610	Fletcher	Joan Eileen	Age 29
611	Fletcher	Cecil George	Age 36
612	Flowers	Harry	Age 32
613	Floyd	Ernest Midlam	Age 59
614	Follis	Albert	Age 55
615	Follis	Annie	Age 53
616	Ford	Henry Thomas	Age 32
617	Forrest	Charles George	Age 75
618	Forrest	William	Age 18
619	Forrest	Laura Ada	Age 76
620	Forrest	Charles William	Age 45
621	Forrest	Edna May	Age 18
622	Foster	Elizabeth	Age 64
623	Foster	Mary	Age 64
624	Foster	Samuel Ambrose	Age 17
625	Foster	George	Age 62
626	Foster	Clara	Age 52
627	Foulds	Terence Leslie	Age 34
628	Foulston	Roy	Age 45
629	Fowler	Maurice Allan	Age 17
630	Fowles	Frederick	Age 59
631	Fox	Daniel	Age 37
632	Francis	Betty	Age 2
633	Francis	Emily	Age 36
634	Francis	Archibald George	Age 64
635	Francis	Walter	Age 19
636	Francis	David William	Age 47
637	Francis	Maud Harriett Lucy	Age 60
638	Franklin	Annie	Age 63
639	Franklin	James Mills	Age 65
640	Free	Sydney William	Age 61
641	Freeman	Arthur Augustus	Age 55
642	Freeman	Gladys Edna	Age 19
643	Freeman	Louisa Harriet	Age 47
644	Freer	Doreen	Age 9
645	Freer	Frederick Arnold	Age 17
646	Freer	Iris	Age 13
647	Freer	Isabella	Age 42
648	Friar	George Thomas	Age 37
649	Frost	James	Age 23
650	Frowen	Albert George	Age 22
651	Frowen	Ernest Henry	Age ?
652	Fry	Vivian Ronald James	Age 18
653	Fry	Edna	Age 16
654	Fry	Elizabeth	Age ?
655	Fryer	Lily	Age 50
656	Fulbrook	Elsie Caroline	Age 70
657	Gadd	Arthur William	Age 62
658	Gadd	Ellen Maria	Age 67
659	Gadd	Florence Louisa	Age 35
660	Galloway	Swanton Agnes	Age 43
661	Gambell	John Alfred	Age 42
662	Gardner	George William	Age 43
663	Gardner	Dorothy	Age 36
664	Gardner	Ethel	Age 42
665	Gardner	Gwen	Age 34
666	Gardner	Phyllis	Age 25
667	Garey	William	Age 46
668	Garner	Albert Herbert	Age 51
669	Gaskin	Annie	Age 62

670	Gaskin	Edward	Age 8
671	Gaskin	Margaret	Age 22
672	Gateley	Robert William	Age 40
673	Gauder	Ernest William	Age 16
674	Gauntlett	Florence Maud	Age 73
675	Gaylord	Arthur Edwin Reginald	Age 61
676	Gaynham	Percy	Age 40
677	Gell	John Vernon Pritchard	Age 62
678	Gennoe	Bertram Ernest	Age 15
679	Gensberg	Charles	Age 39
680	Gibbins	Arthur	Age 67
681	Gibbons	Charles	Age 60
682	Gibbs	Ashley Maria	Age 48
683	Gibbs	James	Age 22
684	Gibbs	Bertha Winnie	Age 48
685	Gibbs	Thomas Charles	Age 23
686	Giblin	John	Age 26
687	Gilbert	Louisa	Age 38
688	Gilbey	Stanley George	Age 32
689	Giles	Thomas Henry	Age 43
690	Gilliver	Lilian Florence	Age 19
691	Gilliver	Rose	Age 22
692	Gilliver	Sarah Ann	Age 62
693	Gilmor	John	Age 61
694	Glover	Albert	Age 18
695	Godson	Harriet	Injured 11 Dec 1940
696	Goldberg	Ann	Age 40
697	Goldberg	Maurice	Age 41
698	Gombrich	Else	Age 60
699	Goodby	John Henry	Age 63
700	Goodchild	Jack Frederick	Age 30
701	Goode	Ernest Alfred	Age 39
702	Goode	Mary Ann	Age 75
703	Goodson	Barbara Ann	Age 2
704	Goodson	Winifred Emily	Age 35
705	Goodwin	Alfred John	Age 34
706	Goody	Rose	Age 15
707	Gorman	John	Age 56
708	Gorth	Frank	Age 60
709	Grady	John	Age 31
710	Grainger	Alfred	Age 66
711	Grainger	Albert	Age 4
712	Grainger	Ellen	Age 34
713	Grainger	Flora Elizabeth	Age 9
714	Grainger	Leonard Charles	Aged 18 mths
715	Grainger	Harold James	Age 35
716	Granner	Henry	Age 58
717	Grant	Mary	Age 19
718	Gray	Alice Laura	Age 42
719	Gray	Derek	Age 14
720	Gray	Robin	Age 42
721	Gready	Bertie	Age 23
722	Greasley	Ann	Age 64
723	Greaves	Gaious	Age 58
724	Green	Ethel Kate	Age 40
725	Green	Arthur	Age 30
726	Green	James Walter	Age 39
727	Green	Mary Josephine	Age 43
728	Green	George	Age 46
729	Green	John Albert	Age 23
730	Greenhill	Mary Ann	Age 74
731	Greenway	Winifred	Age 34
732	Greenway	Jane	Age 71
733	Greer	Reginald Ernest	Age 66
734	Gregory	Harry	Age 72
735	Gregory	Louisa	Age 68
736	Griffin	William Henry	Age 32
737	Griffiths	Mary Eleanor Nellie	Age 55
738	Griffiths	Peter Llewellyn	Age 54
739	Griffiths	Joseph Joshua	Age 60
740	Grimley	Clara	Age 54
741	Grimley	Dorothy Georgina May	Age 18
742	Grimley	William Edward	Age 51
743	Grinsell	Emily Lilian	Age 30
744	Grinsell	Norma	Age 9
745	Groom	William	Age 59
746	Groome	Alice Beatrice	Age 58
747	Grundy	Maud	Age 69
748	Grundy	Joyce	Age 26
749	Guest	John	Age 39
750	Guest	Leonard	Age 24
751	Gumbley	Walter	Age 47
752	Gunn	Mary Elizabeth	Age 45
753	Gupwell	Emma	Age 69
754	Gupwell	Frederick James	Age 72
755	Guscott	Ernest Charles	Age 10
756	Guscott	Dorothy	Age 39
757	Gwinnett	Winifred Violet	Age 29
758	Gwinnett	David Cyril	Age 3
759	Habberley	Ernest Frederick	Age 36
760	Hackett	Harry Reginald	Age 45
761	Hadley	Ada	Age 58
762	Haines	Oliver Alfred	Age 27
763	Hale	Avril Cynthia	Age 8
764	Hale	Ellen Maria	Age 46
765	Hale	William James	Age 66
766	Hale	Stanley Lawrence	Age 12
767	Hall	Amy	Age 64
768	Hall	Walter Reginald	Age 19
769	Hall	Harry	Age 26
770	Hall	John Ernest	Age 52
771	Hall	John Ernest	Age 25
772	Hall	Alice Catherine	Age 15
773	Hall	Lilian Mary Edith	Age ?
774	Hall	Frank James	Age 74
775	Hall	Frank Joseph	Age 46
776	Halpin	Dermot	Age 23
777	Halpin	Julia	Age 28
778	Hamilton	Frederick Douglas	Age 26
779	Hammett	Alice	Age 55
780	Hammett	James Edward	Age 54
781	Hammond	Howard	Age 76
782	Hammond	Louie	Age 62

783	Hammond	Hugh	Age 18
784	Hampton	Frederick Donald	Age 20
785	Hand	George	Age 41
786	Handley	Edith Florence	Age 23
787	Handley	Sarah Ann	Age 70
788	Handley	Edith Maria	Age 57
789	Hands	Bertha Winnie	Age 68
790	Hands	Reginald	Age 17
791	Hanks	Alice	Age 32
792	Hanks	Beryl Ann	Age 2
793	Hannon	Richard	Age 25
794	Harbutt	Ada	Age 53
795	Hardwick	Archibald Thomas	Age 55
796	Hardwick	Marion Frances	Age 13
797	Hardy	Arthur	Age 39
798	Hardy	Valerie	Aged 14 mths
799	Hardy	Vera Mary Elizabeth	Age 30
800	Hare	Ellen	Age 18
801	Hare	John Charles	Age 62
802	Hare	Mary Ann	Age 61
803	Harman	Rowland Thomas	Age 60
804	Harrey	Frederick Edward Hyde	Age 57
805	Harrington	Edith Ellen	Age 59
806	Harrington	Herbert Walter	Age 60
807	Harris	Ivy Priscilla	Age 35
808	Harris	Margaret Rose	Age 6
809	Harris	John Clifford	Age 69
810	Harris	Marianne	Age 66
811	Harris	Adelaide	Age 20
812	Harris	Elizabeth	Age 46
813	Harris	Francis	Age 19
814	Harris	Joan	Age 15
815	Harris	Norman John	Age 9
816	Harris	Richard	Age 47
817	Harris	Walter	Age 12
818	Harris	Harry	Age 60
819	Harris	Ivy Mary	Age 20
820	Harris	Clara Eliza	Age 75
821	Harris	Bert	Age 25
822	Harris	George James	Age 62
823	Harrison	Florence Irene	Age 54
824	Harrison	Robert William	Age 74
825	Harrison	Donald Arthur	Age 17
826	Harrison	Ada Maria	Age 67
827	Harrison	George Joseph	Age 58
828	Harrison	Thomas Edgar	Age 48
829	Harrison	Thomas John	Age 73
830	Harrison	William Frank	Age 23
831	Harrison	John	Age 19
832	Harrison	George	Age 66
833	Hart	Henrietta Madeline	Age 51
834	Hart	Florence	Age 66
835	Hartill	Martha	Age 77
836	Harvey	Basil	Age 45
837	Harwood	William	Age 33
838	Haseler	Helen Mary	Age 67
839	Hassall	Charles Henry	Age 28
840	Hastings	Bertie John Charles	Age 56
841	Hastings	Rose	Age 53
842	Hatton	Thomas	Age 59
843	Hawes	Fanny	Age 48
844	Hawes	Harold James Crisp	Age 52
845	Hawkes	Elsie	Age 53
846	Hawkins	Arthur	Age 56
847	Hawkins	Emily Beatrice	Age 56
848	Hayfield	Henry Edward	Age 64
849	Haywood	Edward Thomas	Age 58
850	Haywood	Polly	Age 58
851	Haywood	Victor William	Age 24
852	Healey	Daniel	Age 41
853	Heath	William Edward	Age 69
854	Heath	Emily Jane	Age 71
855	Heath	Joan Molly	Age 20
856	Heath	Dorothy	Age 21
857	Heath	Sydney	Age 25
858	Heath	Mary Ann	Age 76
859	Hemming	Albert Thomas	Age 24
860	Hemms	William John	Age 56
861	Henley	Alice Gertrude	Age 47
862	Henley	Doris	Age 13
863	Henley	Mary	Age 15
864	Henley	Sheila	Age 6
865	Henson	Cyril John	Aged 18 mths
866	Henson	Frederick John	Age 36
867	Henson	Raymond Harold	Aged 6 Weeks
868	Henson	Dorothy Jean	Age 10
869	Henty	Eileen Margaret	Age 21
870	Henty	Kathleen	Age 52
871	Hewer	Robert Henry Henchley	Age 65
872	Hewitt	Albert James	Age 55
873	Hewitt	Albert Edward	Age 60
874	Hewitt	Audrey Kathleen	Age 2
875	Hewitt	John	Age 52
876	Heynes	Ivy	Age 28
877	Heynes	Louisa	Age 59
878	Heynes	May	Age 30
879	Heynes	Samuel	Age 63
880	Hibbard	Joseph E	
881	Hicken	Gladys	Age 38
882	Hicken	Gladys	Age 19
883	Hicken	Robert	Age 12
884	Hicken	Henry	Age 41
885	Hicks	Rose	Age 20
886	Higgins	Winifred	Age 47
887	Higgins	Leonard	Age 36
888	High	Harry Gilbert	Age 50
889	High	Rosa May	Age 55
890	Higham	Susannah Emma	Age 64
891	Hill	Esther Margaret	Age 72
892	Hill	David William	Age 9
893	Hill	Lucy Jane	Age 64
894	Hill	Frank	Age 43
895	Hill	Hilda Maud	Age 36
896	Hill	Charles Ernest	Age 46

897	Hill	Albert Edward	Age 40	954	Hughes	Nathan Brookes	Age 52
898	Hill	James	Age 58	955	Hughes	Charles William	Age 52
899	Hinton	Annie	Age 77	956	Hughes	Elsie Maud	Age 50
900	Hird	Albert Edward	Age 36	957	Hughes	Ronald Percy	Age 15
901	Hitchen	Catherine	Age 74	958	Hulme	Barbara Nina	Age 19
902	Hobbs	Clarence	Age 36	959	Hulme	Florence May	Age 54
903	Hodges	Charles William Victor	Age 43	960	Hulse	Harry Jerome	Age 67
904	Hodges	Richard Baden Powell	Age 42	961	Hunt	Charles	Age 66
905	Hodgetts	Herbert John	Age 42	962	Hunt	Maud Bevis	Age 60
906	Hodgetts	William	Age 46	963	Hunt	Joseph Henry	Age 56
907	Hodgkins	Harry	Age 60	964	Hyatt	Annie	Age 71
908	Hodgkins	Frederick	Age 73	965	Hyde	Agnes Mary	Age 67
909	Holdaway	Arthur Edmund	Age 36	966	Ilsley	James Thomas	Age 65
910	Holdom	Irene Kitty	Age 30	967	Inman	Charles Henry	Age 50
911	Holdom	Margaret Ann	Age 2	968	Inns	Frederick	Age 83
912	Hollis	Valerie Margareta	Aged 18 mths	969	Isaacs	Florence	Age 53
913	Hollyoake	Kathleen	Age 18	970	Isaacs	Gertrude May	Age 36
914	Holmes	Nellie	Age 53	971	Isaacs	Jean	Age 8
915	Holmes	Thomas	Age 39	972	Isaacs	Peter Philip	Age 4
916	Holmes	Walter	Age 62	973	Islip	Arthur	Age 50
917	Holmes	Albert George	Age 33	974	Islip	Eva	Age 50
918	Holmes	George Henry	Age 22	975	Jacks	John	Age 40
919	Holt	Annie May	Age 55	976	Jackson	Amy Marguerite	Age 66
920	Holyland	Adelaide	Age 47	977	Jackson	Maurice Denton	Age 3
921	Homer	John William	Age 69	978	Jackson	Elizabeth	Age 49
922	Honick	Henry Robert	Age 58	979	Jackson	William Isaac	Age 56
923	Hood	Alice Elizabeth	Age 57	980	Jackson	Joseph	Age 43
924	Hood	Frederick James	Age 32	981	Jackson	William	Age 50
925	Hood	Rosalind Ethel Lilian	Age 30	982	Jacobs	Samuel	Age 60
926	Hood	Winnie	Age 36	983	James	John William	Age 70
927	Hood	Thomas Arthur	Age 57	984	James	Sylvia	Age 18
928	Hook	Ronald Edward	Age 24	985	James	Dorothy Irene	Age 38
929	Hopkins	Arthur	Age 68	986	James	William Henry	Age 36
930	Hopkins	Sarah Ann	Age 63	987	James	Phoebe Harriett	Age 66
931	Hopkins	Walter Joseph	Age 20	988	James	Elizabeth	Age 39
932	Hopkins	Ethel Mary	Age 33	989	Jarman	Florence May Violet	Age 43
933	Hopkinson	Charles	Age 40	990	Jarvis	Herbert	Age 25
934	Horne	Harold	Age 31	991	Jauncey	Charlotte	Age 78
935	Horton	George	Age 33	992	Jenkins	Albert	Age 38
936	Houlson	Ethel Florence	Age 3	993	Jenkins	Geoffrey Thomas	Age 14
937	Houlson	Harold	Age 41	994	Jenkins	Ronald Colin Frederick	Age 17
938	Houlson	Violet Hilda	Age 39	995	Jenkins	William Evan	Age 37
939	Howard	Richard Vincent	Age 54	996	Jenkins	James Hugh	Age 23
940	Howard	Samuel	Age ?	997	Jennings	Benjamin	Age 25
941	Howe	Edward James	Age 69	998	Jennings	Charles	Age 71
942	Hudson	William Alfred	Age 34	999	Jennings	Lionel William	Age 49
943	Hudson	Gladys	Age 37	1000	Jenson	Anne Clarissa	Age 10
944	Hughes	Herbert Victor	Age 77	1001	Jenson	Phillip	Age 12
945	Hughes	Charles Thomas	Age 64	1002	Jenson	Clarice	Age 47
946	Hughes	Peter	Age 5	1003	Jervis	Elizabeth Ann	Age 47
947	Hughes	Audrey Joan	Age 29	1004	Jessop	Emily Lucy	Age 65
948	Hughes	Alice	Age 77	1005	Jevons	Alfred George Isaac	Age 41
949	Hughes	George Owen	Age 64	1006	Jinks	May	Age 74
950	Hughes	Maud	Age 48	1007	Johnson	Annie	Age 71
951	Hughes	Emma	Age 57	1008	Johnson	Mary	Age 28
952	Hughes	Nellie	Age 21	1009	Johnson	John Henry	Age 63
953	Hughes	Neville	Age 16	1010	Johnson	Gladys Winifred	Age 34

1011	Johnson	Benjamin	Age 64
1012	Johnson	Annie Steedman	Age 67
1013	Johnson	Gordon Donald	Age 8
1014	Johnson	Frederick	Age 70
1015	Johnson	Lily	Age 37
1016	Jones	Charles	Age 52
1017	Jones	Thomas Francis	Age 15
1018	Jones	Clara	Age 76
1019	Jones	Leonard	Age 36
1020	Jones	Islwyn Michael	Age 29
1021	Jones	Thomas Howard	Age 17
1022	Jones	Thomas Isaac	Age 27
1023	Jones	Ernest Paul	Age 45
1024	Jones	Arthur	Age 28
1025	Jordon	Pamela	Aged 5 mths
1026	Joseph	Alfred Reuben	Age 37
1027	Jukes	Agnes	Age 53
1028	Jukes	John Albert	Age 19
1029	Kaufmann	Bernard	Age 13
1030	Kavanagh	Peter	Age 21
1031	Kavanagh	Harold Alexander	Age 30
1032	Keasey	Daisy	Age 48
1033	Keasey	Hilda	Age 28
1034	Keasey	Marjorie	Age 26
1035	Keeling	William	Age 49
1036	Keight	Ernest Reuben	Age 30
1037	Kelly	Edward	Age 18
1038	Kelly	John Edward	Age 41
1039	Kelway	Kathleen Dorothy	Age 11
1040	Kemp	Jane Amenda Olive	Age 38
1041	Kemp	Albert	Age 30
1042	Kendrick	Dennis George	Age 17
1043	Kendrick	Emily Beatrice	Age 45
1044	Kendrick	George	Age 52
1045	Kendrick	John	Age 53
1046	Kendrick	Leslie Samuel	Age 25
1047	Kendrick	William George	Age 28
1048	Kennedy	Emma Llewellyn	Age 76
1049	Kennedy	Ada Winifred	Age 25
1050	Kennedy	Maureen	Age 2
1051	Kenny	Rose Victoria	Age 46
1052	Kenny	James	Age 27
1053	Kent	Albert Edward	Age 63
1054	Kent	Philip	Age 68
1055	Kettlewell	Thomas Sykes	Age 25
1056	Kidd	Roland Garner	Age 63
1057	Kidd	Thomas Brand	Age 63
1058	King	Maud	Age 32
1059	King	Robert	Age 32
1060	King	Robert	Aged 14 mths
1061	King	Arthur	Age 79
1062	Kirby	Wilfred	Age 34
1063	Kirk	Alfred	Age 44
1064	Kite	Philip George	Age 34
1065	Knight	Lily	Age 58
1066	Knowles	Albert Bertram	Age 35
1067	Knox	Bridie	Age 32
1068	Knox	Joseph	Age 3
1069	Knox	Marjorie	Age 6
1070	Lacey	Emma	Age 65
1071	Lake	Florence Annie	Age 33
1072	Lambert	Elizabeth	Age 84
1073	Lambert	Edgar	Age 24
1074	Land	Fred Raymond	Age 17
1075	Lane	William Henry	Age 46
1076	Lane	Gladys	Age 32
1077	Lane	Samuel Richard	Age 46
1078	Langford	Nellie	Age 24
1079	Langley	Mary Ann	Age 53
1080	Langley	George Henry	Age 38
1081	Larbi	Ahmed	Age 54
1082	Larkin	Thomas	Age 35
1083	Lawley	John William	Age 37
1084	Lawlor	Elizabeth	Age 32
1085	Lawrence	Esther May	Age 37
1086	Laws	Margaret Campbell	Age 80
1087	Lawson	Dora Mary	Age 19
1088	Laxton	William Henry	Age 67
1089	Layton	Horace Alfred	Age 23
1090	Lea	Aubrey Edgar	Age 25
1091	Lea (Otherwise Davies)	Gilbert	Age 56
1092	Lee	William Alfred	Age 38
1093	Lees	William	Age 50
1094	Leigh	Marjorie Kaihleen	Age 19
1095	Lemmon	Jean Agnes	Age 8
1096	Lemmon	Ramon	Age 10
1097	Lemmon	Maria	Age 48
1098	Lemmon	Stanley William	Age 18
1099	Lemmon	John William	Age 49
1100	Lemon	Edwin Thomas	Age 50
1101	Leonard	John	Age 77
1102	Lewis	Margaret	Age 73
1103	Lewis	Thomas	Age 65
1104	Lewis	Joan	Age 8
1105	Lewis	George Reynolds	Age 59
1106	Lewis	Thomas	Age 51
1107	Lewis	Harold Gilbert	Age 25
1108	Lewis	Ernest	Age 38
1109	Lewis	John	Age 63
1110	Lewis	William John	Age 77
1111	Liddall	Amelia	Age 41
1112	Lilley	Alfred Ernest	Age 79
1113	Lilley	Ellen	Age 75
1114	Lilley	Ellen	Age 49
1115	Lilley	Joseph Ernest	Age 51
1116	Lilley	Phyllis Ellen	Age 20
1117	Lilley	John	Age 2
1118	Lilley	Kathleen	Age 32
1119	Lilley	Kathleen	Age 5
1120	Lilwall	Patty	Age 65
1121	Lines	Alan Colin	Age 8
1122	Lines	Annie Elizabeth	Age 62
1123	Lines	Margaret	Age 6

1124	Ling	Joseph Edward	Age 30
1125	Linton	Leslie Bernard	Age 27
1126	Lister	Elizabeth	Age 44
1127	Lister	Maurice	Age 34
1128	Little	John Michael	Age 37
1129	Llewellyn	Edward Edgar Mannock	Age 19
1130	Lloyd	Rene Llewella	Age 34
1131	Lloyd	Clara Jane	Age 69
1132	Lloyd	Katharine Ann	Age 83
1133	Lloyd	Violet	Age 33
1134	Lloyd	Valerie Doreen	Age 6
1135	Lloyd	Suzanne	Age ?
1136	Lloyd	Lewis	Age 70
1137	Loftus	Edith	Age 31
1138	Lombard	Charlotte	Age 80
1139	London	Herbert William	Age 63
1140	Long	Arthur Ernest	Age 67
1141	Long	Hazel Nellie	Age 2
1142	Long	Dennis Henry	Age 12
1143	Long	John Ernest	Age 24
1144	Long	Katie Ellen	Age 53
1145	Long	Leonard William	Age 32
1146	Long	Samuel John	Age 60
1147	Longford	Ada	Age 43
1148	Longford	James Thomas	Age 43
1149	Longman	William	Age 34
1150	Lord	Ernest Edward	Age 38
1151	Louch	Leonard Robert Charles	Age 53
1152	Lough	Grace	Age 32
1153	Lough	Thomas	Age 32
1154	Loveday	Ernest George	Age 42
1155	Loveday	Audrey	Age 10
1156	Lovedee	Edith Alice	Age 43
1157	Lovsey	Arthur John	Age 20
1158	Lownes	William James	Age 30
1159	Lucas	Alice	Age 58
1160	Lucas	John William	Age 32
1161	Lugg	Hubert Victor	Age 35
1162	Lydiatt	Agnes Mary	Age 40
1163	Lydiatt	Dennis Thomas Charles	Age 8
1164	Lynch	James	Age 28
1165	Lynes	May	Age 33
1166	Lyness	Thomas	Age 78
1167	Maclean	Alexander Murchison	Age 54
1168	Maclean	Donald	Age 18
1169	Maclean	Ian Alister	Age 20
1170	Maclean	Mary	Age 15
1171	Maclean	Mary Muir	Age 46
1172	Macnaughton	Elizabeth Mabel	Age 42
1173	Maddox	George	Age 59
1174	Maddox	Leslie Arthur	Age 31
1175	Mahon	Henry	Age 33
1176	Maiden	Elsie	Age 19
1177	Maiden	Herbert	Age 41
1178	Maiden	Elsie Louise	Age 53
1179	Maiden	Irene Eva	Age 21
1180	Malin	Alfred Thomas	Age 62
1181	Malvern	Cyril	Age 33
1182	Mancini	Anthony Paul	Age 16
1183	Manley	Albert Kenneth	Age 5
1184	Manley	Brenda	Aged 18 mths
1185	Manley	Beatrice May	Age 30
1186	Manley	Cyril James	Age 4
1187	Manley	Gilbert Terrence	Aged 3 mths
1188	Mann	Clara Amelia	Age 78
1189	Mann	Florence Alice	Age 58
1190	Mann	Annie Elizabeth	Age 56
1191	Mansfield	Clara	Age 45
1192	Mansfield	Charles Henry	Age 55
1193	Mapp	Constance Edith	Age 19
1194	Marburg (Otherwise Lloyd)		
		Suzanne	Age 5
1195	Mark	Euphemia Mary	Age 59
1196	Mark	Phoebe Ann	Age 90
1197	Markland	Joseph	Age 24
1198	Marklew	William	Age 57
1199	Marriott	Walter John	Age 65
1200	Marris	Daniel	Age 48
1201	Marsh	James	Age 24
1202	Marson	Patricia Valerie	Aged 13 mths
1203	Marson	Violet	Age 42
1204	Marsters	Gertrude	Age 65
1205	Marsters	Thomas Lewis	Age 65
1206	Martin	James	Age 46
1207	Martin	Albert Edward	Age 17
1208	Martin	Agnes Elizabeth	Age 26
1209	Martin	Arthur	Age 17
1210	Mason	James Henry	Age 49
1211	Mason	Eric Leslie	Age 37
1212	Masters	Alice Helen	Age 42
1213	Masters	Doris Elizabeth	Age 18
1214	Masters	Philip	Age 6
1215	Masters	Colin Thomas	Age 2
1216	Masters	Jean Anne	Age 1
1217	Masters	May	Age 27
1218	Matthews	Bridget	Age 21
1219	Matthews	Mary Jane	Age 65
1220	Matthews	Arthur Bernard	Age 63
1221	May	Frank	Age 47
1222	Mayall	Arthur John	Age 36
1223	Maybury	William	Age 65
1224	Mccarthy	Thomas John	Age 29
1225	Mccarthy	Anne	Age 5
1226	Mccarthy	Desmond	Age 8
1227	Mccarthy	Ellen Nellie	Age 15
1228	Mccarthy	Honora	Age 3
1229	Mccarthy	John	Age 10
1230	Mccarthy	Mary Josephine	Age 6
1231	Mccarthy	Patrick	Age 4
1232	Mccarthy	John Peter	Age 42
1233	Mcclean	Frederick William	Age 26
1234	Mcdonald	John	Age 35
1235	Mcgrail	James	Age 30

1236	Mcgrail (Otherwise Burnett)		
		Rose Elizabeth	Age 35
1237	Mcgrail (Otherwise Burnett)		
		Mavis L	Aged 6 mths
1238	Mcgreevy	Joseph	Age 18
1239	Mcguirk	Henry Edward	Age 19
1240	Mchugh	Bernard Thomas	Age 51
1241	Mclaughlin	Annie Selina	Age 60
1242	Mcpherson	David	Age 27
1243	Mead	Leonard Arthur	Age 33
1244	Meakin	Frederick Thomas	Age 36
1245	Meakin	Susan Elenore	Age 37
1246	Meakin	Alfred Harold Charles	Age 43
1247	Meanwell	Alfred Edward	Age 37
1248	Mellor	Ernest	Age 39
1249	Melville	Mary	Age 82
1250	Merrett	Albert Edward	Age 57
1251	Metcalf	Kate	Age 18
1252	Metcalfe	Matthew	Age 34
1253	Middleman	Christopher	Age 27
1254	Miller	Benjamin John	Age 57
1255	Miller	Minnie	Age 26
1256	Mills	Charlotte	Age 50
1257	Mills	Harry Bertram	Age 62
1258	Mills	Alice Louise	Age 64
1259	Mills	Edith	Age 49
1260	Mills	George Edward	Age 73
1261	Mills	Allen William	Age 34
1262	Millward	Gladys Annie	Age 22
1263	Millward	Mary	Age 73
1264	Millward	Beatrice Louise	Age 49
1265	Milner	Douglas Donovan	Age 17
1266	Milroy	Alice Maud	Age 71
1267	Minikin	Herbert Price	Age 68
1268	Minor	William Charles	Age 58
1269	Minott	Sylvia	Age 6
1270	Mitchell	Emma Ethel	Age 52
1271	Mitchell	Kathleen	Age 20
1272	Mitchell	William	Age 27
1273	Mitchell	Frank Stanley Noel	Age 40
1274	Mitchell	Amy	Age 32
1275	Mitchell	Albert Edward	Age 39
1276	Mitchell	Diana Winifred	Aged 3 mths
1277	Mitchell	Patricia Margaret	Age 5
1278	Mitchell	William Philip	Age 59
1279	Mitchinson	William Alfred	Age 25
1280	Mitton	Thomas	Age 18
1281	Mogg	Brenda	Age 13
1282	Mogg	Rosalind	Age 11
1283	Mogg	Thomas Charles	Age 45
1284	Mohan	John	Age 30
1285	Moody	Edith Ellen	Age 43
1286	Moody	Barbara	Age 15
1287	Moore	Dorothy	Age 45
1288	Moore	June	Age 13
1289	Moore	William	Age 47
1290	Moore	Henry	Age 35
1291	Moore	Thomas Anthony	Age 28
1292	Moorhouse	George Kaye	Age 19
1293	Moran	Sheila	Age 11
1294	Morgan	Maureen Patricia	Age 5
1295	Morgan	John William	Age 60
1296	Morgan	Harry	Age 57
1297	Morgan	Elsie	Age 26
1298	Morgan	Selina Elizabeth	Age 75
1299	Morgan	David John Edwin	Age 18
1300	Morley	Roland	Age 53
1301	Morrall	Doris Ida	Age 46
1302	Morrall	Thomas Edward	Age 46
1303	Morris	Lilian Florence	Age 53
1304	Morris	William Ernest	Age 33
1305	Morris	Walter	Age 56
1306	Morsley	Richard William	Age 54
1307	Mortimer	Eva	Age 62
1308	Moseley	Clifford	Age 36
1309	Moseley	Arthur	Age 33
1310	Moseley	Arthur	Age 31
1311	Moss	Ellen	Age 50
1312	Moss	Elsie	Age 31
1313	Mould	George Herbert Neville	Age 14
1314	Mountford	Ernest Hope	Age 67
1315	Mountford	Edith	Age 52
1316	Mucklow	Joseph	Age 67
1317	Muddyman	Edward	Age 59
1318	Mugleston	Edward Stanley	Age 35
1319	Mulhall	Christopher	Age 19
1320	Mullervy	John	Age 30
1321	Mullins	Edwin	Age 36
1322	Mullins	Sarah	Age 79
1323	Mulliss	Charles George	Age 48
1324	Munn	William Henry	Age 27
1325	Murcott	Joyce	Age 16
1326	Murray	John	Age 20
1327	Murray	Esther	Age 16
1328	Mutchell	Alfred Edward	Age 46
1329	Nash	Linda Florence	Age 29
1330	Nash	Leslie Josiah	Age 28
1331	Navarre (Otherwise Wright)		
		Alexander	Age 42
1332	Neal	Mary	Age 72
1333	Neale	Herbert John	Age 18
1334	Neil	Joseph Harold	Age 40
1335	Nel	Adrian	Age 30
1336	Nend	Louisa	Age 17
1337	Neville	Evelyn Mary	Age 39
1338	Neville	William Allen	Age 17
1339	Nevitt	Richard	Age 72
1340	Newman	Amelia	Age 35
1341	Newman	Joyce	Age 9
1342	Newman	Kenneth	Age 5
1343	Newman	Phyllis	Age 10
1344	Newton	Arthur James	Age 58
1345	Newton	Charles Arthur	Age 31
1346	Nicholls	Henry	Age 44

1347	Nokes	Ada Kathleen Leonora	Age 32
1348	Nolan	Jerrard	Age 27
1349	Nolan	Mary Ann	Age 71
1350	Nolan	William	Age 43
1351	Nolte	Ada Annie	Age 52
1352	Norgrove	Harry	Age 30
1353	Norman	William	Age 62
1354	Norridge	Arthur Francis	Age 66
1355	Norris	Florence Gertrude	Age 54
1356	Norris	William	Age 57
1357	Northern	Mary Elizabeth	Age 42
1358	Norton	Edith	Age 60
1359	Nowell	John Alfred	Age 39
1360	Nunn	George	Age 54
1361	Nutting	Jane	Age 38
1362	Nutting	Lilian Joan	Age 13
1363	O'donell	Lilian	Age 37
1364	O'leary	Jeremiah	Age 39
1365	O'neill	Christopher Joseph	Age 45
1366	O'neill	John Joseph	Age 1
1367	O'neill	Margaret	Age 5
1368	O'neill	Neal	Age 5
1369	O'neill	Thomas	Age 4
1370	Onions	John	
1371	Orme	Joseph	Age 69
1372	Orme	Alice May	Age 15
1373	Orme	Thomas Joseph	Age 18
1374	O'rourke	Thomas	Age 38
1375	Osborn	Peter John	Age 4
1376	Osborn	Winifred Gladys	Age 35
1377	Osmond	Florence Louisa	Age 55
1378	Overend	Hubert	Age 43
1379	Owen	Maud Beatrice	Age 73
1380	Owen	Walter Thomas	Age 45
1381	Owen	Ada	Age 23
1382	Owen	Howard	Age 30
1383	Page	Thomas	Age 64
1384	Page	Mabel Florence	Age 52
1385	Page	Horace Albert	Age 40
1386	Painter	Ellen	Age 59
1387	Painter	Marjorie	Age 30
1388	Palfreyman	Jack	Age 30
1389	Palmer	Leonard James	Age 47
1390	Palmer	Harry James	Age 32
1391	Palmer	Eliza	Age 63
1392	Palmer	Norman	Age 20
1393	Pardoe	Christine	Age 5
1394	Pardoe	Joyce	Age 25
1395	Pardoe	May Gertrude	Age 46
1396	Parfitt	Douglas John	Age 17
1397	Parish	George Kitchener	Age 25
1398	Parish	Eliza	Age 75
1399	Parker	Evelyn May	Age 19
1400	Parker	Beatrice Alice	Age 50
1401	Parker	Philip Henry	Age 53
1402	Parker	Harry	Age 23
1403	Parker	Richard William	Age 58
1404	Parker	Richard William	Age 25
1405	Parker	Joseph	Age 34
1406	Parker	Ivy Grace	Age 34
1407	Parker	Jean Lilian	Age 4
1408	Parker	Daphne Audrey	Age 18
1409	Parker	Leonard William: Air Raid Warden	
1410	Parkes	Martha	Age 63
1411	Parr	Gwendoline	Age 18
1412	Parsons	Amy	Age 68
1413	Parsons	Charles Henry	Age 61
1414	Parsons	Alexander Raymond	Age 30
1415	Parsons	Dennis	Age 16
1416	Parton	Albert	Age 46
1417	Parton	George	Age 52
1418	Parton	Henry	Age 32
1419	Partridge	Phoebe	Age 33
1420	Patrick	Beatrice Maud	Age 35
1421	Patrick	Maureen	Aged 11 mths
1422	Patrick	Mary Jean	Age 5
1423	Patrick	Albert Edward	Age 30
1424	Paul	Horace	Age 17
1425	Payne	Frank	Age 51
1426	Payne	Lawrence	Age 60
1427	Payne	Douglas Harry	Age 36
1428	Payne	Edgar Charles	Age 43
1429	Payne	Ernest William	Age 25
1430	Payne	William	Age 40
1431	Paynter	Gladys Edith	Age 54
1432	Paynter	Henry James	Age 55
1433	Peake	Doris Patricia	Age 14
1434	Peake	Elizabeth	Age 44
1435	Peake	William Edward	Age 51
1436	Pearce	Elsie June	Age 19
1437	Pearce	James	Age 55
1438	Pearson	Beatrice Mary	Age 25
1439	Pearson	Frederick Charles	Age 39
1440	Pearson	William Charles	Age 65
1441	Pearson	Ann	Age 4
1442	Pearson	June Mary	Age 6
1443	Pearson	Vera	Age 35
1444	Peat	Nellie Martha	Age 46
1445	Pemberton	Frances Emily	Age 57
1446	Pemberton	Gwendoline Evelyn	Age 28
1447	Pendleton	Elizabeth Ann	Age 59
1448	Pendrey	Roland Ernest	Age 41
1449	Penson	Catherine	Age 72
1450	Perry	Daisy	Age 49
1451	Perry	Jane	Age 79
1452	Perry	Eliza Ann	Age 66
1453	Perry	Charles Arthur	Age 35
1454	Phillips	Raymond James	Age 23
1455	Phillips	Edith Annie	Age 49
1456	Phillips	Elsie Elizabeth	Age 54
1457	Phillips	Gladys	Age 32
1458	Phillips	Albert Edward	Age 43
1459	Phillips	Albert Arthur	Age 33
1460	Phillips	Ethel Annie	Age 32

1461 Phillips	Janel Alice	Aged 10 mths
1462 Piccioni	Angela	Age 6
1463 Piccioni	Gina Edvige Ernesta	Age 6
1464 Piccioni	Phyllis Maud	Age 46
1465 Piccioni (Otherwise Townsend)		
	Doris Mary	Age 36
1466 Pickering	Ernest	Age 30
1467 Pickering	Ronald	Age 9
1468 Pierpoint	Amy	Age 53
1469 Pierpoint	Cornelius	Age 52
1470 Pitcher	Iverina May	Age 23
1471 Pitman	George Stanley	Age 26
1472 Pitt	Sarah Ellen	Age 72
1473 Pitt	William	Age 74
1474 Pitt	Alfred	Age 63
1475 Pittaway	Arthur	Age 63
1476 Plant	Norman	Age 20
1477 Plumpton	Jemima	Age 77
1478 Pollock	Elizabeth	Age 17
1479 Poole	Matilda	Age 70
1480 Pooley	Lily	Age 49
1481 Poolton	George Edward	Age 31
1482 Potter	William James	Age 37
1483 Powell	Gordon Harry	Age 12
1484 Powell	Kathleen May	Age 42
1485 Powell	George Edward	Age 38
1486 Powell	Edith Maria	Age 63
1487 Powell	Frederick George	Age 62
1488 Powell-Tuck	Ethel Clara	Age 46
1489 Poxon	Samuel Morley	Age 52
1490 Pratt	Joan Winifred	Age 25
1491 Pratt	Herbert Charles	Age 38
1492 Pratt (Otherwise Robinson)		
	Patricia Irene	Age 10
1493 Pratten	Evelyn May	Age 45
1494 Prest	Cicely	Age 73
1495 Price	Wilfred Thomas	Age 38
1496 Price	Walter Robert	Age 39
1497 Price	Douglas Ernest	Age 20
1498 Priestman	Lily Edith	Age 60
1499 Priestman	Lucy Elizabeth	Age 72
1500 Prince	Beatrice Wilhelmina Maude	Age 40
1501 Prince	Jack Delworth	Age 43
1502 Prince	Norman Delworth	Age 12
1503 Prince	Sylvia Olive Janet	Age 13
1504 Pritchard	Susannah	Age 70
1505 Pritchard	Pauline	Age 6
1506 Proctor	Frederick Leslie	Age 25
1507 Pugh	Emma	Age 63
1508 Pugh	Mabel	Age 34
1509 Purser	Cecil Edwin	Age 41
1510 Purshouse	Albert Edward	Age 39
1511 Pym	Joan Irene	Age 16
1512 Pym	Kenneth Arthur	Age 13
1513 Quercia	Joseph	Age 37
1514 Quiney	Bryan George	Age 3
1515 Quiney	Elizabeth Jane	Age 44
1516 Quiney	George	Age 50
1517 Quiney	Olive	Age 16
1518 Quinn	Norman	Age 12
1519 Quinn	Louisa	Age 61
1520 Quinn	Irene May	Age 19
1521 Quinn	Hilda Nora	Age 47
1522 Quinn	Eric Francis	Age 26
1523 Rabone	Frederick Mitchell	Age 73
1524 Radd	William	Age 35
1525 Radford	Ernest James	Age 32
1526 Rainsford	Annie May	Age 20
1527 Rainsford	George Henry	Age 20
1528 Rainsford	George	Age 41
1529 Ralph	Joseph Henry	Age 52
1530 Randall	Arthur Allister	Age 65
1531 Ranger	Frederick Thomas Victor	Age 58
1532 Ravyts	Jeanne	Age 34
1533 Ray	June	Aged 1 mth
1534 Rayworth	Iris	Age 21
1535 Rayworth	John Stewart	Aged 11 mths
1536 Rea	May	Age 44
1537 Rea	Norman Philip	Age 53
1538 Reacord	Charles Henry	Age 61
1539 Reddall	John Norman	Age 33
1540 Rees	John	Age 64
1541 Reeves	William	Age 69
1542 Reid	Alfred	Age 48
1543 Reid	Elizabeth Ann	Age 52
1544 Rendle	Elsie	Age 41
1545 Resuggan	John Henry	Age 54
1546 Reynolds	Leonard	Age 30
1547 Reynolds	William	Age 57
1548 Reynolds	Thomas George	Age 26
1549 Rhone	Florence Ada Lucy	Age 64
1550 Richards	Ronald	Age 17
1551 Richards	Alice Margaret	Age 61
1552 Richards	Charles Douglas	Age 22
1553 Richards	William Frederick	Age 70
1554 Richards	May	Age 46
1555 Richardson	Louisa	Age 73
1556 Rickards	George Samuel	Age 41
1557 Ridgway	Howard Percy	Age 55
1558 Riley	Albert	Age 59
1559 Riley	Janetta	Age 53
1560 Riley	Joan Lilian	Age 16
1561 Riley	Nora Vera	Age 19
1562 Riley	Albert Harry	Age 37
1563 Riley	Douglas	Age 7
1564 Riley	Jean	Age 3
1565 Riley	Laura Elizabeth	Age 21
1566 Rimell	Albert Leslie	Age 24
1567 Roach	Frank	Age 40
1568 Roberts	Annie Avarina	Age 19
1569 Roberts	Arthur	Age 52
1570 Roberts	Annie Mary	Age 19
1571 Robinson	Hilda Daisy	Age 61
1572 Robinson	Frances Patricia	Age 37

1573	Robinson	Peter Maxwell	Age 4
1574	Robinson	William Henry	Age 34
1575	Robinson	Georgina Amelia	Age 71
1576	Rockett	Kate	Age 43
1577	Rockett	Beryl Kathleen	Age 16
1578	Rockett	Horace Frederick	Age 41
1579	Roddy	Nellie	Age 57
1580	Roddy	Thomas	Age 59
1581	Rodway	William Alfred	Age 47
1582	Rodway	Harold	Age 59
1583	Rodway	Minnie	Age 48
1584	Roe	Sarah Ann	Age 75
1585	Roe	William	Age 76
1586	Roe	William John	Age 44
1587	Rogers	Hannah Matilda	Age 53
1588	Rogers	Elizabeth	Age 60
1589	Rogers	Edith	Age 13
1590	Rogers	Elsie	Age 13
1591	Rogers	John William	Age 18
1592	Rogers	Alfred Thomas	Age 43
1593	Rogers	Barbara May	Age 11
1594	Rogers	Mary Ann	Age 53
1595	Rogers	Sybil Barbara	Age 30
1596	Rogers	Minnie	Age 65
1597	Rogers	Richard Lewis	Age 73
1598	Rogers	Annie	Age 78
1599	Rollason	Maurice Stanley	Age 17
1600	Rollings	Harry	Age 25
1601	Rooke	Sarah	Age 72
1602	Rooke	Eliza	Age 70
1603	Roper	Edward	Age 29
1604	Rose	Josephine	Age 20
1605	Rose	Kathleen	Age 22
1606	Rose	Harold	Age 42
1607	Rose	Nellie	Age 51
1608	Rosenberg	Emmie Eliza	Age 62
1609	Rosenberg	Isaac	Age 64
1610	Ross	Rebecca	Age 30
1611	Round	Martha	Age 87
1612	Round	Emma Elizabeth	Age 28
1613	Rowan	Frederick	Aged 9 mths
1614	Rubery	James	Age 32
1615	Rudge	Albert Arthur	Age 44
1616	Rumbold	Arthur	Age 35
1617	Russell	William	Age 53
1618	Russell	Joan Gertrude May	Age 14
1619	Russell	William	Age 38
1620	Rutter	Edwin	Age 72
1621	Ryland	Edith	Age 77
1622	Rymill	William	Age 27
1623	Sallis	Felix	Age 48
1624	Salmon	Ella Alice Louisa	Age 47
1625	Sambrook	Clara	Age 74
1626	Sambrook	John	Age 66
1627	Sambrook	Ronald	Age 16
1628	Sanders	Hilda Maud	Age 29
1629	Sanders	Thomas	Age 57
1630	Savage	William James	Age 25
1631	Savage	Denis Sidney	Age 16
1632	Savin	David Thomas	Age 7
1633	Savin	Kenneth Joseph	Age 2
1634	Savin	Raymond John	Age 4
1635	Savory	Frederick Lionel James	Age 31
1636	Scott	Kenneth Sidney	Age 11
1637	Scott	Sidney	Age 32
1638	Scott	Edith Elizabeth	Age 35
1639	Scott	Elizabeth Jane	Age 58
1640	Scott	Annie Elizabeth	Age 30
1641	Scott	Ernest	Age 62
1642	Scott	James	Age 48
1643	Scott	William Henry Richard	Age 34
1644	Scragg	Alfred	Age 35
1645	Scriven	Elsie Mabel	Age 44
1646	Scriven	Audrey Jean	Age 10
1647	Scriven	Lily	Age 33
1648	Scrivener	Albert George	Age 50
1649	Scrivener	James Henry	Age 33
1650	Scrivens	Florence	Age 47
1651	Sealey	Minnie	Age 42
1652	Seaton	Rosetta	Age 75
1653	Sellek	Mark William	Age 40
1654	Severn	Luke	Age 79
1655	Seymour	Barbara Florence	Age 2
1656	Seymour	William Alfred	Age 32
1657	Seymour	William Barry	Aged 9 mths
1658	Seymour	Divinia Edith	Age 73
1659	Shakespeare	William Henry	Age 37
1660	Shakespeare	Charles Henry	Age 18
1661	Shamsudi	Allah Ditta	Age 50
1662	Shapter	Charles Edward	Age 18
1663	Sharp	Clara	Age 72
1664	Sharp	Herbert Walter Thomas	Age 29
1665	Sharpe	Dennis H	Age 14
1666	Sharpe	Edith Maud	Age 45
1667	Sharpe	John	Age 16
1668	Sharpe	Jesse	Age 18
1669	Sharpe	Alfred	Age 52
1670	Sharples	Harry	Age 20
1671	Shaw	Marion	Age 59
1672	Shaw	Louis	Age 57
1673	Shaw	Brian	Aged 8 mths
1674	Shaw	Edward	Age 41
1675	Shaw	Joan	Age 19
1676	Shaw	Joan	Age 14
1677	Sheffield	George	Age 25
1678	Sheffield	Ida	Age 26
1679	Sheldon	William	Age 23
1680	Sheldon	Leslie	Age 20
1681	Shenton	Annie Amelia	Age 54
1682	Shepherd	Dorothy Louise	Age 49
1683	Shepherd	Lorna	Age 12
1684	Shepherd	Thomas Henry	Age 46
1685	Shepherd	Amy	Age 65
1686	Shepherd	Cyril	Age 24

1687	Shepherd	Howard	Age 33
1688	Shepherd	John	Age 7
1689	Shepherd	Molly	Age 29
1690	Shepherd	William Charles	Age 23
1691	Shepherd	Joseph Charles Lea	Age 23
1692	Sherrin	Thomas Edward	Age 38
1693	Sherwood	William John	Age 67
1694	Sheward	Will	Age 15
1695	Shingler	Monica Agnes	Age 60
1696	Shipley	Eunice Lilian	Age 11
1697	Shotton	Alfred	Age 28
1698	Showell	William Arthur Harry	Age 31
1699	Shutt	Annie	Age 58
1700	Shutt	John	Age 59
1701	Shuttleworth	Eric	Age 17
1702	Silk	William	Age 23
1703	Simmons	Eric Samuel	Age 20
1704	Simpson	Harold Sidney	Age 25
1705	Simpson	Elizabeth Rose Edith	Age 44
1706	Simpson	Sidney	Age 54
1707	Simpson	Frank Philip	Age 65
1708	Simpson	Joseph Ernest	Age 29
1709	Sinclair	Louise	Age 62
1710	Singh	Mehnga	Age 44
1711	Singleton	Alfred John	Age 74
1712	Skermer	Drucilla	Age 47
1713	Skermer	Leonard	Age 6
1714	Skermer	Patricia	Age 10
1715	Skermer	Reginald	Age 12
1716	Skermer	William James	Age 31
1717	Skett	Mary	Age 59
1718	Skinner	Leonard Richard	Age 64
1719	Skinner	Reginald George	Age 49
1720	Slater	Lydia	Age 59
1721	Slater	Leslie	Age 35
1722	Slater	Walter Byron	Age 42
1723	Sleet	Betsy	Age 57
1724	Sleet	Charles	Age 25
1725	Sleet	George	Age 60
1726	Smallwood	Annie	Age 50
1727	Smallwood	Edith	Age 14
1728	Smallwood	Gladys	Age 12
1729	Smallwood	Hilda Mary	Age 17
1730	Smallwood	Thomas Edward	Age 47
1731	Smart	Alice Frances	Age 67
1732	Smart	Muriel Dorothy	Age 36
1733	Smart	William Charles	Age 69
1734	Smith	Ida Mary	Age 20
1735	Smith	Violet Annie	Age 42
1736	Smith	Anthony John Mackenzie	Age 3
1737	Smith	Albert Ellis	Age 18
1738	Smith	Catherine	Age 38
1739	Smith	Frederick	Age 40
1740	Smith	John Kemp	Age 26
1741	Smith	William Arthur	Age 75
1742	Smith	Annie	Age 34
1743	Smith	Edward Arthur	Age 54
1744	Smith	George William	Age 64
1745	Smith	William Albert	Age 28
1746	Smith	Geoffrey William	Age 2
1747	Smith	Anthony John	Aged 18 mths
1748	Smith	Edith Alice	Age 24
1749	Smith	Ralph	Age 35
1750	Smith	Ada	Age 39
1751	Smith	Ernest Evatt	Age 28
1752	Smith	Rose Ellen	Age 32
1753	Smith	Ethel Dora	Age 26
1754	Smith	Florence	Age 53
1755	Smith	Alice Marie	Age 34
1756	Smith	June	Age 18
1757	Smith	Sidney John	Age 35
1758	Smith	Florence Lilian	Age 58
1759	Smith	Wallace	Age 65
1760	Smith	Ernest Henry	Age 69
1761	Smith	Florence Hannah	Age 26
1762	Smith	John	Age 41
1763	Smith	Evelyn Gladys	Age 42
1764	Smith	William	Age 78
1765	Smith	Alice	Age 20
1766	Smith	Alice	Age 52
1767	Smith	Florence	Age 29
1768	Smith	Irene	Age 3
1769	Smith	Elsie	Age 46
1770	Smith	Horace Charles	Age 55
1771	Smith	John	Age 21
1772	Smith	Arthur John	Age 44
1773	Smith	Harry	Age 55
1774	Smith	Hilary Margaret	Age 5
1775	Smith	Alfred	Age 33
1776	Smith	Frank Pearson	Age 60
1777	Smith	Sheila	Age 2
1778	Smith	John James	Age ?
1779	Smith	Mary Ann	Age 70
1780	Smith	Harriet Ann	Age 25
1781	Smith	Albert Edward	Age 32
1782	Smith	John James	Age 51
1783	Smith	Walter Alfred	Age 25
1784	Smith	Alfred John	Age 30
1785	Smith	Alfred Ernest	Age 58
1786	Snow	John Beverley	Age 49
1787	Soden	Colin	Age 7
1788	Sollors	William Frederick	Age 67
1789	Spalton	Joseph Newbould	Age 55
1790	Sparrow	Reginald William	Age 38
1791	Speed	Annie Elizabeth	Age 62
1792	Speed	Sarah Florence	Age 30
1793	Speller	Eustace Lionel	Age 43
1794	Spencer	William Beasley	Age 71
1795	Spencer	Arthur Edward	Age 54
1796	Spink	James	Age 52
1797	Spooner	Harry	Age 29
1798	Spooner	Rose	Age 70
1799	Sprague	Frank	Age 45
1800	Squires	John Gordon	Age 19

1801	Stafford	Alfred Smith	Age 36
1802	Stagg	Clara Beatrice	Age 61
1803	Stanley	Albert Edward	Age 56
1804	Stanyard	Rosanna	Age 67
1805	Staples	Drusilla	Age 57
1806	Starkey	George	Age 61
1807	Steedman	Elsie	Age 51
1808	Steedman	Joan	Age 16
1809	Steedman	Vera	Age 13
1810	Steedman	Edna	Age 11
1811	Stephens	Mary Teresa	Age 68
1812	Stevens	William Thomas	Age 36
1813	Stevenson	Gertrude May	Age 30
1814	Stevenson	Henry	Age 34
1815	Stevenson	William	Age 37
1816	Stimpson	Alfred Edward	Age 51
1817	Stringer	Bertram	Age 37
1818	Strophair	Anita Josephine	Aged 10 mths
1819	Strother	Richard Edward	Age 55
1820	Stryke	George	Age 16
1821	Stuckey	Harriet	Age 63
1822	Summerfield	William	Age 54
1823	Sumner	William Joseph	Age 29
1824	Swadkins	Harry	Age 55
1825	Swadling	Ernest	Age 18
1826	Swales	Henry	Age 21
1827	Sweet	Herbert James	Age 55
1828	Swindale	Florence	Age 25
1829	Swindale	Kathleen Ethel	Age 2
1830	Swindale	Michael John	Aged 4 mths
1831	Swingler	Henry	Age 20
1832	Talbot	Emma Eliza	Age 57
1833	Talbot	Harry	Age 58
1834	Tandy	Phyllis Valentine	Age 20
1835	Tankard	Laura	Age 81
1836	Tankard	Mary Ann	Age 82
1837	Tanner	Isabella	Age 85
1838	Tarnosky	Ida Mary	Age 45
1839	Tatchell	Bertha May	Age 47
1840	Tavinor	Herbert	Age 63
1841	Taylor	Sarah Ann	Age 58
1842	Taylor	Florence	Age 28
1843	Taylor	Gordon	Age 6
1844	Taylor	John	Age 2
1845	Taylor	Norman	Age 5
1846	Taylor	Olive Aline	Age 20
1847	Taylor	William Charles	Age 58
1848	Taylor	Dorothy Rose	Age 37
1849	Taylor	Joan Ethel	Age 14
1850	Taylor	Sidney Arthur	Age 26
1851	Taylor	Samuel	Age 68
1852	Taylor	William	Age 67
1853	Taylor	Henry	Age 36
1854	Taylor	Sarah Elizabeth	Age 69
1855	Teague	Bertha Annie	Age 58
1856	Teague	Joan Margaret	Age 18
1857	Teague	Mary Dorothy	Age 29
1858	Teague	Nellie Edith	Age 23
1859	Teale	Bryan	Age 2
1860	Teale	Dorothy Jane	Age 24
1861	Teale	Kenneth John	Aged 7 mths
1862	Teale	Patricia	Age 6
1863	Teale	William Joseph	Age 25
1864	Tennant	Alice Maud	Age 64
1865	Tennant	Susannah Jane	Age 68
1866	Terrell	Charlotte	Age 53
1867	Terry	Norman	Age 19
1868	Tetley	Samuel Frank	Age 28
1869	Thomas	John Penry	Age 20
1870	Thomas	Evan Owen	Age 39
1871	Thomas	Daniel Smedley	Age 15
1872	Thomas	Trevor	Age 35
1873	Thomas	William Henry Charles	Age 27
1874	Thomas	Thomas John	Age 26
1875	Thomas	George Lionel	Age 37
1876	Thompson	Edith Elizabeth	Age 34
1877	Thompson	Annie Elizabeth	Age 57
1878	Thompson	Edwin	Age 64
1879	Thompson	Mary	Age 57
1880	Thrasher	George	Age 71
1881	Tilly	Arthur	Age 24
1882	Tilt	Samuel	Age 40
1883	Timmins	Harry	Age 66
1884	Timmis	Kate Alice	Age 47
1885	Tims	Edmund Percy	Age 37
1886	Tirrell	Albert	Age 50
1887	Tomkinson	Gertrude Ellen	Age 34
1888	Tongue	Charles Arthur	Age 26
1889	Tonks	Ivy Catherine	Age 35
1890	Tooth	Gladys	Age 34
1891	Tovey	Hannah	Age 60
1892	Towers	Thomas	Age 74
1893	Townley	Alma Eileen	Age 21
1894	Townley	James	Age 55
1895	Townley	Jessiemine	Age 54
1896	Townsend	Mary Ann	Age 62
1897	Townsend	Albert Edward	Age 36
1898	Townsend	Doris Mary	Age ?
1899	Tozer	Augustus Cyril	Age 35
1900	Tranter	Peggy	Age 4
1901	Tranter	Gordon	Age 7
1902	Tranter	Rose	Age 26
1903	Traves	John Henry	Age 50
1904	Trentham	Susannah	Age 66
1905	Trickett	Reginald Louis	Age 54
1906	Troman	Nellie Elizabeth	Age 51
1907	Tropman	Sidney Charles	Age 39
1908	Trueman	Evelyn Annie	Age 24
1909	Trull	Gladys Bertha	Age 26
1910	Tuby	Gladys Anita	Age 59
1911	Tucker	John Ernest	Age 29
1912	Tucker	Ernest Edward	Age 36
1913	Tudor	Dorothy	Age 4
1914	Tudor	Elsie Annie	Age 25

1915 Tudor	George	Age 30
1916 Tudor	Georgina	Age 2
1917 Tulk	Brian Keith	Age 9
1918 Tulk	Frederick Ivor Harris	Age 50
1919 Tunney	Florence	Age 70
1920 Tunney	John	Age 44
1921 Turland	Margaret Victoria	Age 34
1922 Turland	John Alfred	Age 4
1923 Turland	Maureen	Age 3
1924 Turland	Hilda Kate	Age 30
1925 Turland	Alfred Ernest	Age 35
1926 Turnell	Amy Vera Dumolo	Age 29
1927 Turner	Arthur Richard	Age 28
1928 Turner	James Francis	Age 27
1929 Turner	Harry Rowland	Age 12
1930 Turner	Kathleen	Age 47
1931 Turner	Maud Gladys	Age 48
1932 Turner	William Thomas	Age 57
1933 Turner	Mary	Age 89
1934 Turvey	Norah Isabel	Age 50
1935 Tustin	Frank Thomas	Age 34
1936 Tyler	Elsie	Age 49
1937 Tyler	Elizabeth Ann	Aged 6 mths
1938 Tyler	Stanley Horace	Age ?
1939 Tyler	Henry John	Age 79
1940 Ullaha	Rafie	Age 45
1941 Underhill	Edgar Albert	Age 74
1942 Unitt	Benjamin Stanley	Age 25
1943 Upton	Mabel Charlotte	Age 58
1944 Van Asten	June	Age 4
1945 Vann	Emma	Age 62
1946 Vaughan	Winifred Elizabeth	Age 32
1947 Vaughan	Ada	Age 64
1948 Vaughan	Hilda	Age 33
1949 Vaughan	Agnes Boyd	Age 34
1950 Vaughan	Conrad	Age 3
1951 Vaughan	George	Age 38
1952 Vaughan	Jane	Age 8
1953 Vaughan	Noreen	Age 10
1954 Vaughan	Thora	Aged 12 mths
1955 Vaughan	Michael Roy	Age 18
1956 Vaughan	Robert Daniel	Age 9
1957 Vicary	Adrian John	Age 20
1958 Villers	Sidney	Age 34
1959 Vine	George	Age 27
1960 Viney	Emily Mary	Age 48
1961 Vogan	Lily	Age 16
1962 Vogan	Molly	Age 36
1963 Vogan	Thomas	Age 40
1964 Vowles	Ivor	Age 42
1965 Wadhams	Emily Elizabeth	Age 59
1966 Wadhams	William	Age 59
1967 Waight	Elsie	Age 52
1968 Wainwright	Arthur Frank	Age 30
1969 Wainwright	Brian John	Aged 11 mths
1970 Waite	Thomas	Age 35
1971 Wake	Walter Harry	Age 56
1972 Wakeling	Alfred James	Age 56
1973 Wakeling	Mabel	Age 57
1974 Wakeman	Eileen Florence	Age 12
1975 Walden	Arthur	Age 34
1976 Walden	Alfred William	Age 2
1977 Walden	Carol Ann	Aged 2 mths
1978 Walden	Melville	Age 4
1979 Walden	Nora	Age 27
1980 Waldron	Phyllis June	Age 18
1981 Waldron	Henry Charles	Age 65
1982 Walewski	Waclaw	Age 25
1983 Walker	Gertrude	Age 36
1984 Walker	Douglas Henry	Age 17
1985 Walker	Isaac Rufus	Age 52
1986 Walker	Margaret Audrey	Age 43
1987 Walker	Edith Sarah	Age 58
1988 Walker	Arthur Albert	Age 35
1989 Walker	John Henry	Age 30
1990 Walker	John	Age 17
1991 Walker	Elizabeth	Age 65
1992 Wall	Dora Eleanor	Age 20
1993 Wall	Sarah Helena	Age 43
1994 Wall	William Edward	Age 47
1995 Wall	Charles Henry	Age 50
1996 Wallace	James Charles Thomas	Age 20
1997 Wallace	Henry Clement	Age 29
1998 Wallington	Albert Edward	Age 38
1999 Wallington	Albert George	Age 10
2000 Wallington	Charles	Age 16
2001 Wallington	Edith	Age 37
2002 Walmsley	Alfred Ed Ward	Age 39
2003 Walmsley	Doris	Age 16
2004 Walmsley	Caroline	Age 77
2005 Walsh	Daniel	Age 28
2006 Walton	Walter William	Age 59
2007 Ward	Ann Matilda	Age 62
2008 Ward	Charles William	Age 40
2009 Ward	Thomas	Age 75
2010 Ward	Spencer Littleton	Age 34
2011 Waring	Ivy May	Age 16
2012 Warner	Shirley Barbara	Age 3
2013 Warner	Patricia Rose	Age 4
2014 Warr	Rose	Age 32
2015 Warren	Mary Jane	Age 70
2016 Warwick-Mcclave		
	William Frederick	Age 21
2017 Waterhouse	Austin	Age 35
2018 Waters	Edith	Age 55
2019 Waters	Edith Gertrude	Age 22
2020 Waters	Harry Seymour	Age 53
2021 Waters	Winifred Mary	Age 24
2022 Waterson	Fanny Elizabeth	Age 34
2023 Waterson	Jean Elizabeth	Age 12
2024 Waterworth	Sarah Jane	Age 75
2025 Watkins	Alice	Age 23
2026 Watkins	Alice May	Age 61
2027 Watkins	George	Age ?

2028	Watson	Annie	Age 23
2029	Watson	William	Age 62
2030	Watson	William Howard	Age 19
2031	Watson	Henry	Age 50
2032	Watton	Jesse	Age 46
2033	Watts	George	Age 40
2034	Weaving	Annie	Age 45
2035	Webb	Thomas Walter	Age 68
2036	Webb	Algernon	Age 64
2037	Webb	James Frederick	Age 44
2038	Webb	Samuel	Age 47
2039	Webster	Roy William	Age 18
2040	Weeks	Arthur John	Age 45
2041	Welch	Nancy	Age 44
2042	Welch	James	Age 23
2043	Welding	Harold	Age 45
2044	Wells	Arthur Pinfield	Age 48
2045	Wells	Doris Eileen	Age 22
2046	Wells	Nellie Susannah Whiteman	Age 59
2047	Welsby	Clara	Age 72
2048	Welsby	Herbert	Age 69
2049	West	Bertram Edward	Age 66
2050	West	Florence Eunice Bessie	Age 40
2051	Westley	Thomas	Age 39
2052	Westwood	Arthur Thomas	Age 46
2053	Westwood	Arthur Edward	Age 37
2054	Wheeler	John Francis	Age 53
2055	Wheeler	William Joseph Patrick	Age 34
2056	Whitbread	Frederick William	Age 58
2057	White	Howard	Age 33
2058	White	Mary Ann	Age 48
2059	White	William	Age 39
2060	White	David Oliver	Age 27
2061	Whitehead	Thomas	Age 62
2062	Whitehorn	Wilfred Thomas	Age 17
2063	Whitehouse	Adelaide	Age 90
2064	Whitehouse	William John	Age 41
2065	Whitehouse	James Henry	Age 41
2066	Whitehouse	Leonard	Age 25
2067	Whitehouse	Mabel Eliza	Age 74
2068	Whitehouse	Lizzie	Age ?
2069	Whitlock	Arthur	Age 38
2070	Whittingham	George	Age 20
2071	Whittingham	Rose	Age 17
2072	Whittingham	Harold	Age 34
2073	Whitworth	Norman	Age 26
2074	Wiedemann	Herbert Joseph	Age 11
2075	Wilcox	Walter	Age 58
2076	Wilford	Kathleen Annie	Age 17
2077	Wilkes	Irene	Age 31
2078	Wilkins	Alice	Age 20
2079	Wilkins	Alice Maud	Age 52
2080	Wilkins	Frances	Age 12
2081	Wilkins	Joan	Age 10
2082	Wilkins	William	Age 52
2083	Wilkinson	Edith	Age 50
2084	Wilkinson	Ralph George	Age 50
2085	Wilkinson	Henry	Age 29
2086	Williams	William	Age 49
2087	Williams	Alfred Neander	Age 72
2088	Williams	David	Age 47
2089	Williams	Mary Ann	Age 70
2090	Williams	Ernest George	Age 52
2091	Williams	Frederick	Age 58
2092	Williams	Charles Henry	Age 66
2093	Williams	Lily Mary	Age 24
2094	Willmore	Stanley Walker	Age 37
2095	Willmott	Alfred George	Age 72
2096	Wills	Dora	Age 36
2097	Wilson	Samuel	Age 58
2098	Wilson	John	Age 60
2099	Wilson	Stanley Frederick	Age 17
2100	Windsor	Dorcas Hilda	Age 45
2101	Windsor	Margaret	Age 73
2102	Windsor	Mary Jane	Age 65
2103	Winfield	Jessie	Age 53
2104	Winkett	William Wilberforce	Age 57
2105	Winter	Joseph	Age 52
2106	Winwood	William George	Age 84
2107	Witts	Leonard	Age 18
2108	Wood	Alfred John	Age 23
2109	Wood	Lucy	Age 49
2110	Wood	Charles Henry	Age 32
2111	Wood	Alice	Age 57
2112	Wood	Frank Howard Job	Age 39
2113	Woodard	Reginald	Age 27
2114	Woodbridge	Alice Lilla	Age 28
2115	Woodbridge	David Leonard	Age 30
2116	Woodbridge	Leonard	Age 5
2117	Woodcock	Gertrude	Age 63
2118	Woodcock	Charles Henry	Age 63
2119	Woodhall	Maggie Sarah	Age 57
2120	Woodhall	William Benjamin Gold	Age 57
2121	Woodley	Harold Frank	Age 45
2122	Woodley	John Charles	Age 30
2123	Woodward	Robert Alfred	Age 63
2124	Woolaston	Elizabeth	Age 71
2125	Woolley	Gertrude Annie	Age 48
2126	Wootton	Arthur Howard	Age 26
2127	Wormall	May Louise	Age 64
2128	Worrell	Ellen Louisa	Age 67
2129	Would	Harold Temperton	Age 31
2130	Wren	Mary	Age 5
2131	Wright	Thomas Edgar	Age 44
2132	Wright	Thomas Edgar	Age 18
2133	Wright	Christy	Age 31
2134	Wright	William Frederick	Age 45
2135	Wright	Frederick George	Age 37
2136	Wright	Alexander	Age ?
2137	Wrigley	Annie	Age 48
2138	Wyatt	Wilfred Victor	Age 48
2139	Wynne	Frank Wilson	Age 57
2140	Wynne	Rose	Age 58
2141	Yarnold	Edgar	Age 46

2142	Yates	Mary	Age 75
2143	Yates	Dorothy Eileen	Age 10
2144	Yates	Edna Joan	Age 19
2145	York	William	Age 73
2146	Yorke	Charles	Age 56
2147	Young	Daisy	Age 24

Additional names added to memorial since unveiling
Collated by June Eastlake

2148	Bagshaw	Edward Orlando	Age 49
2149	Beech	Kenneth	Age 17
2150	Belcher	Thomas	Age ?
2151	Bell	Daniel Hubert	Age 37
2152	Biddulph	William John Sydney	Age 61
2153	Bidmead	Horace	Age 40
2154	Briant	Arthur Mcalister	Age 62
2155	Brogan	James	Age 16
2156	Bunford	Ruby Maureen	Age 7
2157	Cartwright	Cecil	Age 30
2158	Clarke	John Thomas	Age ?
2159	Collingswood	Sydney Thomas	Age 30
2160	Collins	William Robert	Age 45
2161	Cooper	Horace Edward	Age 31
2162	Cox	George	Age 64
2163	Danks	William Thomas	Age 39
2164	Davis	Arthur Reginald	Age 17
2165	Davis	Eric	Age 38
2166	Day	Ellen	Age 54
2167	Denham	Alfred Albert	Age 31
2168	Duggan	Nellie	Age 25
2169	Eccleston	James	Age 22
2170	Eden	Frederick William	Age 53
2171	Edwards	J.H.	Age ?
2172	Egginton	Ernest	Age 19
2173	Evans	Lily	Age 24
2174	Foster	Beatrice	Age 51
2175	Fuller	Harold Joseph	Age 41
2176	Goolding	Annie	Age 62
2177	Grant	Arthur	Age 26
2178	Green	Arthur Leonard	Age 19
2179	Haddon	George William	Age 40
2180	Harrison	Edward	Age 16
2181	Harrison	George	Age 58
2182	Harrison	Kenneth	Age 17

2183	Hawkins	William Charles	Age 22
2184	Haycock	Harry Cyril	Age 36
2185	Henn	William	Age 39
2186	Holt	Albert Henry	Age 31
2187	Hooper	John Walter	Age ?
2189	Inwood (G.C.)	George Walter	Age 34
2190	Jenkins	Richard Gwilym	Age 57
2191	Jones	Kenneth Bertram	Age 15
2192	Kelly	Kathleen	Age 29
2193	Kelly	Thomas	Age 41
2194	Lawrence	F.G.	Age 24
2195	Long	Donald Roland	Age 15
2196	Matthews	Elizabeth	Age 57
2197	Meakin	Doris	Age 35
2198	Morris	Howard Fisher	Age 19
2199	Newall	Jesse Arthur	Age 16
2200	Orton	Howard Charles	Age 52
2201	Pearce	Emily	Age 69
2202	Rawlins	Edith Ellen	Age 38
2203	Reed	Wallace Nelson	Age 46
2204	Rhodes	John	Age 45
2205	Richards	Howard Walter	Age 41
2206	Richards	John Garbett	Age 32
2207	Robinson	Kenneth Edward John	Age 20
2208	Roper	Maurice Edward	Age 43
2209	Sanderson	William John	Age ?
2210	Selvey	George Alien	Age 32
2211	Senior	Eric	Age 29
2212	Silk	Robert Bernard	Age 17
2213	Spooner	Joseph Henry	Age 26
2214	Stockley	Eric Norman	Age 16
2215	Taylor	Albert Edward	Age 34
2216	Teagle	G.E.	Age 20
2217	Thompson	Albert Edward	Age 58
2218	Walker	John James	Age ?
2219	Whitehouse	Joseph Frederick	Age 39
2220	Williams	Doreen	Age 26

Name spellings corrected on Tree of Life Memorial

148	Beale	Stanley William	Age 20
1323	Mulliss	Charles George	Age 48
1643	Scott	William Henry Richard	Age 34
1684	Shepherd	Thomas Henry	Age 46